Authoritarian Regimes
in Latin America

Jaguar Books on Latin America Series
William Beezley and Colin MacLachlan, Series Editors

I Saw a City Invincible: Urban Portraits of Latin America
   Edited by Gilbert M. Joseph and Mark D. Szuchman

Between Two Worlds: Mexican Immigrants in the United States
   Edited by David G. Gutiérrez

The Indian in Latin American History: Resistance, Resilience, and Acculturation
   Edited by John E. Kicza

Contemporary Indigenous Movements in Latin America
   Edited by Erick D. Langer with Elana Muñoz

Authoritarian Regimes in Latin America: Dictators, Despots, and Tyrants
   By Paul H. Lewis

U.S.-Mexico Borderlands: Historical and Contemporary Perspectives
   Edited by Oscar J. Martínez

Work, Protest, and Identity in Twentieth-Century Latin America
   Edited by Vincent C. Peloso

The Third Wave of Modernization in Latin America:
Cultural Perspective on Neo-Liberalism
   Edited by Lynne Phillips

Tropical Rainforests: Latin American Nature and Society in Transition
   Edited by Susan E. Place

Where Cultures Meet: Frontiers in Latin American History
   Edited by Jane M. Rausch and David J. Weber

Rank and Privilege: The Military and Society in Latin America
   Edited by Linda A. Rodríguez

The Church in Colonial Latin America
   Edited by John F. Schwaller

Colonial Spanish America: A Documentary History
   By William B. Taylor and Kenneth Mills

Drugs in the Western Hemisphere: An Odyssey of Cultures in Conflict
   Edited by William O. Walker III

Where Cultures Meet: Frontiers in Latin American History
   Edited by David J. Weber and Jane M. Rausch

Confronting Change, Challenging Tradition: Woman in Latin American History
   By Gertrude M. Yeager

Authoritarian Regimes in Latin America

Dictators, Despots, and Tyrants

Paul H. Lewis

AN SR BOOK

ROWMAN & LITTLEFIELD PUBLISHERS, INC.
Lanham • Boulder • New York • Toronto • Oxford

An SR Book

ROWMAN & LITTLEFIELD PUBLISHERS, INC.

Published in the United States of America
by Rowman & Littlefield Publishers, Inc.
A wholly owned subsidiary of The Rowman & Littlefield Publishing Group, Inc.
4501 Forbes Boulevard, Suite 200, Lanham, Maryland 20706
www.rowmanlittlefield.com

PO Box 317, Oxford, OX2 9RU, UK

British Library Cataloguing in Publication Information Available

Library of Congress Cataloging-in-Publication Data
Lewis, Paul H.
 Authoritarian regimes in Latin America : dictators, despots, and tyrants / Paul H.
Lewis.
   p. cm. — (Jaguar books on Latin America series)
 "An SR Book."
 Includes bibliographical references and index.
 ISBN 0-7425-3738-2 (cloth : alk. paper) — ISBN 0-7425-3739-0 (pbk. : alk. paper)
 1. Authoritarianism—Latin America. 2. Latin America—Politics and government.
I. Title. II. Jaguar books on Latin America.
JL966.L49 2006
320.98—dc22
                                            2005012718

Printed in the United States of America

♾™ The paper used in this publication meets the minimum requirements of
American National Standard for Information Sciences—Permanence of Paper for
Printed Library Materials, ANSI/NISO Z39.48-1992.

For Anne

~

Contents

~

Abbreviations and Acronyms

AAA	Argentine Anti-Communist Alliance
AD	Acción Democrática
ALN	National Liberating Alliance (Argentina)
ALN	National Liberation Alliance (Brazil)
ANAP	National Association of Small Peasants
ANAPO	National Popular Alliance
AP	Acción Popular
APRA	American Popular Revolutionary Alliance
ARENA	National Renovating Alliance
CDRs	committees for the defense of the revolution
CGE	General Economic Confederation
CGOCM	General Confederation of Mexican Workers and Peasants
CGP	General Confederation of Professionals
CGT	General Confederation of Workers
CGU	General University Confederation
CNA	National Agrarian Confederation
CNC	National Confederation of Peasants
CNOC	Cuban National Labor Confederation
CNOP	National Confederation of Popular Organizations
CNT	National Confederation of Workers
COB	Central Obrera Boliviana
COMIBOL	Mining Corporation of Bolivia
CONCAMIN	National Confederation of Industrial Chambers

CONCANACO	Confederation of National Chambers of Commerce
COPEI	Comité de Organización Política Electoral Independiente
CORA	Corporation for Agrarian Reform
CORFO	Corporación de Fomento
CPC	Confederation of Production and Commerce
CROM	Regional Confederation of Mexican Workers
CTC	Confederation of Cuban Workers
CTC	Cuban Labor Confederation
CTM	Mexican Workers' Confederation
CTP	Confederation of Peruvian Workers
CTRP	Workers' Confederation of the Peruvian Revolution
CTV	Confederation of Venezuelan Workers
DINA	National Intelligence Directorate
ELN	National Liberation Army (Bolivia)
ELN	Army of National Liberation (Colombia)
EP/FA	Encuentro Progresista/Frente Amplio
ERP	People's Revolutionary Army
ESG	Superior War School
FAR	Revolutionary Armed Forces
FARC	Armed Forces of the Colombian Revolution
FEB	Brazilian Expeditionary Force
FMLN	Farabundo Marti National Liberation Front
FRAP	Popular Revolutionary Action Front
FSB	Falange Socialista Boliviana
FSLN	Sandinista National Liberation Front
FSTMB	National Federation of Bolivian Miners
FSTSE	Federation of Unions of Workers in the Service of the State
GOU	Group of United Officers
IADB	Inter-American Development Bank
IAPI	Argentine Institute for Production and Trade
IMF	International Monetary Fund
INRA	National Institute for Agrarian Reform
ISI	import-substituting industrialization
JAPs	*juntas de abastecimiento y precios*
MAPU	Movement of United Popular Action
MDB	Brazilian Democratic Movement
MIR	Movement of the Revolutionary Left
MNR	Movimiento Nacional Revolucionaria

MOPOCO	Popular Colorado Movement
MTT	Militia and Territorial Troops
OAS	Organization of American States
OLAS	Organization of Latin American Solidarity
ORI	Integrated Revolutionary Organization
PAN	National Autonomist Party
PCB	Bolivian Communist Party
PCC	Communist Party of Cuba
PCP	Peruvian Communist Party
PDS	Social Democratic Party
PIR	Partido de la Izquierda Revolucionaria
PMDB	Party of the Brazilian Democratic Movement
PNR	National Revolutionary Party
POR	Partido Obrero Revolucionario
PRI	Institutional Revolutionary Party
PRIN	Revolutionary Party of the Nationalist Left
PRM	Mexican Revolutionary Party
PSD	Social Democratic Party
PSP	Popular Socialist Party
PSP	Social Progressive Party
PT	Labor Party
PTB	Brazilian Labor Party
RADEPA	Razón de Patria
SIN	National Intelligence Service
SINAMOS	National System of Social Mobilization
UCR	Radical Civic Union
UDN	National Democratic Union
UES	Union of Secondary School Students
UP	Popular Unity
VPR	Vanguarda Popular Revolucionária

Introduction:
Authoritarianism in Latin America

Strong, colorful personalities who impose their will upon laws, constitutions, courts, and congresses are an enduring feature of Latin American politics. This has been the rule, beginning with the violent *caudillos* (regional bosses) of the early nineteenth century and continuing to the "hyperpresidential" systems of the present. Strong men have shaped the region's history, usually as dictators, sometimes as leaders of one-party regimes, and, in rare cases like Brazil, as emperors.

Personal rule triumphs when institutions are weak. It emerged in Latin America when the old social order of the Spanish and Portuguese colonial empires broke down and the mass of people were still unready for democracy. In Spanish America the wars of independence were protracted and bloody. In their wake they left mainly anarchy for approximately half a century as *caudillos* fought among themselves for supremacy in the new republics. National consolidation gradually came about in one country after another, either by one *caudillo* dominating all his rivals and becoming a national dictator, or by a group of *caudillos* agreeing to form a political machine that would control the government and share out the spoils. But whether they became dictatorships or oligarchies, the sixteen Spanish American republics that won their independence in the early nineteenth century failed to achieve institutional stability. As of 1900 they had written ninety-nine different constitutions.

The twentieth century brought very little improvement for Latin America in general. Cuba and Panama gained their independence, bringing the number of Spanish American republics up to eighteen, but the group as a whole still experienced a total of eighty-four constitutions. The twentieth century also saw the rise of mass politics: first the middle classes and then the urban workers and rural peasants demanded the suffrage and a greater share of the national income. Group interests were expressed through ideologies, and each ideology contained a plan for organizing the economy and distributing wealth. New political parties emerged to promote their followers' interests, and in conformity with Latin American tradition each party tended to produce a charismatic leader determined to force his agenda on the country. Where politics became too polarized and violent, the military was encouraged to step in and impose solutions. Both populist and reactionary dictators, often drawn from the army, were commonplace throughout Latin America during this century.

The general approach of this book is chronological, in order to place these regimes in their historical context as stages in Latin America's political development, but I also will try to classify the different regimes as to their ideological orientation and internal processes. Chapter 1 ("The Undemocratic Culture") starts by tracing the origins of Latin America's seemingly endemic authoritarianism to its Iberian heritage. It briefly describes the centuries-long struggle of Spain to overthrow Moorish rule on the peninsula, which resulted in a militaristic society and an intolerant, crusading religion. After the discovery and conquest of the New World, those traits were carried over into colonial society. Both the Spanish colonies and Portuguese Brazil were hierarchical societies that were administratively and economically controlled by their respective mother countries, leaving their inhabitants with little opportunity to learn the skills of self-government. The large landed estate worked by slave labor (variously known as a *latifundio*, *hacienda*, or *fazenda*) was also carried over from the Iberian Peninsula. It helped to reinforce the colonial hierarchy and, after Independence, became the basis of a new authoritarian system in which *caudillos* ruled. Chapter 1 describes how the *caudillos* emerged, the sources of their power, and the unwritten political rules of the era they dominated.

The *caudillo* era was characterized by almost constant warfare among petty local chieftains, during which the old colonial administrative divisions broke up into smaller states. Chapter 2 ("Three Deviant Regimes"), however, describes three exceptions to this general picture of near anarchy. Paraguay fell under the rule of a strange tyrant, Dr. Francia, who had imbibed the revolutionary ideas of Rousseau and Robespierre. He eliminated the old elites, sealed off his country from the outside world, built up an army, and created a centrally controlled Creole socialist economy. Chile also found stability through a domineering leader, Diego Portales. Unlike Francia, he was a conservative, and rather than govern as a tyrant he created a Conservative Party political machine that gave power to the old landed elites. Chile escaped both military dictatorship and anarchy by becoming an oligarchy: rule by the few instead of by one man. Brazil was unique too. It became a monarchy because its independence movement was led by the son of Portugal's king. Pedro I and his son, Pedro II, enjoyed what no *caudillo* or oligarch could claim: the right to rule as the legitimate heir of the monarchy. That helped to preserve stability in a very large country whose regional differences might otherwise have led to its breakup.

Chapter 3 ("National Dictators") describes how *caudillo* anarchy eventually gave way to highly centralized national dictatorships throughout much of Spanish America. Mexico under Porfirio Díaz and Venezuela under Juan Vicente Gómez are the two classic examples. Other Spanish American republics, such as Argentina, Colombia, and Uruguay, followed Chile's path in developing oligarchic systems. So did Brazil after the monarchy was overthrown in 1889. Those are described in chapter 4 ("Liberal Oligarchies"). Both chapters 3 and 4 bring us forward in time to the last three decades of the nineteenth century and the first two decades of the twentieth. During those fifty or so years the doctrines of liberalism held sway in Latin America, particularly their economic prescriptions. This was a time of rapid economic growth, fueled by foreign investment and foreign trade. Cities grew rapidly, great improvements were made in transportation and communications, industry began to appear, and the urban middle and working classes began to assume numerical importance. Liberalism did not greatly influence political practices, however, which is why these chapters refer to "liberal dictatorships" and "liberal oligarchies." Nor did the benefits of economic growth and internal improvements trickle down sufficiently to alleviate the poverty of the lower classes. Those failures would lay the groundwork for the great social and political upheavals that are described in chapters 5 and 6.

Chapter 5 ("The Masses Enter Politics") describes the Mexican Revolution of 1910 and the 1952 Bolivian Revolution. Both were huge social upheavals, signaling the violent entry of the masses into politics. I also describe the struggles to give power to the lower classes in Peru, starting with the *aprista* movement and ending with the emergence of the Shining Path guerrillas. Chapter 6 ("Corporatism") relates how Getúlio Vargas of Brazil and Juan Perón of Argentina tried to incorporate the working classes into mainstream politics by adopting certain aspects of Mussolini's fascist corporate state.

Rafael Leónidas Trujillo of the Dominican Republic, Anastasio Somoza of Nicaragua, and Alfredo Stroessner of Paraguay—the subjects of chapter 7

("Tyranny and Succession")—were "throwbacks" to the late-nineteenth-century age of all-powerful "liberal" tyrants. They were able to rule for decades by promoting economic growth, organizing the citizenry into tightly controlled political parties, and creating police states using modern technologies of repression. Each of these three tyrants hoped to train a son to succeed him in power, but only Somoza was able to accomplish that.

Chapters 8 and 9 deal with the Cold War threat of Communism in Latin America and the reaction to it from the Right, which usually took the form of a counterrevolutionary military dictatorship. Chapter 8 ("The Marxists") attempts to give an account of the Cuban Revolution: its causes and the phases through which it evolved. Naturally, Fidel Castro is the central figure of that revolution, but I also discuss Ernesto "Che" Guevara's attempt to create a "new socialist man" by eliminating material incentives to work. That attempt ended with the failure in 1970 to achieve a "ten-ton sugar harvest." After bringing Cuba up to the present, I devote the remainder of the chapter to the career of Chile's Salvador Allende. I describe his rise to the presidency, his attempt to socialize the economy, and his downfall. To some it may seem curious that I have included Allende in a book about autocrats and oligarchs, since he was elected president, but there are good reasons for doing so. As the candidate of the Socialists, Communists, and liberation theology Catholics, Allende received under 37 percent of the vote in 1970, far short of a majority or a mandate. A majority of Congress then elected him president, but only after he signed an agreement with the opposition Christian Democrats promising to respect the constitution. Once in office he forgot his agreement and attempted to rapidly expropriate all the country's large businesses and farms, silence the press, and impose Marxist education in all the schools. While doing so, he ignored orders to desist from both the Supreme Court and Congress. I would argue that Allende and his Popular Unity coalition, which never had majority support, were attempting to rule autocratically as a "red oligarchy."

Chapter 9 ("Counterrevolutionaries") describes the military regimes that held power in Brazil (1964–1985), Chile (1973–1989), Uruguay (1973–1985), and Argentina (1976–1983). I compare these dictatorships according to (1) the conditions of their respective countries on the eve of the military's takeover; (2) the goals they set out to achieve; (3) the factional rivalries that emerged among the officers; (4) the methods they used to suppress opposition; (5) the reforms they attempted, and their relative success; and (5) their eventual breakdown, leading to the military's retreat to the barracks.

The 1980s saw a general trend toward democratic government throughout Latin America. Elections tended to replace violence, as both the soldiers and the revolutionaries seemed chastened by the excesses of military rule. Chapter 10 ("The Prospects for Democracy") poses the question of whether this trend will continue, thus eliminating Latin America's deeply rooted authoritarian tradition. To help answer that question I look at three democratically elected presidents—Carlos Menem of Argentina, Alberto Fujimori of Peru, and Hugo Chávez of Venezuela—whose frequent high-handedness in office should serve to moderate our fondest hopes with a healthy dose of skepticism. Of course no one has a crystal ball to predict the future, and everyone wishes the Latin Americans well, but traditions are hard to shake off.

~

CHAPTER ONE

The Undemocratic Culture

Latin America's authoritarian culture has several roots. One of those is traceable to the Iberian Peninsula, to the hierarchical, autocratic, and crusading character of Spanish and Portuguese society. A second root goes back to the nature of colonial society, which was based on conquest and the subsequent exploitation of slaves. A third root is to be found in the independence movement itself, which in Spanish America was both protracted and destructive—leaving behind, in most cases, anarchy and banditry. In this chapter we shall consider each of these "root causes" of authoritarianism.

The Iberian Heritage

In 711 Islamic Moorish invaders crossed the Strait of Gibraltar and swept through the Iberian Peninsula. The few Spanish and Portuguese who escaped this onslaught retreated, either to the mountains of northwest Spain or beyond the Pyrenees, where they combined with French forces to check the Moors at Poitiers in 732. Driven back into Iberia, the Moors went on the defensive as the Spanish Christians began an eight-century-long struggle known as the Reconquest to recover their land. The series of wars was interrupted by brief periods of peace, and at times the Christian forces fought among themselves, but on the whole those eight centuries constituted a relentless crusade to expel the Moors. The struggle ended in 1492 with the fall of the last Muslim stronghold in Granada.

In the meantime, the Reconquest had formed Spain's distinct national character. Eight centuries of warfare, beginning as guerrilla skirmishes and developing gradually into set battles by organized armies, naturally produced a society based on military norms. The successful military leader rose above his fellow countrymen and claimed aristocratic status. Moreover, as a crusade the Reconquest took on a deeply religious character. From the beginning it was a fight against Islam, to eliminate the Muslim "usurpers" from the land and restore the Catholic faith as the only true religion of Spain.[1]

A religiously inspired army and a militant faith were the twin pillars of Spanish nationalism. In 1474 the political consolidation of Catholic Spain culminated in the marriage of Isabella of Castile with Ferdinand of Aragon, producing a powerful centralized state capable of pushing the final stages of the Reconquest to a successful end. In 1480 Their Catholic Majesties launched the Inquisition, which would impose both religious and political conformity.[2] Small wonder that the fall of Granada in 1492, ending the long crusade, was followed by a triumphal burst of intolerance. The Jews were expelled from Spain within a few months, and the Muslims shared their fate a decade later.

The Colonial Experience

Besides the fall of Granada and the expulsion of the Jews, 1492 also saw Columbus begin his voyage that would lead to the discovery of America. Thus, literally, a whole New World appeared for Spain's militant, crusading society to conquer. At its height, Spain's empire spread over a continent and a half, from California to Tierra del Fuego.

The conquering Spaniards were first attracted by the hope of finding great deposits of precious metals, since many of the artifacts used by the Indians were made of gold and silver. They struck it rich in places like Mexico and Peru. Playing on rivalries among the Indian tribes, they toppled empires, plundered the conquered people, and forced them to work in the mines. To reward these *adelantados* (adventurers) and also attract more settlers to expand the empire, the Spanish Crown offered huge *encomiendas* (grants of land) that included the owner's right to the labor of the Indians residing there. In addition to mineral wealth, the colonies soon began producing lucrative cash crops such as tobacco, sugar, cotton, and indigo, all worked by forced labor.

Such an exploitative economy naturally led to a steeply hierarchical society with relatively little opportunity to rise out of the caste one was born into. At the very bottom of this social pyramid were the conquered Indians.

While nominally protected from abuse under Spanish law, in practice they were indistinguishable from slaves. Labor conditions on large estates and in the mines were brutal in the extreme, and women and children as well as the men were forced to work beyond their strength. Contact with the Spaniards also resulted in the rapid spread of diseases against which the Indians had acquired no resistance. During the course of the empire the Indian population declined greatly, especially in the Caribbean region, where it became necessary to import black slaves from Africa to maintain an adequate labor force.

Just above the Indian and African slave population were the "free" Indians and Africans. Those Indian tribes that had collaborated with the Spaniards in their conquest were exempted from the *encomienda* system. Nevertheless, they could be called upon, under a system known as the *repartimiento*, to provide a certain number of able-bodied men to work for a limited period of time on public projects, or on the large estates during the planting or harvesting seasons. The men would be paid wages, although at a lower rate than that for truly free labor. Like the *encomienda*, the *repartimiento* was often abused. Also just above the slave class were manumitted blacks, or freedmen. They were often found in the towns, and their freedom was quite restricted. They were excluded from public office and most craft guilds, although they could practice certain mechanical trades. Some freedmen were employed in the mines, and they could enlist as common soldiers in the army or colonial militia.[3]

Since women constituted only a small percentage of those Spaniards who immigrated to the New World (they were never more than 10 percent of the European population), the men commonly took many concubines from among the Indians and blacks. And, occasionally, there were unions between these two latter groups. The result was a middling mass of free people of mixed blood, socially inferior to the supposedly "pure" Spaniards but superior to the slaves or freedmen: *mestizos*, the offspring of a Spanish male and an Indian female; mulattos, the offspring of a Spaniard and an African; and *zambos*, the product of an Indian and African union. They formed the majority of the urban population, composing what might be considered the lower middle class of Spanish colonial society: shopkeepers, skilled tradesmen, small farmers, foremen. Some among them composed the criminal and vagabond elements of the cities.

Near the top of the colonial pyramid, but not at the peak, were the Spanish *criollos* (Creoles). These were the landowners, the large merchants, the upper clergy, the militia officers. Whatever their occupation, their status was traceable to the large landed estate—the *latifundio*—that grew out of the original *encomienda*. The *latifundio* was an old institution, developed originally by the Romans and brought by them to Spain, from whence it was replicated in the New World. Originally, a *latifundio*, worked by slave labor, was intended to provide a Roman, or a Spanish, family with economic self-sufficiency. In Spanish America, however, it was usually organized for producing a cash crop; and so, in a sense, it took on certain features of a capitalist enterprise. Unlike a true capitalist enterprise, however, there was no pressure on the owner to be efficient or maximize profits. On the contrary, *latifundios* had only to provide the owner and his family with a sufficient income to live well. That could be done even if only a small part of the estate was cultivated, using primitive methods and a slave labor force.

The important thing was to keep the *latifundio* in one piece, if the landowning family was to retain its elite position in society. This was achieved through the practice of entail, which prevented it from being divided among the owner's heirs. The rule of primogeniture awarded possession to the eldest son—or, if there was none, to the nearest male blood relative. The other sons would perhaps become large merchants marketing the *latifundio*'s produce, or members of the Catholic Church hierarchy, military officers, or lawyers. Women were carefully married into other *latifundio*-owning families, or else they became nuns. Thus, the *latifundio* was more than just an economic institution. It also provided the family with status and power and produced a system of interlocking elites.

Nevertheless, with rare exceptions, *criollos* were excluded from the pinnacle of the colonial pyramid. The governing class was appointed by the Crown and was reserved for *peninsulares*: Spaniards from Spain. In the first place, while *criollos* were anxious to be considered as "pure" Europeans, in Spain they were considered to be racially and socially inferior. It was assumed that at some time or another Creole families had been "tainted" by Indian or African blood. Given the small number of Spanish women who immigrated to the colonies, there were grounds for those suspicions. More important, however, the Spanish monarchs had been centralizing power in their hands ever since Ferdinand and Isabella had united the crowns of Aragon and Castile. The monarchy was absolute in Spain and it intended to keep a tight rein on its overseas possessions as well. Consequently, almost all of its administrative officials in the colonies were native-born Spaniards. They were not to marry or own property in the colonies, and they were moved about frequently so as not to acquire sentimental ties to the people they governed.

All governmental authority flowed from the Crown. Legally speaking, since Queen Isabella had financed Columbus's voyages, all of Spain's territories in America were the property of the Crown. As we have seen, the Crown was generous about giving large land grants to the conquerors and their descendants, but it always reserved the rights to subsoil wealth. Mining concessions would be granted to individuals or companies, but one-fifth of the output belonged to the monarch. The Crown also retained the right to regulate trade with the New World, grant monopolies, restrict certain economic activities (such as colonial manufacturing), restrict the circulation of subversive books or pamphlets, and levy taxes. All of this was done through the Casa de Contratación (Board of Trade), whose regulators and tax collectors were appointed and removed by the Crown.

Colonial governance was centered in the Council of the Indies, which legislated in the Crown's name. It sought to control the colonies through viceroys (literally, "vice-kings"), of which there were two: one for New Spain (Mexico, the Caribbean islands, Central America, and the North American southwest) and one for Peru (South America, plus Panama).[4] Like the Crown, viceroys had wide-ranging appointive powers, and also considerable latitude in interpreting the Crown's wishes. Because the viceroyalties were so extensive, it was necessary to divide them into smaller administrative units whose top officers were appointed by the Crown, not the viceroy. In addition to these, there were judicial bodies called *audiencias*, whose presidents also exercised governing jurisdiction over certain territories. The judges of the *audiencias* were also Crown appointees and reported directly to the Council of the Indies. Further down the administrative hierarchy were the minor local officials: *corregidores*, who policed the Indian communities; provincial governors; and *alcaldes mayores*, who were the chief municipal officials. In this way the Crown, acting through the Council of the Indies, created a system of checks and balances that enabled Spain to retain a modicum of control over the colonies without allowing any one official to acquire too much power. It was not an efficient system. Months might pass before the Council of the Indies approved a petition. On the other hand, given the great distance from Spain, it was relatively easy for colonists to evade the law. Indeed, corruption was rife.

Nevertheless, there was little opportunity for the Spanish colonists to practice self-governance. Only at the very bottom of the administrative pyramid, in the *cabildos* (municipal councils), were the Creoles allowed any role in legislation. Even there, the *cabildo* was hemmed in by rules laid down by the Council of the Indies. Councilmen and other local officers were chosen either by the provincial governor or the Crown. Sometimes these offices were for sale, and in some cases they became hereditary. Even when serious crises called for *cabildos abiertos* (extraordinary meetings) to give the local Creoles a chance to voice their opinions, attendance was upon invitation only. Rather than a school for democratic self-governance, the *cabildo* was the oligarchic preserve of wealthy local families.

Contrast this situation to that of the English colonists in North America. Those settlers in the New World were often religious and political dissidents who rejected the Crown's authority in matters of conscience. They came from a mercantile society with a larger middle class and more social mobility. Custom and the common law guaranteed them certain rights, and the House of Commons in Parliament existed to check the absolutist pretensions of monarchs. There was also a tradition of ordinary men performing local civic functions. This sort of political culture was transferred to the New World, and then amplified. All of the colonies had elective assemblies, and in some cases even elective governors, judges, and administrative officials. Some of those elected came from quite humble backgrounds. Thus, when independence finally came, the English colonists in North America were better prepared to undertake the challenges of forming a new government. On the other hand, the Spanish American colonists, having been deprived of any governing experience, soon fell into anarchy.

The Independence Struggles

Economic deterioration led to Spain's loss of control over America; and its economic decline, in turn, is traceable to its expulsion of the Jews and Moors. Those groups had constituted the bulk of the Iberian Peninsula's merchants and artisans—the very people who might have helped Spain to compete with the new rival trading nations: England, Holland, and France. Also, rather than concentrate on developing new industries, Spain turned its energies to providing the spiritual inspiration and military might for the Catholic Counter-Reformation. Indeed, to finance the Counter-Reformation's wars the Spanish Crown imposed heavy taxes on all commerce.

By the middle of the seventeenth century Spain's economic decline was evident, and with that there appeared increasing difficulties in its mercantile relations with the colonies. From Spain's viewpoint, the colonies' role was to provide the mother country with precious minerals and commercial crops, while also acting as captive markets for the mother country's industrial goods. This was a closed system in which the colonies were not to sell to or buy from any country other than Spain. The problem was that Spain couldn't provide the necessary industrial goods to fulfill its role in this system. Instead, it purchased them from England, France, or Flanders and then transshipped them to the New World. Thus, much of the wealth that Spain extracted from America went out again to its commercial and military rivals. Moreover, the American colonies soon discovered that they could obtain the industrial goods they were buying from Spain more cheaply by dealing directly with the producing countries. Smuggling became common.

Along with economic decline went Spain's deterioration as a military power. England began to gain supremacy on the high seas as a naval power. English pirates plundered the Spanish fleets bringing wealth from America and also sacked and plundered the colonies' cities. Unable to defend the colonies effectively, Spain tried to prepare them to defend themselves by sending out officers to organize and train local standing armies. As usual, *peninsulares* tended to monopolize the officer corps, while the poorer sort of Creoles, *mestizos*, and mulattos made up the ranks of enlisted men. New, and heavy, taxes were imposed on the colonists to support these units. In addition, wealthy Creoles were urged to raise militias as support troops for the new colonial armies. These militias were drawn from the clients or poor relatives of the Creole elites. Over time the original distinction between the regular armies and the militias came to be blurred as Spain was increasingly unable to spare professional officers for the colonies and had to appoint *criollos* to the command of regular units as well.

By the end of the eighteenth century the elements for a revolt against Spanish rule were coming together in a volatile mix. First, the mercantilist system had broken down, and smuggling was widespread as the advantages of direct trade with England, and other modern trading states, became obvious. Attempts by the Spanish government to crack down on contraband and to make its administrative controls more effective only caused resentment. Second, Spain's evident inability to protect its colonies made it seem contemptible. Third, despite ineffectual attempts by censors, revolutionary writings by Voltaire, Rousseau, Locke, and others were circulating, calling into question the traditional authority of monarchs and bishops. Fourth, there were the examples of the French and American revolutions. Especially the latter offered a blueprint for achieving independence. Still, the volatile mix needed a spark to make it explode.

That came in 1808, when Napoleon Bonaparte invaded the Iberian Peninsula, made King Ferdinand VII of Spain his prisoner, and placed Joseph Bonaparte, his brother, on the throne. To Napoleon's surprise, popular revolts against the usurper broke out all over Spain. French troops found themselves harried by guerrilla forces, and meanwhile the various resistance leaders formed a regency government with its capital in Cádiz. Shortly afterward the Creoles in America were invited to send representatives to the regency's Cortes, or parliament. This was the moment that Creole radicals had waited for. To cover their real intentions, they too proclaimed their loyalty to the deposed king, while at the same time refusing to recognize the legitimacy of the government in Cádiz. In one colony after another the royal authorities were overthrown, to be replaced by patriotic revolutionary councils. Sensing the danger, the Cádiz authorities ordered the colonial armies to put down the rebels. Some obeyed, but others sided with the Creole patriots. The wars for independence exploded throughout the length of Spain's American empire in 1810, from the Mexican countryside to the city of Caracas and the port of Buenos Aires. Spain hung on tenaciously to its territories, especially the richest colonies: Mexico, Peru, and New Granada. Guerrilla warfare punctuated by huge bloody battles characterized the fighting. Both sides plundered and devastated those populations unfortunate enough to be in the path of their armies. The fighting went on for many years, destroying property, trade, government, the educational system, and the physical infrastructure of the former colonies.

The patriot forces were drawn from the pre-independence armies and militias that Spain had organized, and they were lucky to find brilliant officers like Simón Bolívar and José de San Martín to lead them—but that was not enough to ensure success. It was necessary to recruit the help of local landowners, with their personal militias, or even bandit gangs whose main interest in fighting lay in the opportunities for plunder. Another peculiarity of the rebel armies was the unwillingness of many of these militia units to fight outside of their local districts. Patriotism in the former Spanish colonies was mainly local; the inhabitants had little sense of loyalty to people in the next town or province. This kind of attitude was deliberately fostered by Spain, which—until the last half of the eighteenth century—had even forbidden the colonies to trade with each other. Thus, the patriot armies were constantly changing their makeup as they marched from one district to another.[5]

The independence wars thus nurtured that nineteenth-century Latin American phenomenon, the *caudillo*. The breakdown of civilization, the spread of chaos, the inability to conceive of a national interest, the parochial outlook, and the easy recourse to plunder that blurred the distinction between guerrilla warfare and banditry produced the local political buccaneer who acted on his own initiative without permission from his nominal commander. With no central authority to rein him in, he could consolidate his local power and enrich himself by pillaging and eliminating his immediate rivals. The wars legitimized him, made him a prestigious local figure with an armed band at his command. The longer they went on—in Mexico they lasted until 1821, and in Peru until 1825—the tighter became the *caudillo's* hold on local power. With the winning of independence, he emerged as the protagonist of the postwar era.

The Breakdown of Order

The wars of independence produced a political vacuum in Spanish America. Eliminating the Crown's authority did not usher in democracy because the *criollo* elites were determined to consolidate their privileges by adding political power to their economic and social advantages. Beneath them was a mass of very poor, illiterate people unprepared for—and in many cases excluded from—the rights and duties of citizenship.

The new republics were really artificial states. What little infrastructure there had been under Spain was destroyed by the wars, and much of the capital needed to rebuild fled with the *peninsulares*. Outside of the areas within easy reach of the capital cities or major ports, most of the "citizens" of these republics lived in small, isolated communities. These were like independent fiefdoms, dominated by the local *latifundio* owner, or *hacendado*. In many parts of Spanish America slavery continued until midcentury; and even where labor was nominally free, much of the rural population was tied to the *latifundio* through the practice of debt peonage. This latter system was based on the peons' dependence on the *latifundio's tienda de raya* ("company store") for some of their necessities. Since peons had little knowledge of money and usually bought on credit, their miserably low wages were insufficient to keep them out of debt. An indebted peon could not leave until he paid off his debt. If he ran away he could be pursued and brought back, with the cost of his capture added to the debt. If he died, his debt was passed on to his children.[6] Often peons worked for no wage, but simply for the right to cultivate a small plot of land for their families' subsistence. To ameliorate the harsh reality of this servitude, *hacendados* tried to instill a sense of mutual obligation in their dependents through the practice of *compadrazgo*, whereby they became godfathers to the peons' children. The *hacendado* thus became a *patrón*, offering his peons jobs and protection in return for their personal loyalty. This variant of feudalism was the base for *caudillo* power.

Society continued to be a rigid hierarchy; but the elites no longer had the authority of a hereditary monarch to legitimize privilege, so the new states soon were torn apart by power struggles. Simón Bolívar tried to create an extensive state, Gran Colombia, out of the old viceroyalty of New Granada, which would include present-day Colombia, Venezuela, Ecuador, and Panama. Then he tried to unite this with Peru and Bolivia (formerly, Upper Peru) and even convoked the first Pan-American conference as a first step toward eventually bringing all the Spanish Americans together in a broad federation. Nevertheless, centrifugal forces generated by localism and the personal ambitions of his lieutenants overwhelmed all his plans. Venezuelans, resentful at being governed from distant Bogotá, revolted under the leader-ship of General José Antonio Páez while Bolívar was liberating Peru. When Bolívar hurried back to restore order, Peru and Bolivia took advantage of his absence to declare their independence. As things fell apart Bolívar assumed dictatorial powers for life, hoping to keep Gran Colombia together through his personal prestige and sheer will. It was no use. In 1829 Páez rose up again, declared Venezuela's independence, and drove Bolívar into exile. The Great Liberator of South America died the following year, just after Ecuador with-drew from Gran Colombia.

Bolívar had considered recruiting a European prince to head Gran Colom-bia, in order to create some sort of legitimate authority—or, if there were no acceptable candidates, assuming the crown himself. Republican sentiment ruled out this option in Gran Colombia; but in Mexico the chief leader of the independence movement, General Agustín de Iturbide, had himself pro-claimed as Agustín I, emperor of Mexico. His empire included all of what is currently Central America, down to Panama, and most of today's American west, including California, Texas, and Utah. Mexican liberals soon revolted, under the leadership of General Antonio López de Santa Anna, one of Itur-bide's former supporters. Driven into exile in early 1823, Iturbide tried to make a comeback the following year but was captured and executed. With his fall from power, five of the six Central American provinces (formerly, the Captaincy-General of Guatemala) seceded from Mexico and created the Central American Federation. This latter also became torn apart by cen-trifugal forces and finally broke up in 1840 after almost a generation of con-stant warfare between those who wanted more autonomy for local govern-ments and those who hoped to create a larger, more centralized state. In 1836 Texas, the Yucatán Peninsula, and the state of Zacatecas also seceded from Mexico, in response to the national government's attempt to impose a cen-tralist constitution. The Zacatecas revolt was quickly put down, but the Yu-catán's physical isolation enabled it to go its own way for more than a decade, until an uprising by the Mayan Indians drove the white landlords to seek the central government's protection. Texas was lost forever.

In southern South America Chile declared its independence from Peru, while to the east the old viceroyalty of La Plata also disintegrated. The port city of Buenos Aires wanted a centralized, unitary state with itself as the cap-ital, but the provinces insisted on a loose federation, and some of them, like Bolivia and Paraguay, demanded their complete independence. Across the La Plata estuary, the frontier zone called Banda Oriental (later, the Republic of Uruguay) also rejected the authority of Buenos Aires and sought its inde-pendence under the leadership of José Artigas.

Thus, the old Spanish viceroyalties broke up along the lines of their provincial subjurisdictions. Since Spain had done little to encourage inter-colonial trade or communications, the few roads that it built were intended to facilitate the movement of mineral and agricultural wealth to the ports, and little else. Given the rugged mountain terrain of most of Mexico, Central America, and the Andean region—plus the vast deserts or jungles that cut off whole regions, like Texas, the Yucatán, southern Peru, Paraguay, and Argentina's western provinces, from the viceregal capitals—it is hardly surprising that larger political units were unsustainable.

Ragtag armies invaded capital cities, pillaged the treasury, set up shaky governments, and were driven out again. Now and then a *caudillo* would temporarily keep his rivals at bay and there would be an uneasy peace, which was only to collapse once more in a new round of warfare. Mexico had fifty-two different governments and thirty-six different heads of state in its first fifty years of independence (1822–1872). One man, General Antonio López de Santa Anna, occupied the presidency eleven times himself and moved many other men in and out of that office, according to his whims. Colombia's record was almost as bad: twenty-five governments, ten constitutions, and twenty-three heads of state in fifty years. Peru fared even worse, with thirty-five different governments, twenty-five different presidents, and nine constitutions. Nor were these unusual cases. Argentina, Costa Rica, El Salvador, Guatemala, Nicaragua, Uruguay, and Venezuela all had more than twenty different governments in their first fifty years of independence from Spain. Bolivia, Chile, Ecuador, and Honduras had more than fifteen different governments. Only Brazil and Paraguay were islands of relative stability in this sea of anarchy, for reasons that I will explain in the next chapter.[7]

Sources of *Caudillo* Power

To establish his power as a local "strongman" a *caudillo* needed certain resources: (1) an armed following that was personally loyal to himself; (2) an economic base, which in those times could only be found in the ownership of a large landed estate; and (3) spoils with which to reward his followers and keep them loyal. How to acquire the first two depended, originally, on a *caudillo*'s social background.

In their social origins, *caudillos* fell into two broad categories. Many arose from the old Creole landed elite and had served as officers in the colonial militia. They recruited personal followings from their upper-class relatives, the dependents who worked on their estates, and their former comrades in the independence wars. Alternatively, many *caudillos* came from more modest backgrounds, rising through the ranks of the patriot forces on the basis of their personal courage and skill as military leaders. Often they were *mestizos* or mulattos, and a few were even full-blooded Indians. Some had been bandits during colonial times and had been recruited into the patriot forces as guerrilla fighters—a nominal change of status that still allowed them to pillage and plunder. Their prestige as fighters and their ability to deliver booty kept their followers loyal. After the wars ended they established themselves as *latifundistas* (*hacendados*) by seizing the property of departed enemies and passing out parcels of it to their lieutenants.

Most of the *caudillos* in the La Plata region—such as José Artigas, who fought for Uruguay's independence; Martín Güemes, the *caudillo* of Salta; Francisco Ramírez (Entre Ríos); Juan Bautista Bustos (Córdoba); and Facundo Quiroga (La Rioja)—were men of great wealth from large landowning families and had proved their ability to lead as militia officers. In many cases their fathers and grandfathers had held commissions in the colonial army or militia. Bustos and Ramírez even traced their family roots back to Spanish aristocracy. Even Estanislao López, the man who ruled Santa Fe, and Félix Aldao, of Tucumán, belonged to the respectable Creole middle class, with connections to the elite. Both López and Aldao had fathers who were officers in the Spanish colonial army and both had themselves served in the militia.[8]

The man who would emerge as the leading *caudillo* of this whole region, Juan Manuel de Rosas, was particularly well connected. His father was an *estanciero* (large rancher) and Spanish colonial infantry captain; his paternal grandfather was an army officer as well. On his mother's side he was related to the Anchorenas, the wealthiest landowning family in Buenos Aires Province. His mother had herself inherited an *estancia*. Moreover, Rosas married into an upper-class Buenos Aires *estanciero* family. Unlike many of the future *caudillos* of his generation, he did not join the army or militia, nor did he take any part in the independence struggle. Indeed, he appears to have preferred the colonial system, with its emphasis on order and unity. He spent the war years on the family *estancia*, learning the ranching business. At the age of twenty he left home and, in partnership with a couple of friends, opened up Buenos Aires' first meat-salting business. He quickly made a fortune and began investing in land, eventually becoming one of the largest proprietors on the pampas.[9]

Rosas's prestige rested upon the fact that, unlike many of the *estancieros*, he actually ran his own estates, adopting the life of a gaucho and excelling in all the qualities that made for leadership on the pampas: courage, strength, good horsemanship, decisiveness, and—if necessary—cruelty and ruthlessness. He won the admiration of the leading *estanciero* families by showing the way to economic success and by organizing the gauchos on his estates, whom he dressed in red ponchos and formed into a disciplined cavalry, to defend the countryside against raids by Indians and outlaw bands. With his extensive kinship and business connections throughout the *estanciero* elite, and his gaucho cavalry, the Colorados del Monte, Rosas gained control of Buenos Aires Province and with it Argentina's only port and outlet to the sea. From that commanding position he was able to establish himself as the most powerful of the country's *caudillos*.

Even so, Rosas did not unite the country into a nation. As governor of Buenos Aires he tyrannized the province, using his army, police, and paramilitary thugs—the Mazorca—to terrify, pillage, exile, and murder his opponents, both real and suspected; but his relations with the other twelve provinces of the Confederation of the United Provinces of the Río de la Plata remained informal. Rosas refused to call a convention to write an official constitution, for that might restrict his freedom of action. He preferred instead to use his control of the port to keep the other governors dependent on him and give him a de facto monopoly of the power to decide the confederation's economic and foreign policies.

The *caudillos* who struggled for power in Mexico came from a greater variety of backgrounds. General Anastasio Bustamente, a leading figure in the postwar Conservative Party and thrice president of the republic (1830–1832, 1837–1839, 1840–1841) was an upper-class Creole from Michoacán. He originally studied to be a medical doctor, but when Fathers Miguel Hidalgo and José Morelos began the movement for independence with an Indian insurrection he, like General Agustín de Iturbide, joined the royal army to help put them down and won notoriety for his harsh methods. He switched to the patriot side when Iturbide did, and for the same reason: because Liberals had come to power in Spain and threatened to implement social reforms in the colonies. Nicolás Bravo, who also held the presidency briefly three times (1839, 1842–1843, 1846–1847), was another powerful *caudillo* from a large landowning family with an extensive kinship and clientele network. Unlike Bustamente, he originally joined the insurgents under Morelos, although he later turned Conservative.

Most Mexican *caudillos* were not from the landed elite, however. Indeed, some of them were from truly humble backgrounds. Vicente Guerrero, who took over the patriot insurgency in the south after Morelos was captured, was an uneducated *mestizo*. After losing a close presidential election in 1828 he revolted and seized the office by force. He made the mistake of naming Bustamente as his vice president, however, and fell victim to a coup the following year. He then tried a second revolt, in 1831, but was defeated by Bravo's forces and was executed on Bustamente's orders. Another *caudillo* from a poor background was Juan Álvarez, a Hispanicized Indian from the then-remote southwestern region around Acapulco. The orphaned son of a small farmer, he joined Morelos's guerrillas, and then followed Guerrero. After independence he became a Liberal and a champion of the peasantry, defending the Indians' lands against encroachment by the regional *latifundistas*. At the same time, having confiscated considerable land for himself, he also discouraged the land-hungry peasants from invading private estates. By skillfully balancing the interests of the elites and the masses Álvarez secured the support of both, won statehood for his region (known as Guerrero), and became the new state's governor and military commandant.[10]

Even the dashing, colorful general Antonio López de Santa Anna, who dominated Mexico's politics during the republic's first fifty years, came from rather modest beginnings. He was born in 1794 in Jalapa, a town near the port of Vera Cruz, and his parents were recent Spanish immigrants. His father was a merchant and minor colonial official who tried, unsuccessfully, to convince his son to follow him in business. Though only a member of the colonial middle class, the older man had sufficient connections to people higher up to enable his son to become a cadet in the royal army. Like Iturbide and Bustamente, Santa Anna first sided with the royalists, then switched to the patriot side, even supporting Iturbide as emperor. Eighteen months later he helped to depose Iturbide upon discovering that he was to be dismissed as commander of the Vera Cruz garrison.

Whether *caudillos* started out as landed gentry or whether they were upstarts who grabbed power during the independence wars, they understood that their authority ultimately required the possession of a large estate. The *latifundio* "was the indispensable foundation" of *caudillo* power: the "source of personal wealth, focus of manpower, place of retreat, and fortress in defeat." "The networks of clients and alliances may have differed in detail" from place to place, but they "were the same in nature and function" everywhere.[11] Santa Anna was no exception to this. As soon as Mexico won its independence he began acquiring property around Vera Cruz. In 1825 he married the daughter of a well-to-do Vera Cruz merchant, and with her dowry he considerably increased his holdings. His principal *latifundio*, called Manga de Clavo, would cover some 483,000 acres of land and surround the road between Jalapa and Vera Cruz. To this he added two other large estates in the district, giving him a predominant position in one of Mexico's most strategic areas, for now he controlled access to the country's chief port, whose customs house was the source of most of the central government's revenues. "Whoever controlled movement between the capital and Vera Cruz held the purse strings of Mexico."[12]

As a regional *caudillo*, Santa Anna built a client base by giving jobs in the state and municipal governments, as well as contracts in the port, to his friends and financial backers. In addition, his military prestige made him popular with peasants and rural smallholders. These, plus the peons on his estates and the soldiers in his garrison, formed the core of his military strength. But Santa Anna needed to build alliances beyond his regional base in order to pursue his ambition to be the first man in Mexico. He acquired some prominence by helping to oust Iturbide and then by backing Guerrero's revolt in 1828. Now he was identified with the Liberals. His big break came in 1829, when Spain landed troops near Tampico in an attempt to retake Mexico. Although outnumbered, Santa Anna led a spirited attack that drove the attackers back to their ships and ended the invasion. From this he emerged as a national hero.

Pleading ill health, Santa Anna remained at Manga de Clavo when Bustamente overthrew Guerrero, nor did he come to Guerrero's aid when the latter revolted a year later; but in 1832 he led a Liberal revolt against Bustamente. He filled his war chest by diverting all of Vera Cruz's customs receipts and capturing government convoys carrying money to the capital. After ousting Bustamente he made himself president—the first of eleven times that he would claim that office. Administration bored him, however, so he soon stepped aside and allowed his civilian vice president, Valentín Gómez Farias, to run the government. But Gómez Farias's anticlericalism provoked a violent reaction from devout Catholics, so to preserve order Santa Anna took back the presidency and sided with the Conservatives. From then until 1855 Santa Anna would be in and out of the presidency, often ruling through puppets. He switched his allegiances easily and cynically, sometimes backing the Liberals, sometimes the Conservatives.

Other parts of the old viceroyalty of New Spain bred their own *caudillos*, many of them from humble backgrounds. Francisco Morazán, president and chief supporter of the ill-fated Central American Federation (1823–1840), was the son of a French West Indian merchant who moved to Honduras but never prospered. Morazán received only a primary school education—and that thanks only to his uncle, a parish priest. He started out as a merchant himself, but when Central America broke away from Mexico he entered politics, displayed a natural aptitude for political and military strategy, and became head of the federation in 1829. Thereafter he was almost continually occupied with putting down revolts by secessionists. Morazán's nemesis, Rafael Carrera, was a dark-skinned Guatemalan *mestizo* with pronounced

Indian features who came from even further down the social scale. Born in a Guatemala City slum, at age fourteen he joined the Conservative Party militia that was fighting Morazán's Liberal/Federalist forces and rose to the rank of sergeant. Mustered out in 1832, he worked on various *latifundios* as a peon before finally marrying the daughter of a small farmer and settling down to raise pigs.

Carrera was catapulted from obscurity to prominence by a cholera epidemic that struck Guatemala in 1837. The epidemic was especially severe in the Indian villages, where people crowded together under poor conditions. When the government tried to quarantine these villages the Indians panicked and turned violent. Their revolt was encouraged by the local priests, who, resentful at the Liberal government for its attacks on the Church, told the Indians that the authorities were deliberately poisoning them so as to seize their lands. The government responded by drafting all able-bodied men with military experience into the militia and ordering them to enforce the quarantine. Carrera was conscripted; but instead of attacking the Indians he went over to their side and offered to lead their revolt. They accepted him, and he quickly proved to be an excellent leader.

The uprising released the Indians' long-suppressed hatred of the white *criollos* in a hurricane of savage violence. The *criollos* appealed to Morazán to intervene. For over a year Carrera and his men carried on an effective guerrilla warfare against the federation's regular forces. Meanwhile, Morazán's strength was being sapped by other revolts in Honduras and Nicaragua. Finally, in desperation, he seized Guatemala City, hoping to crush Carrera, only to find himself surrounded and trapped. After ferocious fighting, Morazán's troops escaped, but with heavy losses. Morazán resigned as president soon after and the federation quickly fell apart. He made one last attempt to restore it by invading Costa Rica from exile in 1842 but was betrayed by his own men and shot. As for Carrera, he now became the undisputed dictator of Guatemala and would remain so until his death in 1865. Deeply conservative, with a hatred of all that liberalism stood for, he took Guatemala out of the Central American Federation, restored the Catholic Church to all of its former privileges, and defended the Indian communal lands from the greed of *latifundistas*. He also protected the latter against Indian land invasions, having acquired considerable acreage himself. But if the elite were allowed to continue enjoying their social and economic superiority, political power clearly rested with Carrera and his old Indian and *mestizo* military comrades, who now constituted the army's officer corps.

Turning to the Andean republics, almost all of Colombia's major *caudillos* were drawn from the upper classes of society.[13] The three principal ones—

Generals Tomás Cipriano de Mosquera, José Hilario López, and José María Obando—were all connected to the elite of Popayán. Mosquera was a Conservative; López and Obando were Liberals. Among them, they served for part of six different presidential terms, all of which were cut short by rebellions.

By contrast, the first generation of Venezuelan *caudillos* were illiterate *mestizos* from the eastern interior *llanos* (plains) who had risen to fame—and fortune—by following Bolívar. Of these, the leading figure was José Antonio Páez. He was a light-skinned *mestizo* whose father was a minor employee in the Spanish Crown's tobacco monopoly. He had no education and, until adulthood, could barely write his name. He fled to the *llanos* at age seventeen, after killing a man in a fight. There he worked as a cowboy, married a woman with a small ranch, and supplemented his income by leading a band of cattle rustlers. When the independence wars broke out he converted his band into a guerrilla force on the patriot side and soon proved himself to be an exceptional leader. He expanded his forces by promising to redistribute the enemy's lands after the war. He also imposed strict discipline on his men, which earned him the gratitude and trust of Venezuela's elites. At the latter's urging he pulled Venezuela out of Gran Colombia and became the country's dominant political figure, in or out of the presidency, from 1830 to 1847. He acquired several *latifundios* after the war, some of which were worked by slaves, and was accepted into Venezuela's upper class as their indispensable protector and leader of the Conservative Party.

José Tadeo Monagas, who replaced Páez as Venezuela's strongman after 1847, was another uneducated *mestizo* from the *llanos*. He had been a subleader under Páez in the struggle against Spain. Afterward, when Páez began hobnobbing with the Caracas elites and ignoring his promises to his old comrades in the interior, Monagas skillfully played on their disappointments and led two unsuccessful revolts, in 1831 and 1835. Páez suppressed both revolts by raising troops from among his own peons and winning over most of the local *caudillos*, who followed him out of personal loyalty. Once he had a preponderance of force on his side Páez graciously offered his old lieutenant a pardon and even allowed him and his officers to retain their properties.

While these tactics preserved the status quo, they also revealed how weak the central government was, for it had no regular army to speak of. Without Páez's personal prestige, it would have been helpless. As it was, the government had no funds for a long campaign. Indeed, after putting down the 1835 revolt, Páez was forced to ask Monagas's wife for a loan so that he could pay for the return of his soldiers to Caracas.[14]

To everyone's surprise, Páez stepped down from the presidency in 1847 and picked Monagas to succeed him. By that time a new generation of *llaneros* had grown up, with little personal knowledge of Páez or sense of loyalty to him. They were, however, attracted to Monagas's demagogic promises of a new distribution of land and offices. Once in office, the new president quickly packed the top military and government posts with his followers and then turned on Páez, who now discovered that his old popular base had deserted him. Monagas ruled until 1851, then turned over the presidency to his brother, José Gregorio Monagas, who returned it to him in 1855. The Monagas brothers claimed to represent the newly formed Venezuelan Liberal Party, as opposed to Páez's Conservatives, but their only liberal act was to end slavery. Otherwise, their rule was noted for an exceptional degree of corruption and administrative ineptitude. Their obvious intention of creating a Monagas dynasty drove their fellow Liberals to patch up relations with the Conservatives and launch a successful revolt in 1858 that ended such plans.

With the Monagas brothers out of the way, the two rival parties resumed their power struggles, as the Conservatives called for a strong central government and social order, and the Liberals demanded a federal constitution and social reform. The "Federal War" lasted until 1863, and even saw a brief return by Páez to power at the head of a Conservative government. But the Liberals finally succeeded in putting their leading general, Juan Falcón, into the presidency, only to discover that he had no aptitude for governing. Chaos returned, and with it one last fling at power for José Tadeo Monagas, who returned this time as a Conservative, in 1868. With that, the alarmed Liberals rallied behind another leader, Antonio Guzmán Blanco, a wealthy financial expert turned military leader, whose father had been one of the party's original founders. In the meantime, José Tadeo Monagas died and was succeeded by his inept son, Ruperto. Guzmán Blanco brought all the Liberal factions together and, in April 1870, drove Ruperto Monagas and the Conservatives from power for the last time. As we shall see in a subsequent chapter, his presidency brought a long period of prosperity and reform to Venezuela.

Ecuador's first great *caudillo*, General Juan José Flores, who dominated the political system until 1845, was an illiterate mulatto from the Venezuelan coast. He arrived in the country with Bolívar's army. After achieving Ecuador's independence in 1830, he proved to be the only man strong enough to force the contending Quito and Guayaquil factions to remain united. He overstepped his bounds, however, when he secretly colluded with Spain to turn Ecuador into a monarchy under Spanish tutelage, with himself as king. Driven into exile, Flores continued to conspire against every succeeding Ecuadorean government and managed to reduce the country to anarchy until an old opponent of his, Gabriel García Moreno, restored order.

García Moreno was a self-made man from Guayaquil who had risen from a very modest background to become a lawyer and marry into one of Ecuador's aristocratic families. He started out in politics as a Liberal publisher of a chain of anti-Flores newspapers, but after a period of exile in France he made a complete turnabout in his politics, returning to Ecuador in the 1850s as a devout Catholic and inflexible Conservative. He made his peace with Flores and together they launched a successful invasion of Ecuador in 1861. García Moreno became president and made Flores the army's commander. The two men worked together efficiently, suppressing both internal opposition and foreign threats until Flores's death in 1863. After completing one constitutional term, García Moreno stepped aside temporarily, only to grab power again in 1869 by a coup. This time he shored up his rule with the authority of the Catholic Church. He restored all the old privileges of the clergy. Religion courses were mandatory in the public schools, and teachers had to be approved by the Church's authorities. Furthermore, the Vatican received large annual financial gifts. This pro-clericalism reached its peak in 1872, when García Moreno dedicated the country to the Sacred Heart of Jesus. Although he also promoted many useful public works, including a railway system and a network of improved roads, his obvious intention of perpetuating himself in power drove some of the younger Liberals to plot his assassination. On 6 August 1875 he was attacked by a machete-wielding group in front of the Presidential Palace and hacked to death.

While Flores and García Moreno emerged from humble beginnings, the first leading contenders for power in Peru, General Andrés de Santa Cruz and General Agustín Gamarra, were upper class in their origins. Gamarra, twice president of Peru (1829–1833, 1839–1841), was a white Creole officer in the royal army who switched to the patriot side after San Martín invaded. Santa Cruz, president of Peru from 1826–1827, and of Bolivia from 1836–1839, was the son of a colonial army officer and a wealthy Indian princess who was directly descended from one of the Incas. Santa Cruz also served in the royal army, in the same regiment as his father, and like Gamarra he originally fought against independence, only to change sides later on.

Despite their similar backgrounds, the two men were bitter enemies. Santa Cruz had become president of Peru in 1826 as Bolívar's stand-in but resigned the following year in the face of violent nationalist sentiment, led by Gamarra, which demanded an end to Colombian interference in Peruvian affairs. After an honorable exile disguised as a diplomatic mission, Santa Cruz went to Bolivia, where he was asked to head an army being raised to stop an invasion by Gamarra that was aimed at forcibly uniting the two countries. He defeated Gamarra, assumed the Bolivian presidency, and in

1835 turned the tables by invading Peru. Upon defeating Gamarra again he united the two countries under an arrangement called the Confederation of the Andes. Gamarra took refuge in Chile, where he easily persuaded the government that the confederation was a threat to its sovereignty. War soon followed, ending in a Chilean victory, the breakup of the confederation, Santa Cruz's flight into exile, and Gamarra's resumption of power. Then Gamarra was killed in another unsuccessful attempt to invade Bolivia.

Bolivia and Peru thus went their separate ways, but with similar results. Like Peru, Bolivia gradually slid into anarchy. Gamarra's conqueror, General José Ball\u00edván, was a self-taught *mestizo* from a modest background who had fought as a teenager with the patriots. During his presidency he successfully promoted exports of guano and quinine, and some of the proceeds were spent on encouraging science and culture. Ballivián was eventually forced from office in 1848 by another general, Manuel Isidoro Belzú, a demagogue from a poor artisan family of La Paz. Belzú's government made populist appeals to the *mestizos*, as against the Creole elites. After seven years of rule, during which he survived an assassination attempt and forty-two revolts, he turned over the presidency to his son-in-law, General Jorge Córdova, and went to Europe as Bolivia's roving ambassador. Córdova lacked Belzú's political talents, however, and was ousted from power by an aristocratic counterrevolution two years later.

Two colorless civilian presidents followed, the fifth and sixth to occupy the office since Ballivián. Then, in 1864, a military revolt brought General Mariano Melgarejo to power: the most brutal, corrupt, and prehensile figure in Bolivia's long history of tyrants. He was an illiterate, drunken *mestizo* who had risen through the ranks of the army, and his idea of government was that of the typical *caudillo*: an opportunity for himself and his followers to plunder. His only positive act in the seven years that he ruled was to kill Belzú when the latter attempted to seize La Paz while Melgarejo was putting down a revolt in the countryside. Pretending to be captured, he had two men conduct him to the inside of the Presidential Palace; when Belzú came into the room to gloat at his prisoner, Melgarejo took out a pistol and shot him. Then he went out to the balcony, where Belzú had been haranguing a crowd, and, holding up the bloody corpse, demanded: "¿*Belzú o Melgarejo?*" After a few seconds of astonished silence, back came the collective shout: "¡*Viva Melgarejo!*"

Upon seizing the government Melgarejo set about emptying the treasury. When it was empty, he confiscated the Indians' lands and sold them. When those revenues were gone he began selling off large tracts of Bolivia's most valuable lands to its neighbors. Some 60,000 square miles went to Brazil;

Chile received an extremely favorable lease on rich nitrate fields on Bolivia's Pacific coast. When those monies were spent Melgarejo ordered a drastic reduction in the silver content of Bolivia's currency. Finally, his pillaging of the economy provoked a revolt by a strange alliance of Creole elites and impoverished Indians that ended his rule in 1870. Afterward, the Indians reclaimed their community lands.

Unfortunately, Bolivia did not achieve stability after Melgarejo's overthrow. There were five presidents in the next five years, culminating with General Hilarión Daza, one of Melgarejo's officers who had deserted him. As minister of war under President Tomás Frías he repeated his treacherous ways and seized power in 1876. Trained in the Melgarejo fashion of ravaging the economy, he tried to unilaterally alter the contracts with Chile. Relations between the two countries deteriorated until war was declared, in 1879. Although Bolivia was joined by Peru, the War of the Pacific (1879–1882) resulted in a decisive victory for Chile. It was a disaster for Bolivia, however, for the country now lost its coastline and henceforth became landlocked.

The Dynamics of *Caudillo* Politics

Many *caudillos* identified themselves as Conservatives or Liberals. These factions were not based on sophisticated ideologies but tended rather to express cultural differences. In general, Liberals claimed to be modernizers. They tended to favor free trade with England, France, and the United States; they wished to sharply reduce the power and wealth of the Catholic Church, which they considered a barrier to progress; and they favored secular education, religious toleration, and the abolition of slavery. Conservatives rallied around the Church as the backbone of traditional Spanish culture. They also favored protectionism for local artisans against the influx of products from more industrially advanced countries. Layered on top of these divisions were disputes over whether the new constitutions should centralize authority at the national level or permit more autonomy for local governments. For example, Colombia's politics divided originally over Bolívar's attempt to make himself perpetual dictator; Conservatives supported him and Liberals opposed him. After Bolívar departed, other issues kept the two sides at loggerheads. Conservatives wanted to preserve the Hispanic tradition of a strong, centralized state and a militant Church; Liberals favored federalism and a more secular society. Colombian society, including the army, was about evenly split between the two camps, and their clashes were violent.

These two major issues—tradition versus modernity, and centralism versus federalism—were not linked in the same way in all the republics. In

Mexico, Venezuela, and Colombia, Conservatives took the centralist position, hoping thereby to impose order and stability. Liberals responded by demanding federalism as the best way to promote local self-rule. By contrast, in Argentina and Central America, Liberals adopted the centralist position as the way to drag their countries forward, while traditionalist Conservatives demanded freedom for the provinces—or outright secession—in order to preserve their traditions. In Argentina, the liberal modernizers of Buenos Aires called themselves the Unitary Party, because they wanted a centralized state that would involve the country in world trade, secularize the society, and lift the interior provinces out of "barbarism." To entice those provinces into agreeing, they held out the promise of sharing the port's customs revenues. Instead, the conservative provinces rebelled and proclaimed their adherence to the Federal Party.

Caudillos did not always take party labels very seriously. Mexico's Santa Anna, for example, switched sides easily, as it suited his purposes. Beginning as a Conservative supporter of Iturbide, he switched to the Liberals, who eventually made him president. A year later, when the Liberals' anticlericalism made them unpopular, Santa Anna proclaimed himself a Conservative president. Exiled in 1845, he returned the following year at the Liberals' request to command Mexico's armies in the war with the United States. During the war, however, he once again deserted the Liberals for the Conservatives. Scheina explains Santa Anna's ability to attract both parties, despite his political infidelities, in these terms: "Santa Anna and his Mexican rivals commanded feudal armies, which they raised and held together by patronage . . . and coercion. . . . In such an environment, the brave, risk-taking López de Santa Anna dominated."[15] In the end, however, a new generation of Liberals, led by Benito Juárez, Ignacio Comonfort, and Porfirio Díaz, definitively drove him from power.

Argentina's Juan Manuel de Rosas was another political pragmatist. Although he proclaimed himself a Federalist and drove the Unitaries out of the country, his chief complaint against the Unitaries was their proposal to share the port's customs receipts. Once he came to power those revenues stayed in Buenos Aires. Such superiority of resources, plus the ability to control most commerce entering or leaving the country, allowed him to dominate the other *caudillos*. In 1852, however, he was ousted from power by one of his trusted allies, General Justo José Urquiza, who headed a coalition of exiles, Brazilians, and Uruguayans.

In Venezuela, José Tadeo Monagas called himself a Conservative when Páez picked him to be his successor in 1847; but when he ousted Páez and the Conservatives the following year he claimed to represent the recently founded

Liberal Party. Then, in 1868, having been overthrown and exiled by more doctrinaire Liberals a decade earlier, he tried to make a comeback by heading a Conservative revolt. Similarly, General Tomás Cipriano de Mosquera, thrice president of Colombia (1845–1849, 1861–1864, 1866–1867), came to power the first two times as a Conservative and the last time as a Liberal.

In reality, Liberals and Conservatives represented loose coalitions of *caudillos* whose chief concern was spoils. The party leaders were those *caudillos* with the broadest networks of relatives, friends, and clients. Minor *caudillos* attached themselves to those leaders in the expectation of sharing the rewards of victory. Defeat or disappointment might cause them to change sides, however, so the inner logic of *caudillo* politics demanded that the chief *caudillo* "must continuously find new resources of wealth which can be distributed to his following, or he must attach resources which replenish themselves."[16]

This was the internal dynamic of the *caudillo* wars that would eventually bring about order through despotism, in much the same way that absolute monarchies in Europe arose out of the disorder of feudalism. *Caudillo* politics, rather than being pure chaos, followed a certain logic.[17] Like any politician, a *caudillo* had to attract and maintain a following. To establish himself as a leader, he had to be able to distribute patronage, which in those times meant spoils—either in booty or land. During and just following the independence wars the main targets were the Crown's possessions, as well as those of the *peninsulares* and pro-Spanish *criollos*. To these would soon be added the Indians' communal lands and those of the Catholic Church. But once those were seized, *caudillos* could expand only at each other's expense.

In the scramble to grab land, one could not increase his holdings by confiscating the property of friends or kin, and seizing French, British, or U.S. property was very risky too. The only way a *caudillo* could find additional land for himself and his followers was to plunder his political rivals. Ultimately, control of the national government allowed a *caudillo* to raise taxes, collect customs duties, expropriate property, and contract loans—all of which were "replenishable resources."

Even so, it took nearly half a century after independence for most Spanish American republics to suppress *caudillo* anarchy. Political instability and endemic violence caused society to regress to a level resembling feudalism. Irresponsible and ephemeral governments contracted foreign debts that went unpaid, ruining their countries' credit. Capital fled, commerce languished, infrastructure crumbled, educational and cultural institutions declined. All this would end when, sooner or later, one *caudillo* would seize the "replenishable resources" and, with the help of foreign capital, use them to modernize his army, overwhelm his rivals, and impose the "blessings" of orderly despotism.

Notes

1. John A. Crow, *Spain: The Root and the Flower*, 3rd ed. (Berkeley: University of California Press, 1985), 78–79; Jaime Vicens Vives, *Approaches to the History of Spain*, trans. Joan Connelly Ullman (Berkeley: University of California Press, 1970), 45–46.

2. Crow, *Spain*, 150–51.

3. On the colonial social structure, see C. H. Haring, *The Spanish Empire in America* (New York: Harcourt, Brace & World, 1963), 197–203.

4. Two more viceroyalties were created in the eighteenth century. New Granada (1740), with its capital in Bogotá, embraced modern-day Colombia, Venezuela, and Ecuador. La Plata (1776), with its capital in Buenos Aires, had jurisdiction over present-day Argentina, Paraguay, Uruguay, and Bolivia.

5. Haring, *Spanish Empire*, 320; John Lynch, *Caudillos in Spanish America, 1800–1850* (Oxford: Clarendon, 1992), 35, 38, 56, 58.

6. Slavery was abolished in Argentina by the 1853 constitution; it was not completely abolished in Colombia until 1851, in Ecuador in 1850, and in Peru and Venezuela in 1854. On debt peonage, see Wendell C. Gordon, *The Political Economy of Latin America* (New York: Columbia University Press, 1965), 20.

7. Searching for Our Roots, Country Leaders, www.rootsweb.com/~prsanjua; www.mexconnect.com; David Scott Palmer, *Peru: The Authoritarian Tradition* (New York: Praeger, 1980), 37–40; Jacques Lambert, *Latin America: Social Structures and Political Institutions* (Berkeley: University of California Press, 1967), 258–59; David Bushnell, *The Making of Modern Colombia* (Berkeley: University of California Press, 1993), 288–92. Heads of state refers to presidents, interim presidents, juntas, emperors, and regencies. The Dominican Republic, which did not become independent until 1844, also had twenty-five different governments, seventeen heads of state, and six constitutions in its first fifty years.

8. Rubén H. Zorrilla, *Extracción social de los caudillos, 1810–1870* (Buenos Aires: Editorial La Pleyade, 1972); Fernando Sabsay, *Caudillos de la Argentina* (Buenos Aires: Editorial El Ateneo, 2002).

9. John Lynch, *Argentine Caudillo: Juan Manuel de Rosas* (Wilmington: Scholarly Resources, 2001), 1–3; Sabsay, *Caudillos*, 257–58.

10. Lynch, *Caudillos in Spanish America*, 228, 230–34, 358–59.

11. Lynch, *Caudillos in Spanish America*, 130–31.

12. Robert L. Scheina, *Santa Anna: A Curse upon Mexico* (Washington: Brassey's, 2002), 5, 17.

13. David Bushnell, "Politics and Violence in Nineteenth Century Colombia," in *Violence in Colombia*, ed. Charles Berquist, Ricardo Peñaranda, and Gonzalo Sánchez, 24 (Wilmington: Scholarly Resources, 1992).

14. Lynch, *Caudillos in Spanish America*, 293–95.

15. Scheina, *Santa Anna*, 88.

16. Scheina, *Santa Anna*, 175.

17. Eric R. Wolf and Edward C. Hansen, "*Caudillo* Politics: A Structural Analysis," *Comparative Studies in Society and History* 9, no. 2 (January 1967): 168–79.

CHAPTER TWO

∽

Three Deviant Regimes

Three Latin American countries avoided the anarchy that characterized the *caudillo* era. Remote, landlocked Paraguay achieved stability soon after independence under the rule of Dr. José Gaspar Rodríguez de Francia. Francia was a revolutionary who eliminated the old colonial elites, established a primitive type of socialist economy, and based his rule on the support of the peasants. Chile, after a brief period of upheaval, also found stability under strong leadership. Diego Portales was a Conservative who subordinated the military to civilian rule and grounded his regime on the traditional landowning *criollo* elites. Brazil was the third anomaly. Its independence was achieved by a descendant of the Portuguese royal family, who became Pedro I (1822–1831). His legitimacy, and that of his son, Pedro II (1841–1889), was never in question.[1] The revolutionary dictatorship and the conservative oligarchy are two types that recur in Latin America. Brazil's monarchy was unique, but it serves to highlight the differences between legitimate and illegitimate authoritarian governments.

Paraguay under "El Supremo"

Not much is known about Dr. Francia's background and childhood.[2] His father was from Brazil and originally spelled his name as *França*, or sometimes *Franza*. He became a tobacco exporter, married into a prominent Paraguayan family, and rose to the rank of captain in the colonial militia. José Gaspar, born in 1766, was the third of five children. Educated at the Colegio de San

Carlos, a Dominican "prep school," he did so well in his studies that he was one of only two Paraguayans of his generation to attend a university. It is said that his father refused to finance his studies at the University of Córdoba, in Argentina, but that a relative on his mother's side put up the money.

The university was under the strict discipline of the austere Franciscan order. Students lived in cells, ate plain food, and spent long hours in study and prayer. Corporal punishment was meted out even for slight infractions. Francia rebelled against this and became a lifelong hater of the Church and its clergy. Also, he somehow discovered the revolutionary writers of the time: Voltaire, Helvetius, Holbach, Rousseau. Although he earned his doctoral degree in theology he never took holy orders. Still, the Franciscans left their imprint on him. Throughout his life he ate and dressed with extreme simplicity. His solitary, bookish manner was much like that of a monk. He was scrupulously honest, but unforgiving.

Francia returned to Paraguay in 1785, at the age of nineteen, with a background in theology, law, algebra, astronomy, geometry, and French: an immense education by Paraguayan standards. Nevertheless, the best he could do was to find a nonpaying adjunct job teaching Latin at his old school, the Colegio de San Carlos, and wait for a chance at a regular faculty position. He also quarreled with his father at this time. Francia's mother had died three years before, while he was away at the university, but his father had wasted no time in mourning. Instead, he immediately remarried, then separated from his second wife within a year, and was now living with a mistress. There was a bitter scene between the young doctor of theology and his profligate parent, ending with Francia demanding his portion of his mother's estate and threatening to sue unless he got it. With the money he finally received he bought a small farm outside Asunción, Paraguay's capital, and a modest house in town.

Not long after this a position teaching theology opened up at San Carlos and Francia applied for it; but although he was the most qualified applicant the job went to a man with better social connections. Francia also learned that his opponents had spread the rumor that he was a mulatto, because of his Brazilian antecedents. That stung, for indeed he had changed his name from Franza to Francia in order to claim French rather than Brazilian ancestry. Incensed, Francia went to court and compelled the authorities to certify that his family was pure European. Moreover, the court required San Carlos to hold an open competition for the theology post, which Francia won handily in a debate. But he did not keep the job long, for his anticlerical views soon led to his dismissal. He then went to the town of Yaguarón, some thirty-five miles from Asunción, where his father had just been appointed *alcalde* (mayor) by Paraguay's governor. Another quarrel ensued when Francia found that his father was stealing from the town's treasury and from the local Indians. It was the final break in their relations.

Francia ran for a seat on Asunción's *cabildo* (municipal council) in 1798. Once again the old racial slur rose to haunt him. His opponents whispered behind his back that he was a half-breed, and that his doctorate was fraudulent. After losing, Francia went through a peculiar personality change that may have been a nervous breakdown. Previously he had been puritanical and ascetic; now he was seized with a passion for gambling and women. He fathered at least two illegitimate children but refused to have anything to do with them, or to support any of his mistresses. Eventually his health broke, forcing him to retire to his farm for about a year and a half.

After recovering, Francia led a more sedate life, although he continued to have mistresses up to the time he became dictator. Once in power, however, he resumed his ascetic ways, as if the exercise of power compensated entirely for the absence of sex. Meanwhile, having refused the priesthood and failed at teaching, he turned to law to make a living. Soon he was one of the most highly regarded advocates in the colony. Although his manner was cold and somewhat conceited, his honesty was legendary. He cared little for money, would often take a case simply for the principle involved, and seemed to delight in defending poor peasants and Indians against the haughty aristocrats. Indeed, his hatred of the Spanish and Creole upper classes was becoming quite open, adding even more to his reputation as a social misfit. He cared little about that at first, but in 1804 he took a case for the aristocratic Zavala family and during his visits to their house fell in love with their daughter, Petrona. When he asked for her hand, however, Colonel Zavala refused permission on the grounds that, being only seventeen, she was too young to marry. Not long afterward, however, the colonel accepted the suit of a young aristocrat, Juan José Machaín. Worse still, Francia learned that Colonel Zavala had told friends that he would never let his daughter marry a mulatto.

About this time some of the young Creole hotheads were plotting to oust the governor of Paraguay, who had become corrupt and arbitrary. They went to Francia for advice because his reputation as a lawyer, his 300-volume library (the largest in Paraguay), and his habit of going to the roof of his home at night to gaze at the stars through a telescope made rich and poor Paraguayans alike conclude that he was a wizard and an astrologer who could read the future in the heavens. Francia dissuaded them from violence and advised them to appeal to the viceroy in Buenos Aires. He even drafted the petition himself, which proved successful. A new governor, Bernardo Velasco, took over and quickly promoted Francia's career. The former social outcast became attorney general for the province and *alcalde de primer voto* (mayor) of Asunción, the highest local positions a Creole could aspire to. There were still to be setbacks, however. In 1809 Governor Velasco proposed to send Francia as Paraguay's representative to the parliament in Cádiz, where Spanish patriots were trying to organize resistance to Napoleon's invasion of the Iberian Peninsula. Once again the Spanish and Creole aristocrats raised the issue of Francia's mixed blood, demanding that the appointment be postponed pending an investigation into his alleged false statements about his background.

Events in Buenos Aires soon made the investigation moot, for on 25 May 1810 patriots deposed the Spanish viceroy and called upon the provinces of the Viceroyalty of La Plata to join them in forming a new government. They even sent an army in December to help liberate the Paraguayans. But Paraguayans had their own long-simmering resentments against Buenos Aires and therefore repulsed the Argentines in two successive battles. After the second clash, however, the two forces fraternized during a truce and Paraguay's militia leaders were won over to the idea of independence. On 14 May 1811 a barracks revolt ended Spanish rule.

Francia was included in the new patriotic junta because he had more administrative experience than any other Creole in Paraguay.[3] He was thought to be the only man capable of dealing with a new delegation on its way from Buenos Aires to discuss Paraguay's joining an Argentine federation. Thus, when the army and its popular leaders, Fulgencio Yegros and Pedro Juan Caballero, tried to overrule his orders Francia threw them into a panic by resigning. His price for rejoining the junta was the purge of all his enemies and a free hand at the conference table. When the Argentines finally arrived Francia proved to be more than a match for them. The treaty he signed, though full of lofty phrases, promised nothing concrete.

Francia's political stock rose greatly after that, but he still found Yegros and Caballero overruling some of his acts. He resigned again and this time stayed out of the government for almost a year. Yegros and Caballero were soon in trouble, unable to handle finances, keep discipline in the barracks, suppress banditry, or protect frontier villages from Indian raids. Moreover, Buenos Aires had repudiated the meaningless treaty and was sending another diplomatic mission, with the implicit understanding that unless Paraguay gave in there would be a resort to force. Meanwhile, Francia's modest farmhouse outside of town became the center of a growing movement to restore him to the government, with increased powers. Not only was he capitalizing on his reputation as a lawyer for the poor to build up a popular base, but many well-off *criollos* were convinced that he alone was competent to head the state. In November 1812 Yegros and Caballero gave in again and pleaded for Francia to return. This time he received his own infantry battalion and half of the country's arms and munitions.

With Francia back in the junta the administrative machinery began to run smoothly again. His own army officers occupied key positions around the capital, while those of his opponents were sent to the countryside to secure the frontiers and put down bandits. He now moved to consolidate his position by giving people without property the vote and holding elections for a constituent congress. With Francia orchestrating its sessions, the Congress decreed Paraguay's independence, which presented the Buenos Aires diplomats with a fait accompli. The Congress also created a system of two rotating consuls, and Francia and Yegros were to take turns running the administration. By then, however, Yegros was resigned to Francia's superiority and only expressed a wish to retire. So a year later another congress, packed with Francia's supporters, replaced the consul system with a dictatorship, to last for five years. Before that period was up, however, a third congress, meeting in June 1816, granted Francia dictatorial powers for life, with the official title of "El Supremo."

Francia was a nationalist, and his chief interest was to preserve the new republic's independence at all cost. Spanish loyalists, who still formed the social elite, opposed him, and so did many of the Creole elites who had economic ties to Buenos Aires. These latter favored some sort of federation with Argentina. Francia's response was to seal off Paraguay's borders and throw all available resources into defense. Prominent opponents were rounded up and exiled, and their property was seized by the state. Francia also used his dictatorial powers to settle scores with the Catholic Church by taking over its extensive properties as well and closing down the Colegio de San Carlos. With so much property now under state control, Francia was able to buttress his isolation policy with a system of socialist economic planning. State lands were leased to formerly landless peasants, and the government reserved the right to say what should be planted and how much it could sell for. Rent was paid in the form of produce. Leaseholds could not be sublet but were renewable. In a similar manner, the state fostered small industries for essential goods like clothing, leather goods, ink, paper, furniture, and gunpowder. A few imports were allowed, under careful state supervision and at prices that Francia set. Such goods were stored in government warehouses in Asunción; some were designated for the army, and the remainder were to be sold to the public at fixed prices. Exports of gold, silver, or livestock were forbidden, and the export of timber was a state monopoly. Merchants could not sell on credit, and the state collected its taxes up front.

Most of the state's revenues went to the army. The officer corps, ruthlessly purged during Francia's first years in power, was given privileges no other Paraguayan enjoyed, but it was also kept firmly under his surveillance. The barracks around Asunción received his daily inspection. Out of a total force of about 1,200 men in any given year, there were no more than 20 to 25 officers. Francia knew them all personally and decided on their promotions and assignments. None of them exceeded the rank of captain. He continually shifted them around, switching their commands and even putting some of them into quasi-civilian posts as regional administrators. Like the rest of Paraguay, the army was expected to provide for its own needs, from military *estancias* created out of some of the confiscated land.

Francia's radicalism gradually reduced Paraguay to the level of a socialist barracks state. Although the peasant leaseholders were better off than before, the old upper classes and middle-class professionals were ruined. Education was limited to the primary grades, and censorship put an end to the circulation of newspapers and pamphlets. The government's personnel, apart from the army and police, was drastically reduced.

At first there was resistance to this siege economy. Francia's police uncovered a plot in 1820 involving several influential citizens, including some retired military officers, who had been in touch with a secret agent from Buenos Aires. Close surveillance by spies of the homes of prominent Creoles led to more arrests later in the year. Under severe questioning, Colonel Fulgencio Yegros and other leading figures of the independence movement admitted to having planned Francia's assassination. Finally, in July 1821, the police intercepted a letter from a foreign army commander to Colonel Pedro Juan Caballero, offering to coordinate an invasion of Paraguay with an internal uprising against Francia. More suspects were rounded up, after which the principal conspirators from all three plots were sent to the firing squad. Around fifty people were executed over the next several weeks, and their bodies were left to rot all day in the tropical sun as a warning to others.

During the twenty-six years of Francia's dictatorship (1814–1840) Paraguay was ruled like a primitive totalitarian state. In addition to the army and police, Francia had the support of the common people, who acted as his eyes and ears. Convinced, like him, that Paraguay was surrounded by enemies, they turned on internal foes, both real and imagined. There was a ubiquitous atmosphere of terror and suspicion, in which any chance remark might lead to arrest. Those arrested were tortured with savage whippings until they broke down and implicated their families and friends. Although perhaps no more than seventy people were actually executed under Francia, many hundreds died in the malaria-infested jungle prison colony of Tevego or in the dark, windowless dungeons beneath the barracks where prisoners were allowed no exercise, sanitary facilities, or medical treatment. Some were victims of Francia's desire to revenge himself for past grievances. Juan José Machaín, the man who married Francia's only love, died in one of those dungeons; and Colonel Zavala, the girl's father, was sent to the firing squad.

Nevertheless, Francia had his many defenders who claimed that, without him, Paraguay would not have lasted as an independent state. It is also true that he administered the state's business with honesty and prudence. Although taxes were light, there were always budget surpluses, thanks to fines and confiscations. Francia supervised every expenditure, down to the most trivial detail. Apart from military spending, public works were carried out mainly with prison labor. Administrative costs were negligible. There was no legislature, no supreme court, and no cabinet to speak of, apart from a treasury secretary who kept accounts and a personal secretary who took notes and ran errands. The palace staff consisted of a cook, a houseboy, and a couple of maids. Local government was equally simple. Village councillors and *alcaldes* served without pay; in the larger towns army commanders doubled as intendants. Justices of the peace and appellate judges also served without pay, while Francia was the ultimate arbiter in major cases. "El Supremo" drew only a third of his salary and returned the rest to the treasury.

Francia had no interests outside of the exercise of power, to which he devoted himself for long hours every day. He stayed alone, with his four servants, in the old Governor's Palace and led an ascetic life. He never married. Women did not enter his life after he came to power. He had no friends and never accepted gifts. None of his relatives profited by his being in power; in fact, some of them were punished for presuming on their relationship to him. A younger sister lived at the palace for a brief period, but Francia eventually quarreled with her and sent her away.

The severity of this regime should not obscure its popular basis. In breaking the power of the Spanish and Creole elites who had scorned him, Francia also delighted the lower strata of society, who were eager to see their former masters humbled. His miscegenation law of 1814, forbidding any white man from marrying a white woman, was both an act of personal revenge and an egalitarian blow against the old racially based hierarchy of colonial society. Thus, when "El Supremo" finally died, in September 1840, the common people received the news with shock and dismay. So great was their fear of and reverence for the man that they could not refer to him by name but spoke in whispers of "El Difunto" (The Dead Man).

The Portalian System in Chile

Chile, a narrow strip of a country on the western side of South America, situated between the Pacific Ocean and the Andes Mountains, took its first steps toward independence in 1810 when a *cabildo abierto* set up a patriotic junta. The patriots soon broke into quarreling factions, however, and in 1814 a Spanish army drove them across the mountains into Argentina. Some enlisted in General San Martín's army, and three years later they followed him in a brilliantly executed march over the Andes that surprised and routed the Spaniards. Bernardo O'Higgins, a Chilean patriot leader who was San Martín's second in command, became supreme director of the new republic.

O'Higgins proved to be too liberal for the traditional *criollo latifundista* elite that controlled the rich Central Valley around Santiago. He funded public works programs through higher taxes on the rich; he threatened to break up the *latifundios* by abolishing the laws of entail and primogeniture; and he angered the Church by encouraging secular education and religious tolerance. Conservatives rose up in 1823, forcing him to flee to Peru. O'Higgins had given Chile two constitutions (1818, 1822); over the next six years there were three more, for a total of five, as Liberals and Conservatives struggled for power. Finally, in 1829, the Conservatives won the upper hand and installed one of their leaders, Francisco Ruiz Tagle, as president. Ruiz Tagle, in a fateful move, then brought his cousin, Diego Portales, into the government as minister of the interior, foreign affairs, war, and navy.[4]

Diego Portales was born in Santiago in 1793, the son of a royal official who headed the local mint. Like Francia, Portales was originally destined for the priesthood but changed his mind and earned a law degree at the local university. He took no prominent part in the independence movement, although his parents—who favored the patriot cause—were imprisoned by the Spaniards. After independence Portales worked at the mint, and in 1819 he married his cousin. Her death two years later left him emotionally devastated. He moved to Peru and opened a business; but constant political turmoil forced it to close in 1824. Returning to Chile, Portales purchased a monopoly concession on the importation and sale of tobacco, liquor, and playing cards, but political pressure eventually caused the government to rescind its contract, and this business failed as well.

Like Francia, Portales was a man of extreme moods. He could be irritable, caustic, vehement, and domineering; at other times he could be charming and vivacious, fond of singing and playing the guitar. He never loved again after his young wife's death, although he used women for his pleasure and had at least three illegitimate children. Above all, he had a strong will to power.

He ascribed his business failures to the vagaries of politics, so by joining the Conservative cause he aimed single-mindedly at imposing order on Chile, at whatever cost. He started a newspaper in Valparaiso and eventually launched another in Santiago, both of which called for a strong government that could guarantee law and order. It was his hard-hitting propaganda that brought him to the attention of Ruiz Tagle; but once in the government Portales helped oust his cousin for being too conciliatory and had him replaced by José Tomás Ovalle. When Ovalle died the following year Portales maneuvered General Joaquín Prieto, the leader of the successful 1829 revolt, into the presidency. Prieto would head the state for the next ten years, while Portales actually ran the government.

Portales looked to the *latifundista* aristocracy of the Central Valley to give the state a firm social foundation, so land reform was not an option. To make the Catholic Church a second pillar, he restored all of its former privileges and even required government officials to attend daily Mass. Liberal newspapers were closed and leading Liberals fled the country. Those who were caught were imprisoned and in some cases executed.

Like Francia, Portales believed in honesty and efficiency in government. With General Prieto's support, his first task was to reduce the influence of the military, which consisted of little more than *caudillo* bands. He began by purging the officer corps of those suspected of disloyalty. Instead of replacing them, he reduced drastically the military's top echelons and made sharp cutbacks in the bureaucracies of the war and navy ministries. By 1833 the military budget was less than half of what it had been a decade earlier, when military spending had created huge budget deficits and crowded out other needs. Part of the military budget now went to maintain the Military Academy and the Naval School, which Portales created to give officers professional training. Another large slice went to the newly created Civil Guard, based on part-time but compulsory military service for all able-bodied males. With 22,000 men in 1836, compared to the army's 3,000, the guard was an effective counterweight to the professional military, as well as serving as a heavily armed police force to maintain order inside Chile.[5]

The constitution of 1833, though not written by Portales, reflected his principles. It provided for a highly centralized government headed by a strong, indirectly elected president who served a five-year term and was eligible for one reelection. Through his minister of the interior, he appointed all provincial and municipal officials. There was also an indirectly elected bicameral congress. The suffrage was restricted by literacy and property qualifications, but in any case elections usually were manipulated by government-appointed local officials.

Portales did not merely intend to impose a stagnant, reactionary order on Chile. Some of his reforms were clearly forward looking. He modernized the port of Valparaiso, structured the tax system so as to promote agricultural exports, and welcomed foreign capital. Though believing in intellectual conformity, he was sufficiently appreciative of intellect to provide a famous Venezuelan exile, Andrés Bello, with government support to introduce classical studies into Chile's schools and to head a commission to draft a civil code. All of these reforms bore fruit. Political stability and a favorable business climate attracted foreign capital and technology, which in turn helped to create a long period of economic progress. That enriched the *latifundista* oligarchy while at the same time creating a merchant elite in the towns. Since these two leading classes had common interests, the Portalian state rested on a broader base.

Portales's handiwork was put to its severest test in 1836, when Chile went to war against Peru and Bolivia. The war originated in a trade rivalry between Valparaiso and the Peruvian port of Callao. Then, when Andrés Santa Cruz merged Bolivia and Peru to create the Confederation of the Andes, Portales became alarmed at the prospect of a powerful enemy to the north. An attempted invasion from Peru by a group of Chilean Liberal exiles, with Santa Cruz's not-so-secret support, brought on the war. Portales ordered the conscription of all able-bodied males and called for a state of siege, which included the order to execute any exiles who attempted to return. Portales and his staff took the lead in planning the campaign, raising the troops, and outfitting the ships. Portales, however, would not live to see the war carried through to its successful conclusion. He was kidnapped by mutinous soldiers early in June 1837 and put to death. His "martyrdom" turned what had been an unpopular war into a national crusade, and when victory finally came, in 1839, the Portalian state soared in prestige.

The Francian and Portalian States: A Postscript

Both Dr. Francia and Diego Portales were domineering, power-driven neurotics bent on establishing order and preserving their countries' independence through a strong state. In pursuing those ends, however, they created very different states. Francia persecuted the old upper class, seized its property, and made the landless peasants the beneficiaries of his Creole socialism. By cutting off Paraguay from the outside world and converting it into a self-sufficient barracks state, he reduced the living standards of almost everyone else. By contrast, Portales based his regime on the landed upper classes, opened the country to foreign trade, and initiated a long period of economic growth. Chile became an oligarchy run by the rich, for the rich.

The two kinds of states differed in other, equally important ways. Francia ruled in a solitary fashion, aided by a minimal staff. He made all the decisions, large or small, and no detail escaped his attention. Portales never occupied the presidency, although he could have done so if he had wished to. He was not concerned with titles. While he insisted that the state be run his way, he was willing to share some of the power with close collaborators— such as Mariano Egaña, who wrote the 1833 constitution, and Manuel Rengifo, who as treasury minister did much to promote economic progress. Unlike Francia, Portales attempted to leave behind a solid legal and administrative structure that would provide the state with a secure foundation.

Both states survived the death of their creator. After a few years of experimenting with a return to the two-consul system, a Paraguayan congress awarded dictatorial powers to Carlos Antonio López, who ruled from 1844 to 1862. On his death he was succeeded by his son, Francisco Solano López. The two Lópezes retained Francia's socialist economy and even extended it to include most of the landed property in rural Paraguay—although, since the Lópezes and the state were identical, the result was more like a patrimonial despotism. They dropped Francia's isolationist policy, however, on the assumption that increased foreign trade would bring the revenue and technology needed to keep upgrading the military. Under the elder, more cautious López, this program did indeed usher in a period of economic growth: improvement in the port facilities, the renovation of downtown Asunción, the inauguration of South America's first railway line, the installation of a telegraph system, and an iron foundry for the manufacture of weapons. The fatal flaw of one-man rule only became apparent when Francisco Solano López took office. Spoiled, headstrong, and ambitious to the point of megalomania, within three years he embroiled Paraguay in a war with both of his giant neighbors, Brazil and Argentina. Years of preparation for war allowed Paraguay to fight gallantly against overwhelming odds from 1865 to 1870, but in the end it was crushed and López was killed. The victorious allies and the Paraguayan exiles who entered the country with them wrote a new constitution, guaranteeing the right to private property. Over the next decade the state's holdings were sold off, including the peasant leaseholds, while the *latifundio* and *caudillismo* finally made their tardy appearance.

Post-Portales Chile followed a much more successful path. General Prieto finished his second five-year term in 1841, after which the Conservatives elected his nephew, General Manuel Bulnes, to the presidency. Bulnes had led the Chilean forces against the Andean Confederation and returned a war hero. Despite his great popularity, Bulnes refused to act like a *caudillo*. On the contrary, he encouraged a stronger, more independent Congress and judiciary. Throughout the 1840s he presided over a booming economy. Large deposits of gold, silver, and copper were discovered in the northern desert region, while coal was found in the south. Copper alone accounted for more than half the value of all exports and brought in revenues amounting to more than double the government's budget. Agricultural exports rose too, thanks to rapidly growing demand for food in California and Australia. Chile's prosperity brought in more imported goods too, so that Valparaiso became the busiest port on South America's west coast. There were public improvements of every kind. A national university was founded in 1843, with Andrés Bello as its first rector. There also were technical institutes, a normal school for the training of teachers, libraries, and a large number of new public schools. Meanwhile, Chile expanded southward until it reached the Strait of Magellan and Tierra del Fuego, giving it access to the Atlantic.

Bulnes served two five-year terms and then engineered the election of his minister of the interior, Manuel Montt. This time, however, mining interests in the north joined with southern agricultural interests to challenge the Central Valley/Valparaiso elites' monopoly on power. Though defeated, these interests would revolt again at the end of Montt's second term, in 1859. Eventually they opened up the system, since in conjunction with foreign capital and technology they were now the main basis of Chile's continued prosperity. Manufacturing also began to be important after midcentury, adding yet another element to an increasingly heterogeneous economic elite. As a result, the Conservative Party began to splinter, giving the Liberals an opportunity to take over in 1861, first as partners in a fusion ticket, and later on their own. Because the oligarchy was so heterogeneous, liberalization brought no violent upheavals—although the Church suffered defeats about secular education, religious toleration, and civil marriage. Liberalization also resulted in smaller government, reduced presidential powers, a stronger Congress, local autonomy, and the expansion of the suffrage. Finally, a second war against Peru and Bolivia—the War of the Pacific (1879–1883)—resulted in Chile's acquiring the rich nitrate deposits of the Atacama Desert, which started another period of economic expansion. Thus, the transition from Portales's Conservative Republic to the Liberal Republic was carried out without overthrowing the institutional order that Portales laid down. Indeed, the 1833 constitution lasted until 1925.

The Brazilian Monarchy

In 1808 King João VI of Portugal, fleeing Napoleon's invasion of the Iberian Peninsula, moved his court to Rio de Janeiro. Although João subsequently raised Brazil's status from a colony to a kingdom, on equal footing with Portugal, Brazilians resented the haughtiness that the court aristocrats displayed toward them. Worse, royal bureaucrats were now able to supervise matters that previously had been left to the local *fazendeiros*, as the big Creole landowners were known (the *fazenda* was the Portuguese equivalent of the *latifundio*, or *hacienda*). Resentment turned to revolt in the northeastern province of Pernambuco in 1817, and although it was quickly put down it was a warning that centrifugal forces, like Spanish America's *caudillismo*, lay just below the surface.[6]

João found Rio de Janeiro so pleasant that he would have stayed, even after Napoleon was finally defeated at Waterloo, but in 1820 a liberal government in Lisbon demanded that João either return to head a constitutional monarchy or give up the throne. He chose to return but left behind his son, Pedro, with orders to put himself at the head of any movement toward Brazilian independence. In September 1823, when the Lisbon cabinet demanded that Pedro return as well, he issued a formal declaration of Brazil's independence and proclaimed himself emperor. Some of the royal garrisons in the northern provinces revolted, forcing Pedro to hire mercenaries to restore order; but in comparison with most Spanish American countries, Brazil's transition to independence was easily achieved. Moreover, with a legitimate monarch in charge, Brazil avoided the power vacuum that led to *caudillismo* in Spanish America.

Even so, Pedro I was never popular. Although the *fazendeiros* saw the monarchy as a stabilizing factor, liberal sentiment in the towns favored a republic. When a constitutional convention met in 1823 the Liberal delegates tried to limit the emperor's powers and create a more decentralized political system. Pedro dissolved the convention and appointed a royal commission that wrote the 1824 constitution, setting up a centralized system of government with a powerful emperor at its head. There was a bicameral general assembly, whose upper house, the Senate, was appointed for life by the emperor. The lower house, or Chamber of Deputies, was indirectly elected by the municipal *senados*, who in turn were elected by a very restricted number of male voters. The emperor could convoke or dissolve the General Assembly and veto its legislation. He appointed his cabinet and prime minister without consulting anyone. He exercised the right of ecclesiastical patronage, inherited from the Portuguese Crown, and also chose the members of his top advisory body, the Council of State. He regulated provincial and municipal governments more tightly by appointing governors and municipal intendants through his minister of the interior. Finally, the emperor had something called *poder moderador* ("the moderating power"), which gave him the right to intervene—with the approval of the Council of State—anywhere in the governmental structure to preserve the constitutional order.

Pedro's popularity suffered from his high-handedness. He involved Brazil in a fruitless war with Argentina over the Banda Oriental. The army fought badly, there was widespread resistance to conscription, and in the end the British intervened to create the Republic of Uruguay as a buffer state. Britain also forced Pedro to end the importation of slaves, which the *fazendeiros* viewed as an economic death blow. Brazilians of all classes resented Pedro's preference for Portuguese courtiers who openly disdained the local population. His refusal to consult the parliament about his cabinet appointments finally caused local resentment to boil over in March 1831, after he packed his cabinet with cronies. Mob violence broke out in Rio de Janeiro, and the clamor for his abdication rose to such a pitch that even the army's loyalty was shaken. On 7 April 1831, Pedro stepped down in favor of his five-year-old son and left the country.

A regency council was set up to govern for the young boy, who would not reach his legal majority until the age of sixteen. However, without a strong monarch to hold Brazil together, centrifugal forces soon made their appearance, threatening to dismember the country. Over the next ten years there were three revolts in Bahia, two in Pernambuco, two in Maranhão, and one each in Rio de Janeiro, Ceará, Piauí, Mato Grosso, Minas Gerais, and Rio Grande do Sul. Most of these lacked *fazendeiro* support and were therefore containable with the regency's limited resources. The revolt in Rio Grande do Sul was an exception, however. It spread to neighboring Santa Catarina, whereupon the rebels proclaimed an independent republic. These outbreaks were sufficiently alarming that the Regency Council decided to bring Pedro II to the throne early, when he was just fourteen.

Pedro II, unlike his father, was Brazilian born and identified with the country and its people. Not only did he become far more popular, he also proved to have greater political skills. Instead of surrounding himself with Portuguese favorites, he spent long hours in his office studying the issues before the government, consulting with his ministers, dictating memoranda. Although he shared his father's view of Europe as being more civilized, he wanted Brazil to close the gap, and so he became an avid patron of education, science, and the arts. For the same reason, he used his "moderating power" to rotate his cabinets periodically between the two major parties, Liberals and Conservatives, hoping thereby to lay the foundations of a real parliamentary system by giving both parties experience in running the government. During the forty-eight years that Pedro ruled there were thirty-six different cabinets, for an average of one every sixteen months. Twenty-two of those thirty-six were dismissed by Pedro; another thirteen resigned for lack of a majority in the Chamber of Deputies; and one (the last) fell from power along with Pedro himself. Eleven of the cabinet changes came after the emperor dissolved the chamber. As a rule, the newly appointed minister of the interior would dismiss the incumbent governors and intendants and replace them with men from his own party. These men were then charged with seeing that the forthcoming elections resulted in the desired majority in the chamber.

Under Pedro the state gradually developed a more modern bureaucracy, expanded and staffed with talented elements of the urban middle class, as well as lawyers drawn from the younger sons of the provincial *fazendeiro* elite. Pedro also took advantage of a military reform instituted during the regency to attach the elites even more closely to the central government. The Regency Council had abolished the old local militias and *ordenanças* (commands) and replaced them with a national guard. Under Pedro II the officers of this organization, originally intended as a domestic police force, became members of an exclusive corporation. Only men of high social standing could enter its ranks, and although they served without pay they were compensated with titles of nobility and *foros* (special privileges). Eventually, entry into the National Guard's officer ranks was made a hereditary honor. *Coroneis*— colonels of the militia, drawn from the *fazendeiro* class—of long-standing service were invited to further serve the state as the emperor's courtiers or cabinet ministers. All of this helped to solidify loyalty to the Crown, while reducing somewhat competing loyalties to region and kin.

Pedro's modernizing efforts were helped by a long period of prosperity that lasted to the end of the 1870s. During this time Brazil became the leading supplier of coffee on the world market. This resulted in a shift in economic power toward the central and southern states—Minas Gerais, São Paulo, and Paraná—which were especially suitable for coffee growing. There also was a temporary boom in cotton production in the 1860s, due to the American Civil War. Brazil had favorable trade balances, despite a rise in imports caused by prosperity. New, cheap land was being settled in the south as colonization schemes attracted a large inflow of immigrants. A rural middle class began to emerge in the southern states; and, more important, immigration began to increase the size of cities like São Paulo and Rio de Janeiro. Stimulated by a parallel inflow of foreign capital into railroad building, shipping, banking, insurance, and utilities, a new urban middle class of small merchants and industrialists rapidly grew in size and importance.

As the 1880s opened, the imperial system began to show signs of breaking down. The emperor's "moderating power" now seemed anachronistic, especially as it rested upon his manipulation of elections. Liberals also criticized existing suffrage requirements that restricted the ballot to only about

1 percent of the adult population, or about 140,000 people. The Liberal Party, which was strongest in the central and southern states, became more vocal in its demands for an elective Senate and more power for the parliament as a whole. It also wanted more autonomy for state and local governments, and more secular control over education as well as over the registry of births, deaths, and marriages. More extreme liberals, who had split off to form the Republican Party, wanted to replace the monarchy with a democratic federal system much like that of the United States. They also went one step further than the Liberals and demanded a complete separation of church and state as well as the abolition of slavery.

Pedro's chief political support lay in the Conservative Party, based on the traditional *fazendeiro* elite and the Catholic Church. Nevertheless, Pedro leaned more toward the Liberals than toward the Conservatives. He had worked for the gradual abolition of slavery: beginning in 1850 he prohibited the importation of slaves; next he signed the "law of free birth" (1871), which freed the children of slaves; then he decreed (1885) that slaves over the age of sixty were to be free. As a result, he lost the *fazendeiros'* goodwill; and when he took the final step of abolishing all remaining slavery, in 1888, they supported his overthrow a year later. Pedro also turned the Church against him by refusing to outlaw Freemasonry (he himself was a Freemason) and by siding with the Liberals on the issue of secularizing education and the civil registries. But the fatal confrontation that led to his fall came by way of the army, which also should have been one of his pillars of support.

Pedro's military troubles were traceable to the war with Paraguay, in which Brazil bore the brunt of the fighting against Francisco Solano López's well-prepared defenses. The Brazilian troops performed poorly at the beginning, for the empire had never spent much on its professional armed forces, and the burden of combat fell upon the poorly trained National Guard. By the end of the war, training and morale had improved, but now the emperor decided to demobilize the conscripts and their officers. The military's budget for equipment, training, and pay was slashed. This angered those officers who wished to see the military modernized. They resented their outdated weapons, the use of press-gangs for recruitment instead of conscription, and the shortage of courses on military technology and engineering in the military academy. The growing alienation of the military from the government also was influenced by the recruitment of an increasing number of junior and middle-grade officers from the urban lower-middle class, whereas the senior officers were more likely to be from the *fazendeiro* elite. Many of the would-be military modernizers had relatives and friends in the Republican Party, who encouraged their sense of grievance.

All that was lacking was a senior officer to head a revolt, and a chain of command. Marshal Deodoro da Fonseca, a hero of the Paraguayan War, filled the first need. A prickly officer who was often critical of the government's neglect of the military, he established the Military Club in 1887 to encourage a stronger corporate feeling among the officers. The club's vice president was Lieutenant Colonel Benjamin Constant, a military engineer who taught mathematics at the academy. Constant was an ardent believer in the Positivist philosophy of Auguste Comte, with its advocacy of a modernizing authoritarian republic to be headed by scientists. His brother was a leading Republican.

The catalyst that finally triggered the revolt was the government's attempt to remove Deodoro from the scene by assigning him to the frontier territory of Mato Grosso. He went but then returned to Rio de Janeiro a few months later without official permission, just after "the moderating power" had manipulated another election. A disgusted Military Club, which had been led by Constant during Deodoro's absence, urged him to lead a coup—and he accepted. On 15 November 1889 a bloodless barracks revolt ended the empire. The former Pedro II and his family were put aboard a ship twenty-four hours later and sent into permanent exile while Deodoro da Fonseca proclaimed himself president of Brazil's first republic.

Notes

1. The period from 1831 to 1841 was the regency, because Pedro II had not yet reached his majority.

2. The most definitive biography of Francia is Julio César Cháves, *El supremo dictador* (Buenos Aires: Ediciones Nizza, 1958). Also useful are Guillermo Cabanellas, *El dictador del Paraguay, Dr. Francia* (Buenos Aires: Editorial Claridad, 1946), and Francisco Wisner, *El dictador del Paraguay, José Gaspar de Francia* (Buenos Aires: Editorial Ayacucho, 1957). Also, José María Ramos Mejía, an Argentine psychiatrist, wrote a psychological sketch of Francia's "paranoid" personality in "La melancolia del dictador Francia," in *Las neurosis de los hombres celébres en la historia argentina*, pt. 2 (Buenos Aires: Editorial Martín Biedma, 1882).

3. Francia's rise to power and his conduct of the government as dictator are treated in the biographies cited above but also in works written by contemporaries and in more recent scholarly studies. Of the former kind, three are outstanding: John P. Rengger and Marcelino Longchamps, *The Reign of Doctor Joseph Gaspard Roderick de Francia of Paraguay: Being an Account of a Six Years' Residence in That Republic, from July, 1819, to May, 1825* (Port Washington, NY: Kennikat, 1971); John Parish Robertson and William Spence Robertson, *Four Years in Paraguay: Comprising an Account of That Republic under the Government of the Dictator Francia*, 3 vols. (Philadelphia: E. Cary &

A. Hart, 1938); and Charles Ames Washburn, *The History of Paraguay, with Notes and Personal Observations*, vol. 1 (Boston: Lee & Shepard, 1871). Recommended recent studies are John Hoyt Williams, *The Rise and Fall of the Paraguayan Republic, 1800–1870* (Austin: University of Texas Press, 1979), and Richard Alan White, *Paraguay's Autonomous Revolution, 1810–1840* (Albuquerque: University of New Mexico Press).

4. For Portales's biography and his political achievements I have consulted chiefly the following sources: Simon Collier and William F. Sater, *A History of Chile, 1808–1994* (Cambridge: Cambridge University Press, 1996); Liliana de Riz, *Sociedad y política en Chile: De Portales a Pinochet* (Mexico City: Universidad Nacional Autónoma de México, 1979); Francisco A. Encina, *Portales*, vol. 1 (Santiago: Editorial Nacimiento, 1964); Brian Loveman, *Chile: The Legacy of Hispanic Capitalism*, 3rd ed. (New York: Oxford University Press, 2001); William Sater, "Portales Palazuelos, Diego José Pedro Víctor," in *Latin American Lives*, ed. Macmillan Compendium, 818–20 (New York: Macmillan Library Reference, 1996).

5. Hernán Ramírez Necochea, *Las fuerzas armadas y la política en Chile* (Mexico City: Casa de Chile en Mexico, 1984), 36. By 1858 the ratio of guardsmen to the army had increased, 38,000 to 2,077.

6. On the Brazilian monarchy, I have consulted mainly Roderick Barman, *Citizen Emperor: Pedro II and the Making of Brazil, 1825–1891* (Stanford, CA: Stanford University Press, 1999), and E. Bradford Burns, *A History of Brazil*, 2nd ed. (New York: Columbia University Press, 1980).

~

CHAPTER THREE

National Dictators

In most of Spanish America the "Caudillo Era" lasted approximately fifty years, until around the 1870s. Then the last three decades of the nineteenth century saw a gradual trend toward political centralization around strong dictators who, arising out of *caudillo* struggles, managed to eliminate their rivals. As we noted previously, the internal dynamics of *caudillismo* impelled the power contenders to continually extend their sphere of control and seek renewable resources from which to reward their followers. Such a process would by itself tend to result in one *caudillo* dominating the rest, but there were also external forces at work that accelerated the pace of change. The 1870s were a time when western Europe and the United States entered a prolonged period of rapid capitalist industrial growth. This new phase of the Industrial Revolution, characterized by large and highly productive factories, the rapid growth of population as a by-product of technology, and the migration of masses of people from rural areas to cities, created a big demand for Latin America's raw materials and foodstuffs.[1]

The scale of these external demands may be gleaned from a few rough figures. In 1820, at about the time that the Latin American states won their independence, the total value of manufacturing in Europe and the United States was approximately $5.9 billion; by 1894 it had reached almost $26.9 billion. Meanwhile, in the course of the nineteenth century the combined population of Europe and the United States had increased from just over 180 million to about 544 million. Moreover, the impact of population growth was felt mainly in the cities. In Great Britain, less than 17 percent of the population was urban at the start of the century, but by the first decade of the twentieth century that figure had risen to around 70 percent. In the United States and Germany the urban population rose from around 3 percent to about 50 percent in the same period. Translated into markets for Latin American goods, these figures meant high demands for minerals, cotton, wool, hides, sugar, coffee, grains, and meat. With respect to food-stuffs, the increasing use of steamships and the invention of refrigeration during the last decades of the century sped up the transportation of goods and reduced the amount of spoilage.

Not surprisingly, beginning around 1870 most of Latin America began ex-porting raw materials and food on a large scale. Increasingly large amounts of foreign capital were invested in mining, export agriculture, and infrastructure aimed at facilitating the movement of goods from their sources to the ports. Railway lines and improved roads reached back into the interior provinces, where investors were also rehabilitating long-neglected mines and introduc-ing modern agricultural and stock-raising methods. Along with the railroads went telegraph lines, for quicker communication. Ports were improved; ship-ping companies and warehouses were set up; banks and insurance companies made their appearance to finance and cover the risks of international com-merce. Foreign capital also brought in modern utilities: electricity, potable water, streetcars, gas, and telephones. These major industries, in turn, had a rippling effect that encouraged the appearance of smaller, ancillary enter-prises to service them and the growing urban population: repair shops; small metallurgical shops making replacement parts and simple tools; small facto-ries producing processed foods and beverages, paper, soap, furniture, glass, and construction materials. Parallel to this gradual appearance of local in-dustry was the spread of commercial establishments: retail and wholesale merchants, restaurants, bars, hotels, pharmacies, barbershops, and tailors. Many of these new businesses, especially in southern South America from São Paulo to Santiago, were started by immigrants attracted to the opportu-nities offered by the New World. But whether immigrant or native, the oc-cupants of Latin America's growing cities were beginning to form a new mid-dle class that would eventually force politics to change.

Political stability was a necessary prerequisite for attracting foreign capital and making commerce grow. Investors shunned unstable countries where plunder and extortion were the rule. Given the absence of a citizenry with the skills to make democracy a realistic alternative, stability and continuity in Latin America could be secured in this era only in one of two ways: either through a one-man dictatorship committed to modernization and capable of crushing all rivals, or through the cooperation of several *caudillos* willing to establish a political machine that would distribute benefits among them—and crush all rivals. In this chapter we will look at examples of national dictatorships, while the following chapter will describe some examples of national political machines.[2]

Mexico: Porfirio Díaz

Porfirio Díaz, who ruled Mexico from 1876 to 1911, epitomized the new type of national dictator who paved the way for economic progress by imposing order on his country. He remains a controversial figure even today, because although it is undeniable that Mexico's economy grew significantly under his dictatorship, it is also true that this was achieved at the cost of making most poor Mexicans even poorer while the benefits were monopolized by Díaz's friends and some influential foreign investors. This contradiction, which worsened over time, eventually produced the upheaval known as the Mexican Revolution.[3]

The Rise to Power

Díaz was born in 1830, in the southern city of Oaxaca, the sixth of seven children of a *mestizo* couple. The father died when Díaz was three, leaving the family in straitened circumstances. Fortunately, Porfirio's uncle was the parish priest and would soon become Oaxaca's bishop. Because of that, the boy, who had shown promise in the local primary school, received a fellowship to enter the seminary at age thirteen. There, too, his intelligence made him stand out. He seemed headed for a successful priestly career, but in 1846 two events occurred that set him off in a different direction. The first was the outbreak of war with the United States over the annexation of Texas, which stirred the patriotism of many of the seminarians, including Porfirio. The young men volunteered for military service, and although they were never called into battle, their experience with the National Guard awakened in Porfirio an interest in military life. The second event that altered Porfirio's career plans was his being hired to give Latin lessons to the young son of a law professor at Oaxaca's Institute of Arts and Sciences. Marcos Pérez, the law professor, was a Zapotec Indian, an activist in Mexico's Liberal Party, and a close friend of the local Liberal leader, Benito Juárez—another Zapotec. Pérez took a liking to the bright, energetic seminarian and introduced him to Juárez, who himself had once been destined for the priesthood but switched to law instead. Dazzled by the older men's brilliance and dedication to the Liberal cause of modernizing Mexico, Porfirio joined their party and, when Juárez became Oaxaca's governor in 1847, decided to leave the seminary and pursue a career in law. Although his uncle, the bishop, swore never to forgive him, Díaz enrolled in the institute as Pérez's protégé. He took on several jobs to pay his way: carpenter, shop clerk, tutor, librarian, substitute teacher, and law clerk in Pérez's office. He also managed to find time to join the local Freemasons and rose to be the head of the lodge. In time, he became a thirty-third-degree Mason, the highest rank possible (as was Benito Juárez). Since the Masons were extremely influential in the Liberal Party, the young Díaz was already a rising star.

Porfirio's career took another sudden turn in 1853, when General Santa Anna proclaimed himself perpetual dictator, at the head of a Conservative government. Benito Juárez, an old enemy of Santa Anna's, prudently left the country. Marcos Pérez was jailed. Porfirio Díaz went to the mountains with some of his young Liberal friends to begin guerrilla warfare against the government. When, in 1854, General Juan Álvarez, the governor of Guerrero, and his friend, Ignacio Comonfort, revolted against Santa Anna, Díaz's contingent joined them. After Santa Anna fled, in 1855, the returning Liberal exiles immediately launched a reform program, known as La Reforma, designed to break the Conservatives' power once and for all. As General Álvarez's minister of justice, Juárez abolished the military and ecclesiastical *fueros* (special privileges). Miguel Lerdo de Tejada, the finance minister, went even further by drafting a law forbidding the Catholic Church from owning any property other than church buildings and cloisters. These and other reforms, such as universal male suffrage, were then included in a new constitution of 1857. Next came elections, resulting in Comonfort's becoming president. Juárez, meanwhile, had returned to Oaxaca as governor; but he was soon called back to the national scene as president of the Supreme Court—which, there being no provision in the constitution for a vice president, made him next in line to succeed the president.

Conservatives were outraged by the reforms, and especially at the constitution's failure to designate Catholicism as the country's official religion and its failure to prohibit the practice of other religions. In December 1857 a group of Conservative army officers revolted, forcing Comonfort to resign. Juárez escaped to Veracruz, proclaimed himself president, and prepared to fight. Díaz, meanwhile, had been made head of Oaxaca's National Guard; now Juárez appointed him commander and governor of Tehuantepec. There, for the first time, he showed himself to be both a natural military *caudillo* and an astute diplomat. On the military side, he displayed personal courage as well as a talent for tactics. Though he could be a stern disciplinarian and was ruthless toward deserters, he made sure that his officers and men were paid and well provisioned. As governor, he was aware that the local population was deeply religious and decided not to enforce some of the new, harsh decrees that Juárez was leveling against the Church. His tact enabled him to win recruits for his army.

By early 1861 the Conservatives were defeated. Juárez was elected to a full term as president, but he inherited an empty treasury and a huge foreign debt that had mounted during the civil war. This was the era of gunboat diplomacy, so when Mexico declared a two-year moratorium on debt payments, Britain, Spain, and France sent a joint fleet to occupy Veracruz and seize the customs receipts. France had grander designs than merely collecting on its debts, however. Emperor Napoleon III wanted to extend his influence in the New World by placing a puppet, Archduke Maximilian of Austria, on the Mexican throne. His project was facilitated by the connivance of the defeated and desperate Mexican Conservatives, and by the fact that the United States was then distracted by its own civil war. When French troops began marching toward Mexico City the disgusted British and Spaniards withdrew. Díaz, meanwhile, had been elected to Congress, but now he was called back to the army, promoted to brigadier general, and sent to check the French advance. On 5 May 1862 the French army was beaten at Puebla and retreated to Veracruz. But this was only a temporary setback. Reinforced, the French resumed the fight the following year and finally took Puebla and Mexico City. While Maximilian was being proclaimed "Emperor of Mexico," Juárez and his government withdrew to the northern border, where they received official recognition from President Lincoln.

Once the American Civil War was won, the U.S. government began supplying Juárez. At the same time, Napoleon III was becoming alarmed at the growing power of Prussia and decided to prepare for the inevitable conflict by withdrawing French troops from Mexico. The struggle inside Mexico thus began to tilt toward the Liberals again, and their leading general was now Porfirio Díaz. Starting once more as a guerrilla leader, he had gradually built up a formidable army that routed the French and Conservatives in successive battles throughout 1866 and early 1867, at Puebla, Oaxaca, and finally Mexico City. Maximilian, who had ignored Napoleon's advice to flee, was captured and, in June 1867, executed by a firing squad.

Díaz emerged from the war as the Liberals' most prestigious general, yet Juárez received him coldly upon his return to Mexico City in July. He suspected the brilliant young general of having political ambitions, and he was right. Porfirio had a broad network of friends throughout the army, among several local political leaders whom he placed in charge as he liberated territory from the French, and also within the great network of Mexican Freemasonry. Juárez, furthermore, angered the radical wing of the Liberal Party by demanding changes in the 1857 constitution that would enhance the president's powers in dealing with Congress and increase the central government's powers relative to the states. The radical Liberals convinced Díaz to declare himself a candidate when Juárez announced that he was running for reelection later that year. The election was close, and the results were tainted by charges of fraud on both sides, but the Supreme Court sided with Juárez. Nevertheless, the challenge had been serious enough to make him drop his reform plans. But the two men were never friends again.

Four years later they contended again for the presidency, as Juárez decided to seek a third term. This time there was a third Liberal in the race, Sebastián Lerdo de Tejada. Since none of the three men won a majority, the race was thrown into the unicameral Congress to decide, and there Juárez's men and Lerdo's struck a deal: Benito would be president, and Sebastián would head the Supreme Court and be next in line to succeed the aging Juárez. This time Díaz did not accept his defeat peaceably. As commander of the eastern army, he had been preparing to revolt in the event that he lost, and now he issued his *pronunciamiento*. He misjudged his strength, however. Most of the army backed Juárez, so the revolt sputtered out and Díaz had to hide out in the mountains. Fortunately for him, Juárez died the following year. When Lerdo became president, he gave Díaz an amnesty.

After serving a four-year term Lerdo decided to seek reelection, which provoked Díaz to revolt again. Lerdo lacked Juárez's charisma, so this time Porfirio's military and civilian networks worked successfully. Lerdo went into exile and Díaz achieved the presidency he had sought for so long. He would be the arbiter of Mexico's politics for the next thirty-five years, an era that came to be known as the *porfiriato*.

Order and Progress

Latin American liberalism in general, and Mexican liberalism in particular, had become more tough minded since the early days of independence. The old liberalism of Adam Smith and Jeremy Bentham had been predicated on the exercise of "enlightened self-interest" by free, rational citizens willing to engage peacefully in negotiation and compromise. Several decades of violent warfare with Conservatives, whose defense of tradition and "superstition" often proved to have popular support, made Liberals distrustful of the unenlightened masses. If modernization was to be achieved, it would have to be imposed from above. This conclusion by the Liberals was buttressed by the spread of new liberal doctrines that claimed to be more scientific and that emphasized the role of enlightened elites in bringing about progress. One of these new doctrines was Positivism, a pseudoscientific philosophy developed in France by Auguste Comte; another was social Darwinism, whose chief exponent was Herbert Spencer. Latin American liberalism became an amalgam of those two streams of thought in the last three decades of the nineteenth century.

Positivism held that societies operate according to discoverable laws, just as nature does, and that these can be studied empirically. Comte argued that human society had developed through three broad stages: the theological, in which people explained phenomena as being caused by the will of God, or gods; the metaphysical, in which abstract reason attempted to replace theological explanations, for example, by referring to some mythical "state of nature"; and finally, the scientific, in which careful, systematic, empirical research discovers the laws of the universe. The task ahead was to develop the social sciences, so that human laws would reflect scientific knowledge instead of mere prejudice. Social Darwinism, which shared many of Positivism's assumptions, added the idea of evolution and the concept of society as a living organism that evolves according to scientific laws. According to Spencer, societies evolve from a simple and homogeneous form to an increasingly complex and heterogeneous one. As they become more complex, their internal functions become more differentiated and specialized. At the same time, those highly specialized functions become more interrelated and interdependent. Spencer also divided the evolution of human society into two broad phases. Early society was organized for warfare and/or defense. Led by warriors and legitimized by priests, the state emphasized unity and conformity over individualism. In Spencer's terms, this was militant society. Over the centuries, however, weapons became more complex and destructive. To keep up with the enemy it was necessary to develop industry and technology. Industrial society grew up within the womb of militant society, and an entirely new civilization eventually emerged that encouraged science, specialization, and private initiative. As in Marx's utopia, the state would wither away; but in contrast to Marx's vision, greater individualism rather than collectivism would result.

Taken together, these two new philosophies gave Mexican Liberals a mission and a strategy for carrying it out. Colonial Mexico had lived in the theological stage of development, where militant society ruled. The early Liberals had tried to introduce the metaphysical stage but had failed. Now it was time to enter the scientific stage and propel Mexico along the path toward industrial society. But, as Comte and Spencer also taught, progress can come about only through order. Someday Mexico might become a free society, but in the meantime an enlightened, scientific elite would have to modernize the country by force. After all, scientific truth is independent of public opinion.

Since Mexico lacked both capital and entrepreneurs to lead the modernization process, Díaz and his Liberal followers quickly reached the pragmatic conclusion that it was necessary to attract foreign investors. Given Mexico's proximity to the United States, and the fact that the latter was already Mexico's chief trading partner, good relations with the Americans became the cornerstone of Díaz's foreign policy. It also was clear that foreign capital would not come to Mexico unless there was political stability, a favorable legal climate, and an image of financial responsibility.

The process of political pacification proceeded in stages. Díaz started out as a true Liberal. He had opposed both Juárez and Lerdo when they ran for reelection, so after serving a four-year term (1876–1880) he handed the presidency over to his war minister, General Manuel González; but when the latter's term was up, in 1884, the Liberals insisted that Díaz return to the presidency as the country's "indispensable man." He was easily persuaded by them, and once back in office he stayed there through seven more reelections, until the Mexican Revolution ousted him in 1911. Similarly, Díaz also respected the Liberals' commitment to federalism, at first. During his initial term he consulted with state governors when drawing up the official electoral ticket for Congress and when making judicial appointments in their states. Governors, after all, were regional *caudillos* who headed powerful networks of relatives and clients. On his side, Díaz had the backing of the army and also his own network of local *jefes políticos* (political bosses) who were personally loyal to him. And, as the economy improved, there was more patronage for him to distribute.

To improve Mexico's image abroad and raise its credit, Díaz had his agents purchase the foreign debt in the secondary market, for about four cents on the dollar. Meanwhile, laws were changed to attract foreign capital. For example, profits could now be repatriated out of the country. To revive the extractive industry, the mining code was revised to allow private investors to own subsoil resources—although they had to actually work the mines or else ownership would revert to the state. A new land law created a commercial revolution in agriculture by permitting individuals to claim as "vacant" any land to which there was no clear title. Smallholders and Indian communities lost their livelihoods and were often driven into debt peonage, but huge quantities of land were bought up by wealthy Mexicans and foreigners (usually Americans) interested in promoting large-scale export agriculture. Naturally, this provoked rural revolts, but Díaz was quick to snuff them out with his rural police. These *rurales* were a force of some 1,600 hardened men—many of them former bandits—who were stationed around the country in eight corps of 200 men apiece. They were not well trained or disciplined, but they had a reputation for cold-blooded cruelty that frightened all but the most desperate peasants into submission. If a revolt became too much for the *rurales* to handle, Díaz could send in the army.

For the upper classes, however, the Díaz regime was legitimized by a sustained "boom" in investments and exports. In 1884 the total amount of foreign capital invested in Mexico was estimated at 100 million pesos; by 1910 that number had risen to 3.4 billion. About a third of the increase went to railroad construction, which increased from only 700 miles of track in 1880 to over 12,000 by 1910. Railroads facilitated the movement of goods from Mexico City to Veracruz, and from southern Mexico to the U.S. border. They opened up previously isolated regions to development—and also to greater control from the central government. The extractive industry attracted the next-largest amount of foreign investment (about 27 percent). Long-neglected mines were reopened and were worked with modern techniques. Shipments of silver, gold, zinc, copper, and lead accounted for the greatest share of Mexico's exports, which registered a 600 percent growth from 1876 to 1910. Agricultural products—henequen, cotton, coffee, sugar, and rubber—made up most of the remainder, enriching the Mexican *hacendados* and foreign investors.

To further ensure political stability Díaz made peace with the Church. His first wife died in 1879, but he soon remarried. Carmen Romero Rubio was from a well-off Mexican family and was a devout Catholic. They were married in a church ceremony, and she subsequently convinced him that the clergy could help him control the lower classes, if he would conciliate them. Díaz was an anticlerical Liberal, but also a pragmatist. So long as the bishops accepted his authority, he agreed not to apply the Juárez and Lerdo religious legislation to its fullest. He would not, however, allow religion classes in the public schools, would not suppress the Protestants, and would not abandon the Freemasons. Though not enthusiastic, the bishops were sufficiently satisfied to allow their parishioners to take an oath of allegiance to the constitution.

On returning to power in 1884, Díaz began tightening his grip on Mexico. He divided Mexico into eleven military zones that often were large enough to encompass two or three states. These zones were then divided into smaller military regions, and those were subdivided into even smaller subregions. Díaz personally chose the commanders of these divisions, battalions, and regiments, being careful to make sure that they were loyal. Those officers were well paid, given opportunities for graft, and frequently shifted. Thus, the twenty-seven states were crisscrossed by military commands whose top leaders were capable of keeping the governors under control. Díaz also became bolder at interfering in state politics. In most states there were rival family cliques vying for power, so it was possible for him to follow the strategy of divide and rule. By the mid-1890s he had found governors to his liking in most of the states, with the result that these men were "reelected" with the same regularity that he was. Indeed, the entire political system from top to bottom tended toward stasis. Cabinet ministers, senators, congressmen, local *jefes políticos*—all enjoyed increasing longevity in office. Small wonder, then, that in the salons of the Jockey Club, the exclusive social center where Mexico's political, economic, and military elites met to mimic the tastes and manners of Europe's aristocracy, the *porfiriato* was toasted as the model for all developing nations to follow.

Mexico's political system was thus one huge patronage machine. At the top there were cabinet ministries with their undersecretaries and hundreds of federal jobholders. There were hundreds of seats in Congress, 27 state governorships, over 300 district leaders (the *jefes políticos*), thousands of state legislative seats, thousands of municipal officials, and hundreds of judgeships ranging from the Supreme Court to justices of the peace. In addition to these various government posts there were military commands to parcel out. Every appointment, civil or military, had to be approved by Díaz. At election time he would meet with his ministers and governors to go over the official slate. Governors were expected to be well acquainted with local candidates, who in any case were usually their relatives and close friends. Díaz usually did not interfere in state or local politics unless there was some serious disturbance, such as a revolt or a strike. At the federal level, he took care of his own relatives and in-laws, as well as old friends and military comrades. At the very top was a clique of favorites known as the Científicos (Scientists). As especially influential ministers and presidential advisers, these were men strongly influenced by Positivism and who believed in modernizing Mexico. One of them was Díaz's father-in-law, Manuel Romero Rubio, the minister of the interior, who had important business and political connections in the United States. Another was José Limantour, the treasury minister, clever at obtaining foreign loans and producing yearly budget surpluses. A third was Justo Sierra, the education minister. Díaz gave each of them a long leash, but he drew the line when they tried to convince him to establish an official political party that would hold periodic conventions with regular procedures for nominating candidates. As Díaz grew older, the Científicos were looking ahead to ensuring a smooth succession, but Díaz would give up none of his discretionary power.

Díaz believed, as did many others, that he was indeed the indispensable man—the symbol of Mexico's long-sought stability and its commitment to modernization, the necessary negotiator, arbiter, and conciliator who balanced the demands of foreign interests, military needs, and political ambitions. And he worked at this role by maintaining a wide network of correspondence with politicians, military officers, and fellow Freemasons who provided him with information that allowed him to ward off trouble before it escalated. This centrality of a single individual, however, was also the essential flaw in the *porfiriato*. It worked only so long as the "indispensable man" was physically and mentally capable of staying on top of events.

In 1910 Mexico celebrated the centennial of its independence (counting from Father Hidalgo's revolt). Also in 1910 "Don Porfirio," who would turn eighty in September, announced his candidacy for a seventh reelection. Both Mexico and Don Porfirio had changed a great deal since 1876. A middle class of urban professionals, government officeholders, shopkeepers, and—perhaps most significantly—industrialists had emerged. These latter were mainly small entrepreneurs running family businesses: iron- and steelworks in Monterrey, textile factories in Puebla, food and beverage plants in various parts of the country. These entrepreneurs increased in number, thanks to the government's desire to promote national industry through protective tariffs. Still, they had little access to bank credit, for their factories were labor rather than capital intensive and could compete only if they kept down wages. The trouble was that a Mexican labor movement also was beginning to form as miners, railway workers, and industrial workers grew in number and came into contact with socialist and anarchist union organizers. Attempts to strike were met with police violence, which radicalized them. Meanwhile, out in the countryside the number of landless people was growing too. By 1910 over half of Mexico's farmland was owned by a few thousand *hacendados*, many of them foreigners. In northern Mexico the Yaqui Indians revolted when American agribusinesses moved in to claim their "vacant" lands. The first uprising, in 1886, was suppressed by the army, but others followed until finally, in 1902, Díaz ordered whole villages uprooted and sent to the Yucatán to work as debt peons on the henequen plantations. The army also crushed a revolt in western Chihuahua when Indians resisted expulsion from their lands by an American timber company. Ultimately, the most explosive element in the rural scene was the *rancheros* (small farmers) who were being reduced to peonage because they either could not produce a valid title to their land or, in many cases, could not afford the expense to fight their eviction in the courts.

Social pressure was building up from below. It became more intense beginning in 1906, when a global recession shook the Mexican economy, exposing its fragility and undermining public confidence in the regime. Mexico's exports plunged and so did the government's revenues. Unemployment spread and the domestic market for local industry contracted, driving the middle classes to protest. Meanwhile, the "indispensable man" was percepti- bly aging. Close associates noted signs of physical and mental decline: less at- tention to details, lapses of memory, irrational bouts of irritation. His insis- tence on yet another presidential term offended even some of the elites, who perceived that Mexico's economic progress was not being matched by polit- ical modernization. Then, unexpectedly, the whole gamut of opposition to the status quo found a leader in Francisco Madero, the scion of an old ruling clan from the northern state of Coahuila. Echoing a demand that Díaz him- self had once made against Juárez and Lerdo, he called for "effective suffrage and no reelection" and declared himself a candidate for president. At first Díaz refused to take seriously this foreign-educated, overbred aristocrat with a squeaky voice; but as Madero toured the country, drawing huge crowds fired up by his message and his obvious sincerity, it became clear that a serious op- position movement was building up. He ordered Madero placed under house arrest, and although the latter escaped to the United States, Díaz easily coasted to another electoral "victory" in September 1910.

But that was not the end of the campaign. Madero issued a call from ex- ile for an armed rebellion, and within weeks Pancho Villa rose in revolt in the northern state of Chihuahua, while in the south Emiliano Zapata began an insurrection of land-hungry peasants in Morelos. By the beginning of 1911 the revolution had spread throughout Mexico. Not only were the *ru- rales* overwhelmed, but this time even the army proved inadequate. For years corrupt officers had been padding the figures on enlisted men in order to pocket the money budgeted for their upkeep. Now it was discovered that the force levels were about 40 percent less than the official tallies. Moreover, the so-called enlisted men either were demoralized conscripts who had been dra- gooned into service, or were drawn from the *Lumpenproletariat* of vagrants, petty criminals, and social misfits. Such an army lost battle after battle against the revolutionary forces, who drew on the disgruntled middle classes, the urban workers, the ruined *rancheros* and displaced peasants, and reform- ers generally who were fed up with the *porfiriato*. On 21 May 1911 Díaz ac- cepted his defeat and opted for exile in France.

Venezuela: Antonio Guzmán Blanco and Juan Vicente Gómez

Antonio Guzmán Blanco, whose eighteen years of rule seem like a paren- thesis in Venezuela's chaotic nineteenth-century politics, was born into the country's social elite.[4] His father, a prominent politician who helped found the Liberal Party, had acted as a confidential secretary and amanuensis to both Bolívar and Páez. His mother was the daughter of Bolívar's sister. He himself had been an aide-de-camp to General Juan Falcón during the Federal War and was well acquainted with all the other Liberal *caudillos*. When Falcón became president he sent Guzmán Blanco to Great Britain as his financial agent, and when the latter proved successful at raising loans Falcón made him his finance minister. Along the way, Guzmán Blanco compiled a considerable personal fortune out of commissions and under-the-table "sweeteners." When the government fell in 1868 to a Conservative revolt, Guzmán Blanco escaped with his fortune to the Dutch island of Curaçao, where he planned and outfitted a Liberal invasion of the mainland. When he finally landed on the Venezuelan coast in 1870 the Liberal *caudillos* quickly rallied around him and ousted the Conservatives.

As president, Guzmán Blanco still faced the problem of maintaining order in the country, for the *caudillos*, as state political bosses, resented any interference in their affairs. Yet, there was almost continual violence in the countryside as political factions fought to control state and local governments, which were practically the only source of regular (though modest) income. Furthermore, states were often on the verge of war with each other as *caudillos* sought "renewable resources." Unlike Páez, Monagas, or Falcón, Guzmán Blanco had grown up in Caracas, the capital, and therefore had no regional base from which to raise a personal army, other than the meager, ill-equipped federal forces. He did have a reputation, however, as a financial wizard, and this he used to win over a group of *caudillos* who were willing to try his essentially Positivist scheme of creating a stable business climate that would attract capital to Venezuela. In return, he promised to share with them the greater revenues from customs duties that would flow into the treasury from increased trade.

This was the formula that underpinned Guzmán Blanco's eighteen years in power. With greater peace and order came foreign investment, in railroads, ports, shipping, banking, commercial agriculture. As he had predicted, the volume of trade between Venezuela and Europe rose, and as it did there was more money, in the form of federal transfer payments to the states, to grease the cogs and wheels of his political machine. The railways, plus new roads, opened up the interior to commerce. As the *caudillos* came to depend more and more on revenue sharing, they realized that they had an interest in maintaining the system.

Prosperity also gave Guzmán Blanco the wherewithal to increase the number of schools and promote scientific and cultural activities. Much was spent on beautifying the capital by putting up new buildings, refurbishing old ones, improving the streets, building parks, and erecting monuments. Many of those monuments were to himself, but there were also memorials to Simón Bolívar, whose image was rehabilitated as a symbol of national unity. As a typical nineteenth-century liberal, Guzmán Blanco stripped the Catholic Church of its privileges, closed the monasteries and convents, and expelled any clergy who spoke out against him.

His fatal flaw was his mania for France. Thomas Rourke depicts him as "pathetically addicted to French culture, the French language, French perfume, everything French."[5] His fortune was invested in France; his daughters married French noblemen; he owned a palace near Paris. His infatuation with France was so great that he actually tried to govern Venezuela from Paris! Three times he departed Caracas for lengthy stays in Paris, leaving behind a puppet who was supposed to carry out his orders by remote control. The first time was from 1877 to 1879; the second was from 1884 to 1886. Both times he had to hurry back to keep his government from falling apart, because none of his puppets had the confidence of the *caudillos* that he did. The third time he left, just a year after straightening out the last crisis, even his most loyal supporters decided they had had enough of "The Illustrious American," as he liked to be called. His egotism, his ridiculous Francophilia, his pilfering from the treasury, and his increasing indifference to his duties as president moved them to send him a message, informing him that he need not return. And, since Guzmán Blanco preferred real Paris salons to tropical imitations, he didn't bother to try.

His departure, however, plunged Venezuela back into *caudillo* anarchy, for Guzmán Blanco had never really tamed the local bosses—he had only bought them off. One of his generals, Joaquín Crespo, managed to last out a presidential term, from 1892 to 1898, but his picked successor was unable to keep order. In the mountainous state of Táchira, hard by the Colombian border, a provincial lawyer named Cipriano Castro raised a revolt. Having fled to Colombia seven years earlier because of a failed revolt against Crespo, he had recrossed the border with sixty men and wiped out a small contingent of government troops. In a few days his army had grown to 600, and within a couple of weeks he had 2,000 armed followers. Castro had a flair for bold military tactics. His men outmaneuvered and outfought the demoralized federal forces. At the end of October 1899 these rough cowboys from the mountains rode into Caracas and put their leader in the Presidential Palace.

Edwin Lieuwin, a student of Venezuelan politics, calls Cipriano Castro probably the worst of Venezuela's many dictators. Castro was "despotic, reckless, licentious, and corrupt," and his government was "characterized by administrative tyranny, inefficiency, graft, and extravagance, by financial chaos, by almost constant domestic revolt, and by frequent foreign interventions" to collect debts that Castro refused to pay.[6] As the dictator threw himself into debauchery he came to depend more and more on one man in his entourage: General Juan Vicente Gómez.

Gómez's origins are obscure. Thomas Rourke says that he was the bastard child of an upper-class Colombian from Cúcuta, just across the border, and an Indian woman; and that he was adopted by Pedro Gómez, a modest raiser of mules and cattle in Táchira. José Miguel Medrano, a more recent biographer, insists that he was the legitimate eldest child—out of thirteen—born to Pedro Gómez and Hermenegilda Chacón, the daughter of a respectable Cúcuta family. Officially, his birthday was recorded as 24 July 1857, during the last year of José Tadeo Monagas's rule. Medrano bolsters his argument by relating that when Juan Vicente was fourteen, Pedro Gómez sent him to apprentice with a merchant in Cúcuta, because by the law of primogeniture the boy would inherit the ranch. Juan Vicente spent three years with the merchant, and what he learned turned out to be valuable, for when he was only nineteen Pedro died. The young man became an able manager and a shrewd businessman. With the help of his brothers he expanded the size of the ranch, acquired good coffee-growing land adjacent to it, and grew the business so quickly that within ten years the Gómezes were among the largest and richest landowners in Táchira.[7]

Cipriano Castro and Juan Vicente Gómez were neighbors and friends, although their personalities were very different. Castro, the lawyer, was eloquent, colorful, extravagant; Gómez, the shrewd businessman, was a good listener and a good judge of men. He believed that Castro had a political future and decided to back him. Unfortunately, their first attempt at power, against Crespo in 1892, went bad, and Gómez had to join Castro in exile in Colombia. He lost all his property in Táchira and had to start over, but by the time they were ready for their second try at power he had gained back all his wealth. Gómez's part in the revolution was to ensure that Castro's army had a steady supply of provisions: a crucial role, if not a prominent one. Once Caracas was taken, Gómez continued to see that the rebel army was supplied, and at the same time he became the principal man in the new government for dealing with the *caraqueños* (people of Caracas). Gómez was different from the other cowboys, more businesslike, more at home with urban people. Soon Castro named him governor of the Federal District (Caracas), and eventually vice president.

The more that Castro submerged himself in the fleshpots, the more he depended on his steady, efficient friend. He even sent him out to put down the revolts by local *caudillos* that kept threatening the government. Gómez showed himself to be an officer of unusual talent. He was the first Venezuelan *caudillo* to perceive the advantage of using the railroad to move troops quickly and catch the enemy by surprise. He became Castro's best general and, moreover, he began to harbor political ambitions of his own. Castro was not blind to this, but years of dissipation had taken such a toll on his health that he finally was forced to go to Germany to seek a cure for a kidney ailment, leaving Gómez in charge. History then repeated itself. Gómez immediately began replacing all of Castro's ministers and state governors with his own men, and they, in turn, saw to it that elections would return a pro-Gómez majority in Congress. Congress then named Gómez as the new president, and Castro received a telegram telling him that he should stay in Europe.

The "Gómez Era" in Venezuela lasted twenty-seven years, until the dictator finally died peacefully in his bed. During that time Gómez either occupied the presidency himself or put a "front man" in office and ruled from behind the scenes as minister of war and commander of the army. Though corrupt and high-handed, he seemed to have an obsession with maintaining a legal facade for his dictatorship. The constitution was rewritten six times: in 1909, 1914, 1922, 1925, 1928, and 1929. Beneath it all, Gómez managed to centralize all power in himself, to the extent that his approval was necessary for every political office: the cabinet, Congress, judges, state governorships, *jefes políticos*, even minor appointments. The dictator himself ruled the country from his fortified estate in Maracay, a modest town about sixty miles from Caracas, where he lived quietly and alone, except for family and bodyguards. He governed Venezuela as though it were his private *latifundio* and he were the nation's *compadre* (godfather). Although he had come from a large family, he never married—yet he was said to have fathered more than 100 children, and provided for them all. He put his family, friends, and close collaborators into government jobs: his younger brother and his eldest son both served as vice president. Other family members were situated throughout his administration; one was minister of the interior. Others were state governors, *jefes políticos*, army officers, directors of state companies, or managers of the Gómez family properties—which included extensive ranches (Gómez became Venezuela's largest landowner), coffee plantations, and light industries in the areas of textiles, cement, food processing, and meatpacking. When the dictator died in 1935, at the age of seventy-nine, his estate was estimated at over $200 million. It had been built up by property confiscations, under-the-table payments for oil concessions, and "sweetheart" contracts from the government for public works. Throughout his rule Gómez used the National Treasury as if it were his private bank account.

Fortunately for him, his rule coincided with a long period of prosperity for Venezuela. Even before oil was discovered, commerce with Europe and the United States was on the rise. Exports of meat and agricultural products tripled between 1908 and 1913, and imports, mainly of consumer goods, almost doubled. When World War I came, Venezuela's foodstuffs were even more in demand. Gómez kept the country neutral and traded with both sides for as long as possible. Meanwhile, the first successful oil well was drilled in 1914. Oil exports were first recorded in 1918, amounting to 21,000 tons. Ten years later Venezuela was the world's leading exporter of oil, at 15 million tons a year. Gómez has been criticized frequently for allegedly granting foreign—especially U.S.—companies oil concessions on easy terms; but Malcolm Deas argues that he drove better bargains than he usually is given credit for, and that he skillfully played British interests off against the Americans. He created a state oil company (Companía Venezolana de Petróleo) in 1923 to deal with the foreign concessionaires, and a nascent nationalism can be seen in his use of oil revenues to pay off Venezuela's enormous foreign debt.[8]

Oil revenues also were used to modernize the army. The War Ministry received, on the average, about a fourth of the government's annual expenditures. Much of that went to buy the latest military equipment. Gómez also was concerned to provide his officers and men with professional training. At that time Chile's German-trained army had the highest reputation in South America, due to its victory in the War of the Pacific, so Gómez hired Chilean officers to help reorganize his army and navy. The process began with weeding out holdovers from the *caudillo* days and replacing them with younger men trained in the recently created army and navy academies. The most promising academy graduates were even sent to Europe for advanced training. In addition to the academies, the government also created schools for military engineers and schools for noncommissioned officers. All of the officers and noncoms were well paid and enjoyed special privileges. Political criteria were not entirely absent, for it was no coincidence that a preponderance of the top officers were *tachirenses* (men from Táchira). Still, by the 1920s, Gómez had a military establishment that was better trained, better equipped, and able to overwhelm the forces of any of the regional *caudillos*, or any combination of them.

Oil revenues also went to improving Venezuela's infrastructure. Most significant, for political purposes, was the expanded road and railway network that linked all parts of the country to Caracas. Much of the road building was done under the supervision of military engineers. Following closely behind the extension of the road network was the construction of new military bases that gave the federal government and its professionalized army a more effective control of the regions. Whereas Guzmán Blanco had pacified the *caudillos* by bribing them, Gómez definitively established the federal government's superiority, making the *caudillos* obsolete.

Positivist intellectuals correctly credited Gómez, not just oil, with bringing political stability and economic progress to the country. Laureano Vallenilla Lanz, the best known of them, argued in his book *Cesarismo democrático* (1919) that strongman rule of Gómez's sort was the only kind of government that could bring order to Venezuela and establish the conditions for progress. The cold, impersonal northern European races might live peaceably under the rule of law, he explained, but Latin people see no special virtue in individual liberties, freedom of the press, elections, or the alternation of parties in government. Those might work in some distant future, after material progress and education have raised the cultural level; but so far all they have ever produced in Venezuela is anarchy. For the present, Venezuelans require a more personal kind of government: a "democratic Caesar" who understands the needs of the common folk. Vallenilla Lanz became a leading propagandist for Gómez, editing the official newspaper, *Nuevo Diario*, and heading the National Archives. Other Positivist intellectuals worked in the government as well: Pedro Manuel Arcaya, a lawyer and sociologist, became minister of the interior and plenipotentiary to the United States; José Gil Fortoul, a historian, served as minister of education; and César Zumeta, a writer and diplomat, was minister of foreign affairs. Their correspondence with Gómez was full of effusive praise.[9]

Gómez cared little for their opinions, and less for their philosophy, but they gave a certain polish to his regime's facade. The Positivists were correct in singling him out as the crucial linchpin in the system, however, for as Medrano reminds us, Gómez already had been in power for a decade when oil exports began and had "built up a tremendously solid political base, without oil having played an important role."[10]

What the Positivists preferred not to dwell on were the brutalities and injustices that accompanied their vaunted "progress." Gómez had an efficient and ubiquitous apparatus of repression, beginning with the army but also including paramilitary thugs who terrorized known and suspected opponents of the regime. At the national level they were organized into a force called La Sagrada. Most of them were *tachirenses*. Well armed and well trained, they constituted the political police. Below them, reaching down into every town, were other paramilitaries, under the orders of *jefes políticos* appointed by Gómez. Linked to these paramilitaries was an omnipresent network of spies and informers who infiltrated every organization suspected of having any political purpose. That included just about any private club or association. Indeed, Gómez once ordered the closing of a Rotary club in Caracas because he thought it might become a meeting place for his opponents. Spies operated in all the government ministries, throughout the ranks of the army, in the streets, and even among the exiles in neighboring countries.

Those who were arrested for real, or suspected, antiregime activities were brutally treated. Thousands were jailed without trial, put into leg irons, and thrown into a dungeon where they remained for as long as the dictator wished, without any contact with the outside world. Many of the prisoners died from torture, hunger, thirst, or disease.

Positivists also preferred not to dwell on the widespread corruption within the regime, starting at the top with Gómez himself, and his family and friends, and spreading throughout the government and the army, all the way down to the village level. As social Darwinists, they probably cared little about the fact that for the vast majority of the population the benefits of "modernization" failed to trickle down. Because the government saw no need to spend much money on improving education or public health, the average Venezuelan remained illiterate, underfed, and unhealthy. The infant mortality rate was high, and average life expectancy at birth was barely above forty years.[11]

Gómez himself was ambivalent about the "progress" he helped bring about. Venezuela was becoming a more complex and pluralistic society, and the younger generation of students, raised in the post–World War I era, was beginning to reject the cold-bloodedness of Positivism and Social Darwinism. Social revolutionary ideas were circulating in the meetings of the University Student Federation, culminating in a strike in February 1928 at the University of Caracas. The students sent Gómez a telegram, demanding that he step aside and allow free elections. Gómez responded with the police, who arrested some of the student leaders. That provoked even bigger and more violent demonstrations, which led to more arrests. The strike dragged on from February to April, at which point some junior army officers joined the students in planning a revolt. The violence escalated. Eventually the protesters took over a government building, so Gómez brought in the army. Large numbers of students and junior officers were thrown into prison and put to hard labor. Others were exiled.

Gómez pretended to be humbled by the student strike of 1928. He announced that he would not run again when his term expired in 1929. Although a parade of his puppet congressmen went to Maracay to dissuade him, he insisted on retiring to private life. A hand-picked successor—an obscure judge named Juan Bautista Pérez—occupied the presidency for the next two years, until Congress "persuaded" Gómez to come back. He remained in power until his death, on 17 December 1935, but his last years were bitter ones. Aging, sick, and often bedridden, Gómez watched his regime being buffeted by the Depression. Nor had he found anyone in his family with the talent to take his place. In fact, when General Eleazar López Contreras took office as provisional president upon the dictator's death, one of his early acts was to order the Gómez family out of the country. The general also released all the political prisoners, lifted press censorship, permitted the exiles to return, and let the University Student Federation reappear. In the first heady days of the new government an excited mob stormed Vallenilla Lanz's *Nuevo Diario* and destroyed its offices.

Still, Gómez continued to influence Venezuela's evolution through the fact that its military chiefs were all *tachirenses*—and they, in turn, remained the arbiters of the political system, down to 1958. López Contreras had himself "elected" president by Congress in 1936. In 1941 he turned over the office to another general and Gómez protégé from Táchira, Isaías Medina Angarita. In the meantime, the former exiles from the Generation of 1928 had created a new political party, Acción Democrática, and were demanding democracy and social reform. In what seemed to be a repeat of 1928, they were joined by a group of junior officers who managed to oust Medina Angarita in 1945. This was followed by the creation of a governing junta, headed by one of the former student leaders, Rómulo Betancourt. After drawing up a democratic constitution, which was adopted in 1947, the junta scheduled elections in 1948. Acción Democrática's presidential candidate, a famous novelist named Rómulo Gallegos, won—but his administration lasted only nine months. Major Marcos Pérez Jiménez, one of the leaders of the 1945 coup, and a *tachirense*, seized power for himself. He remained as Venezuela's strongman until January 1958, when the military, reacting to popular demonstrations, restored democracy.

Other Liberal Dictators

Porfirio Díaz, Antonio Guzmán Blanco, and Juan Vicente Gómez are the major examples of late-nineteenth-century Latin American dictators who centralized their political systems and—consciously or not—employed the Positivist formula of "order and progress." Their "order" may have been the repressive type, based on the club and the gun; and their "progress" may have materially benefited only a handful of cronies and foreign investors; but the end result was to change forever the configuration of political power and, for better or worse, to integrate their economies into the world market. In doing so, they prepared the ground for the next stage of development, which would bring the lower classes into the political system and would produce a nationalist reaction against liberalism in all its forms, whether Positivism or Social Darwinism.

Meanwhile, there were other, less prominent Liberal dictators in many of the smaller Latin American countries. These deserve a brief mention because, although they applied the same principles of order and progress, they serve to illustrate how common was the combination of autocracy and liberalism throughout the region. Justo Rufino Barrios, who ruled Guatemala from 1873 to 1885, is an excellent case study of a heartless, domineering Liberal. He was determined to modernize his country, regardless of the human costs. Once, when one of his cabinet ministers reminded him of the constitution, Barrios shook his horsewhip at him and exclaimed, "This is the constitution I govern by!"

Barrios was born in 1835 in San Lorenzo, near Quetzaltenango, the capital of Guatemala's "high country" and traditionally a center of liberal sentiment. His youth was spent under Rafael Carrera's Conservative dictatorship, and although he was part of a circle of Liberal students and professors while attending law school in Guatemala City, he did not become active in politics until after Carrera died, in 1865. Then, in 1869, he participated in a failed revolt against Carrera's successor, General Vicente Cerna, and had to go into exile in Mexico. While in Mexico he formed friendships with prominent Liberals like Benito Juárez and the Lerdo brothers. Two years later he was back in Guatemala, as second in command to the insurgent General Miguel García Granados. This time the Liberals triumphed, and General Granados headed the new government. Barrios, however, was the real brains and spirit of the Liberal Party. When Granados tried to pacify the country by seeking a compromise with the Conservatives, Barrios forced him to resign and took over as president.

Once in power, Barrios brooked no opposition to his Liberal reforms. He attacked the Catholic Church, stripped it of its property and traditional privileges, and banned religious processions and the wearing of priestly garb in public. He expelled the archbishop and any other clergy who spoke out against his policies. Like most Latin American Positivists, he welcomed foreign capital as the only way for a poor country to modernize. To encourage it, he sold off public lands to foreign investors—mainly American, German, and British—to build railroads and establish large holdings for export agriculture. Guatemala subsequently experienced a rapid growth in its production of coffee, bananas, and cattle. Barrios also recognized that, in addition to stable government, there had to be an honest and efficient bureaucracy. Much effort was put into training a civil service, professionalizing the police and army, and adopting modern bookkeeping and budgeting procedures.

Above all, Barrios believed that secular education was the way to prepare citizens to participate in a modern commercial society. He ordered public schools to be built in every town and village, including the Indian communities, where resistance to secularization was greatest. Truly, the Indians exasperated him, for they resisted modernization in all its aspects. Among other things, they refused to work on the coffee and banana plantations, which were short of labor. So, in 1878, Barrios promulgated a "vagrancy law" that required every Guatemalan to work for wages. Indians living on subsistence agriculture in their communal villages were rounded up as vagrants and forced to work on the plantations at harvest time, at minimum wages. Soon they were converted into debt peons.

In one aspect Barrios was the mirror image of Carrera, because he wanted to impose governments like his on the rest of Central America. Whereas Carrera often intervened in neighboring countries to put in Conservative presidents, Barrios now intervened to install Liberals. This policy created bad feelings, even among the Liberal beneficiaries, who resented Guatemalan bullying. Annoyed by his neighbors' frequent "backsliding" in politics, Barrios finally announced that he was going to recreate the Central American Federation, with Guatamala City as the capital. At the end of March 1885, he took the first step by invading El Salvador, but a sniper's bullet cut him down on April 2.

Paul Burgess, in his biography of Barrios, sums up the man's essential failing: "The great mistake of Barrios and of so many Latin American statesmen has been that of considering progress and civilization as something which could be imposed from above by decree. The inevitable result is tyranny, and tyranny is essentially demoralizing."[12] The truth of that judgment is evident in the sequel to Barrios's death, for the Liberal Party quickly became corrupted by power. To please powerful capitalist interests, as well as the traditional landed oligarchy, it produced some of the region's most vicious, brutalizing dictatorships. Manuel Estrada Cabrera, who became president in 1898 after Barrios's nephew, José Reyna Barrios, was mysteriously assassinated, was the personification of a decadent Positivism. A protégé of Justo Rufino's from Quetzaltenango, and vice president under Reyna Barrios, he saddled Guatemala with a twenty-two-year reign of terror and exploitation (1898–1920). He continued Barrios's policies of forced labor and encouragement of export agriculture, but without any of the zeal to educate or "improve" the population. His one bow toward education was to create a cult of Minerva, the goddess of wisdom, and build a temple to her in 1919. His increasingly bizarre and repressive policies finally provoked a broad reaction that included students, labor, the nascent urban middle class, the Catholic

Church, coffee planters, and even the army. In April 1920 the Guatemalan Congress declared him mentally unfit and removed him from office.

Barrios's shadow was not quite at its end, however. In 1931 Guatemala's last Positivist dictator took power, General Jorge Ubico. Opponents whispered that he was Barrios's bastard son by the wife of a subordinate. However that might be, Ubico ruled until 1944, during which he combined harsh repression with an ambitious program of internal improvements. He extended roads, electricity, and running water throughout the country. Every provincial capital had its telegraph office, government headquarters, and military barracks. Like Díaz and Gómez, he effectively centralized power. And like Barrios, he enforced a vagrancy law that forced the Indians to labor on the coffee and banana plantations. He also followed Barrios in trying to place Liberal Party dictators in power in the other Central American countries. By 1944, however, decades of commercial growth in Guatemala had produced an urban middle class and working class that demanded a political opening in the system. Joined by students and junior army officers, they forced Ubico into exile and began an era of mass politics.

The career of Ecuador's great Liberal figure, Eloy Alfaro, has many parallels with that of Justo Rufino Barrios. Born in 1842, near Guayaquil, he twice participated in revolts against the Conservative regime of Gabriel García Moreno.[13] He finally took refuge in Panama, where he went into business, prospered, and financed a successful revolt in 1895 that brought the Liberals to power, with himself as president. He quickly began stripping the Catholic Church of the paramount position it enjoyed under the Conservatives, confiscating its property, removing state patronage, secularizing education and official record keeping, and decreeing freedom of religion. The constitution that he wrote in 1896 prohibited a president from serving two consecutive terms, so Alfaro turned over power to a Liberal Party rival, Leonidas Plaza, in 1901. When Plaza then secured the election of one of his followers in 1905, however, Alfaro staged a coup and wrote a new constitution to legitimate his seizure of power. Although the constitution guaranteed the freedom of speech, freedom of press, and freedom of assembly he arrested political opponents and shut down opposition newspapers. Still, he stepped down again in 1911 and returned to Panama. But when his successor suddenly died in office Alfaro launched another invasion of Ecuador. This time, however, he was defeated and imprisoned. While he was awaiting trial in Quito, an angry mob burst into the jail and lynched him.

Paraguay, in the period after the war against Argentina and Brazil, offers a final example of liberal autocracy.[14] After a decade of chaos, in which many rival *caudillos* struggled for power, General Bernardino Caballero secured the removal of the Argentine and Brazilian occupation forces and began the slow process of rebuilding the society and economy. It was a daunting task. The country was devastated: the victors had stripped it of huge tracts of territory, it was saddled with enormous war debts, its economy was in ruins, and half of its population was dead—including almost all of the males between fourteen and sixty. Caballero, who had fought by Francisco Solano López's side until the end, assembled a government composed pragmatically of veterans like himself and former exiles who, calling themselves the Paraguayan Legion, had accompanied the allies' invasion. They operated under the liberal constitution of 1870, a document drawn up by the Legionnaires, which repudiated the old socialist system created by Dr. Francia and the Lópezes. The rights of private property and individual liberty were to be the basis of the new order.

Although he often waved the *lopista* bloody shirt in public, Caballero understood that the only way to acquire the capital to rebuild Paraguay was to sell off the state's property, which included most of the country's land. The land sales that took place between 1883 and 1890 alienated over 16 million acres of state property. In order to attract foreign investors, prices were kept low, but the parcels put up for sale had to be at least 2,000 acres in size. In order to grease the ruling political machine, the land was first sold to Caballero's cronies, who then resold most of it to foreign interests, mainly Argentine and British. By the end of the 1880s some seventy-nine foreign purchasers owned most of the arable or forested land in Paraguay, in holdings that sometimes exceeded the size of the smaller European states. In the process, the yeoman peasant leaseholders whom Francia and the Lópezes had nurtured were turned into debt peons, working for foreigners.

There were protests from some of the war veterans and from a younger postwar generation that decried the corruption that attended the land sales. These dissidents formed the Centro Democrático in 1887, to contest the forthcoming elections. Caballero and his clique responded by organizing an official regime party, the National Republican Association—or Colorado Party, because of its red banners and ponchos. Both parties were ideologically liberal; neither advocated restoring the socialist state. The Colorados were the party of pragmatic compromise, which they justified by pointing to Paraguay's gradual recovery from the war. The Centro Democrático, which eventually renamed itself the Liberal Party, was the party of clean government. When, after years of rigged elections, the Liberals finally overthrew Caballero and his political machine in 1904, they changed very little. Their leading politicians became lawyers for the foreign agribusinesses.

From 1904 to 1936 Liberal factions squabbled over the spoils of office, excluding the Colorados just as the latter had once excluded them. While the

Liberals frittered away opportunities for real reform, however, and the Colorados sulked, another threat of war began to arise—this time from Bolivia. The controversy concerned who would control a vast wasteland called the Chaco. For Bolivia, the Chaco offered access to the Paraná–La Plata river system, and thence to the Atlantic: another route to the sea after Bolivia's loss of its port on the Pacific to Chile. When war finally came, from 1932 to 1935, there was total mobilization on both sides. Against all expectations, Paraguay defeated the larger and better-equipped Bolivian forces, largely because of the fighting spirit of its peasant-soldiers. But the Chaco War had revolutionary consequences for both countries. Officers and men, especially on the Paraguayan side, had bonded during the fighting. Once the war ended, they were determined that the conscripts would not return to their former servitude on the foreign *latifundios*. To the surprise of the outside world, on 17 February 1936 an army revolt overthrew Paraguay's victorious Liberal government and installed in power a dashing war hero, Colonel Rafael Franco, with a mandate for revolutionary reform. Nationalism would now replace liberalism as the dominant ideology, as indeed it was doing elsewhere in twentieth-century Latin America.

Notes

1. On the growth of the economies of western Europe and the United States in the nineteenth century, I have consulted the following sources: Ernest Ludlow Bogart, *The Economic History of the United States* (New York: Longmans, Green, 1915); Clive Day, *Economic Development in Europe* (New York: Macmillan, 1947); Phyllis Deane, *The First Industrial Revolution* (Cambridge: Cambridge University Press, 1965); W. O. Henderson, *The Industrial Revolution in Europe, 1815–1914* (Chicago: Quadrangle, 1961); Charles P. Kindleberger, *Economic Growth in France and Britain, 1851–1950* (New York: Simon & Schuster, 1969); Angus Maddison, *Economic Growth in the West: Comparative Experience in Europe and North America* (New York: W. W. Norton, 1964); and Frederick Austin Ogg, *Economic Development of Modern Europe* (New York: Macmillan, 1923).

2. On the impact of increased trade and liberal ideas on Latin America, see David Bushnell and Neill Macaulay, *The Emergence of Latin America in the Nineteenth Century*, 2nd ed. (New York: Oxford University Press, 1994), chap. 8; Edwin Williamson, *The Penguin History of Latin America* (London: Penguin, 1992), chap. 7; John Lynch, *Caudillos in Spanish America, 1800–1850* (Oxford: Clarendon, 1992), 425–33; Germán Arciniegas, "The Search for Order and Progress in Latin America: From Utilitarianism to Positivism," in *Positivism in Latin America, 1850–1900*, ed. Ralph Lee Woodward Jr., 1–7 (Lexington, MA: D. C. Heath, 1971); John D. Martz, "Characteristics of Latin American Political Thought," in Woodward, *Positivism*, 7–10; and

Arturo Ardao, "Assimilation and Transformation of Positivism in Latin America," in Woodward, *Positivism*, 11–16.

3. On Porfirio Díaz, see Paul Garner, *Porfirio Díaz* (London: Pearson Education, 2001); David Hannay, *Díaz* (Port Washington, NY: Kennikat, 1970); Edwin Lieuwin, *Mexican Militarism* (Albuquerque: University of New Mexico Press, 1968), 1–12; Colin M. MacLachlan and William H. Beezley, *El Gran Pueblo*, 2nd ed. (Upper Saddle River, NJ: Prentice-Hall, 1999), chaps. 3–7; and Leopoldo Zea, "Positivism in Mexico," in Woodward, *Positivism*, 65–77.

4. On Guzmán Blanco, I have consulted Mary Bernice Floyd, "Antonio Guzman Blanco: The Dynamics of Septenio Politics" (Ph.D. diss., Indiana University, 1982); Malcolm Deas, "Venezuela," in *The Cambridge History of Latin America*, vol. 5, *1870–1930*, ed. Leslie Bethell, 670–74 (Cambridge: Cambridge University Press, 1986); and Thomas Rourke, *Gomez, Tyrant of the Andes* (Garden City, NY: Halcyon House, 1936), 26–30.

5. Rourke, *Gomez*, 26.

6. Edwin Lieuwin, *Venezuela* (London: Oxford University Press, 1961), 43–44.

7. On Gómez, I have consulted Rourke, *Gomez*; Deas, "Venezuela"; José Miguel Medrano, *Juan Vicente Gómez* (Madrid: Ediciones Quorum, 1987); Yolanda Segnini, *La consolidación del regimen de Juan Vicente Gómez* (Caracas: Academia Nacional de la Historia, 1982); and Napoleón Franceschi González, *Caudillos y caudillismo en la historia de Venezuela* (Caracas: Eximco, 1979).

8. Deas, "Venezuela," 680.

9. See Elias Pino Iturrieta, *Positivismo y gomescismo* (Caracas: Ediciones de la Faculdad de Humanidades y Educación, Universidad Central de Venezuela, 1978).

10. Medrano, *Juan Vicente Gómez*, 98.

11. Segnini, *La consolidación*, 122.

12. Paul Burgess, *Justo Rufino Barrios: A Biography*, 2nd ed. (Quetzaltenango: "El Noticiero Evangelico," 1946), 126.

13. On Eloy Alfaro, see John D. Martz, *Ecuador: Conflicting Political Culture and the Quest for Progress* (Boston: Allyn & Bacon, 1972), 65–67; and Linda Alexander Rodríguez, "Alfaro Delgado, José Eloy," in *Latin American Lives*, ed. Macmillan Compendium (New York: Macmillan Library Reference, 1996), 26.

14. See Paul H. Lewis, *Political Parties and Generations in Paraguay's Liberal Era, 1869–1940* (Chapel Hill: University of North Carolina Press, 1993).

C H A P T E R   F O U R

~

Liberal Oligarchies

Many Latin American countries managed to transcend the age of *caudillo* anarchy through less brutal methods than dictatorship. We already have seen the example of Chile, which achieved a consensus among its elites by mid-nineteenth century. Other countries were slower to follow this route, but by the end of the century Peru, Colombia, Uruguay, Argentina, and Brazil had developed arrangements for governing that allowed liberal civilian elites to establish a modicum of order and material progress while continuing to limit political participation. Military rule was becoming the exception, rather than the norm, although in most cases the military continued to underpin these oligarchic governments by guaranteeing their stability. New urban elites, middle classes, and workers—a result of economic progress—were making demands for political participation that were increasingly difficult to resist.

These liberal oligarchies tried various types of power sharing. One type was the national political machine in which regional elites agreed to share the spoils of office. Another type involved assigning each party certain geographic districts in which it would rule unchallenged. Yet another type was to allow competition in a multiparty system, but with a restricted, upper-class electorate. Politically speaking, the "liberal" period in Latin America— roughly, the period from 1870 to 1930—continued to exclude the masses from politics. Still, such liberal oligarchies usually kept up a facade of republican rule, allowing freedom of speech and the press, within limits. In this chapter I will present examples of these different oligarchic arrangements.

Multiparty Oligarchies: Chile and Peru

Chile

In Chile, the transition from Conservative to Liberal hegemony was relatively peaceful, partly because of intermarriage between elite families, partly because political leaders were flexible enough to co-opt groups reflecting new sources of wealth, partly because two victorious wars lent prestige to the political system, and partly because all elite groups in Chile recognized a common interest in preserving an economic order that brought them prosperity.

> The political system of that time only included those members of the dominant class whose economic power allowed them to claim their own political space. The direct connection between economic power and political power in Chilean society conferred an oligarchic character on the State from the beginning. The use of democratic forms didn't change that character. The great landlords of Santiago and the south (more than ever devoted to exporting), the great mine owners of the Little North, and the commercial and financial groups linked to the foreign trade of the capital and its port, Valparaiso, were the legitimated actors in this system of domination. . . . A national ruling class, politically unified around a functioning model of a State that guaranteed its domination—first under an autocratic regime, later under a more liberal one—had undertaken the task of directing the society's development.[1]

Cracks in this coalition appeared in the 1880s because of a drop in demand for Chile's agricultural exports. Growers in the south sought to offset their losses by monopolizing the domestic market, for which they demanded protective tariffs. Domestic manufacturers, who were still a small but growing segment of the economy, joined them. Protectionism violated the free trade strictures of classical liberalism, which, following Adam Smith and David Ricardo, warned that free markets wouldn't work if the state interfered with the law of supply and demand. It thus implied a more active state than the classical liberals (as opposed to the Positivists) would allow. President José Manuel Balmaceda, elected in 1886, favored a more active state. He also reflected the beginnings of a nationalist sentiment among some leading citizens, who wanted more regulation of the largely foreign-owned nitrate companies. These companies' decisions over how much to produce and export were thought to have too much impact on government revenues and the economy in general to be left uncontrolled. Congress, on the other hand, was reluctant to attack the main source of Chile's income, or to reverse the trend set back in the 1850s toward hemming in presidential power.

Balmaceda refused to be hemmed in, however. When Congress turned down his requests he began issuing executive decrees designed to circumvent it. By 1891 passions on both sides had escalated to the point where Balmaceda looked to the army to impose his will, while Congress called on the navy to save the constitution. Seven months of civil war ended in Balmaceda's defeat and suicide. With legislative supremacy now firmly established, the period from 1891 to 1920 came to be known in Chile as "the Parliamentary Republic." In addition to weak presidents, it was characterized by a proliferation of parties due to the adoption of proportional representation in elections. In addition to the traditional Conservatives and Liberals, followers of Balmaceda formed the Liberal Democratic Party. There were also the small Independent Liberal Party, the National Party, and two reform parties: the Radicals, an offshoot of the Liberals' left wing; and the pro-manufacturing, pro-protectionist Democratic Party. With seven parties in Congress, it was difficult to form majority governments. Cabinets were made up of unstable coalitions. Between 1891 and 1920 there were more than 100 different cabinets and over 500 different ministers.[2]

The Parliamentary Republic, despite its many parties and ephemeral governments, was still a system in which participation was restricted to the well-to-do. Nevertheless, pressures were growing for political change. The Radicals and Democrats spoke for an expanding middle class of small merchants and industrialists, teachers, small immigrant farmers, and lower-level government workers who wanted universal suffrage and protectionism. Even more disturbing to the oligarchy was the steady rise of a socialist movement, based on workers in the nitrate and copper fields, the railways, factories, and ports. Their class consciousness was sharpened by a severe economic crisis that hit Chile around 1910, when the invention of synthetic nitrates wiped out the county's chief export. The Workers' Federation of Chile, founded in 1909 by Luis Emilio Recabarren, inspired some 293 strikes, involving over 150,000 workers between 1911 and 1920. Recabarren founded the Workers' Socialist Party in 1912, and two years after the triumph of the Russian Revolution in 1917 he established links between the Workers' Federation and the Bolshevik government that resulted in the appearance of the Chilean Communist Party, in 1921.[3]

The Parliamentary Republic ended in 1920 with the election of Arturo Alessandri, a charismatic candidate supported by the Radicals and Democrats for president. Although he promised sweeping reforms, Alessandri—like Balmaceda—was blocked by a resistant Congress. But in January 1925 Chile's army, which was usually passive, broke the stalemate. When Congress, after refusing to act on urgent measures to alleviate the ongoing economic crisis, voted itself a handsome pay raise, the soldiers surrounded the building and dismissed the legislators. At first, Alessandri left the country rather than submit to military dictation, but when he was offered guarantees of a free hand he returned. The remainder of the year (and his presidential term) was devoted to writing a new constitution, Chile's first since 1833. Although it put more power in the president's hands, and also broadened the suffrage, it unfortunately retained the use of proportional representation. Consequently, many narrowly based parties continued to jockey for power in Congress, often fragmenting and making it difficult to obtain legislative majorities. While Chile became more democratic, its democracy remained fragile.

Peru
Like Chile, Peru developed a multiparty oligarchy in the last decades of the nineteenth century.[4] In its case, however, the military preserved a greater influence over politics. Not until 1872 did the first elected civilian president, Manuel Pardo, take office. While mayor of Lima, Pardo had formed the Civilista Party among his aristocratic friends with the aim of getting the soldiers out of politics. As president, Pardo had to deal with a severe budgetary crisis inherited from his predecessor, General José Balta, and Balta's finance minister, Nicolás de Piérola. His remedy, like that of any classical liberal, was to balance the budget by raising taxes and slashing government spending. Bureaucrats were dismissed, military expenditures were drastically cut, and the armed forces' personnel were reduced by almost three-fourths. All of this was unpopular with taxpayers and military officers, and Pardo's anticlericalism earned him the Catholic Church's opposition as well. Not surprisingly, his administration was constantly battered by military revolts, many of which were inspired by Piérola, a born conspirator and demagogue with an itch for power. Pardo survived, however, and to mollify his opponents he chose a military man, General Ignacio Prado, to succeed him in 1876. War broke out with Chile three years later. General Prado left for Europe—to buy weapons, so he said—and never returned, so Nicolás de Piérola seized the presidency by a coup and tried to rally the country. The superior Chilean forces crushed the poorly trained, poorly equipped, and poorly led Peruvians, however, and Piérola had to take refuge in the mountains.

One of the few Peruvian heroes to emerge from the war was General Andrés Cáceres, who had kept up an effective guerrilla campaign against the Chilean invaders. Elected president in 1886, he launched another long period of military rule. To consolidate it, he formed the Constitutionalist Party, which engineered the election of his friend, General Remigio Morales Bermúdez, in 1890. Then Cáceres returned to office in 1894, as the result of widespread electoral fraud. Piérola, meanwhile, had created his own Democratic Party and now claimed to be the champion of civilian rule. In 1895 he and the Civilistas put aside their old feud and ganged up to overthrow Cáceres in a bloody revolt that cost an estimated 10,000 lives.[5]

In his second term Piérola hired a French mission to train, reorganize, and professionalize the military. To a certain extent he succeeded in establishing civilian supremacy, for at least all of the presidents from 1895 to 1914 were civilians. He also instituted direct elections for the presidency. Still, nothing fundamental really changed. Of the seven "civilian" administrations between 1895 and 1914, four were coalition governments of Civilistas and members of General Cáceres's essentially militarist Constitutionalist Party. All four of the contending parties—Democrats, Civilistas, Constitutionalists, and Liberals— were led by either aristocrats, military officers, or wealthy businessmen. Voting was limited to wealthy, literate males. In 1894, when Cáceres won his second term, a mere 4,539 people cast ballots; by 1904 the electorate had increased to only 146,990, out of a population of approximately 5 million. There was no secret ballot, so intimidation at the polls by *jefes políticos* was common. The only change in the old alliance of military officers and civilian oligarchs was that the latter were now the senior partners. The great mass of urban and rural poor were simply ignored.

This period, known in Peru as "the Aristocratic Republic," came to an inglorious end in the second decade of the twentieth century. Population pressure on the land in the Andes highlands, plus the growth of industry and commerce in Lima, created a discontented urban mass of factory workers, slum dwellers, and small entrepreneurs. Strikes became more common, and radical ideas—socialist and anarcho-syndicalist—were circulating. Guillermo Billinghurst, elected on the Democratic Party ticket in 1912, was sympathetic to the protests, but before he could push through a package of labor reforms the old aristocracy/military alliance replaced him with Colonel Oscar Benavides. New elections in 1915 brought José Pardo, son of the Civilista Party founder, to the presidency. Labor unrest continued, and university students joined in. The 1919 elections saw Pardo's handpicked successor defeated by an independent, Augusto B. Leguia. Facing the prospect of a hostile majority in Congress, and fearing that Pardo was about to annul the election results, Leguia sought support from the old military hero, General Cáceres. A coup ensured that the transition would take place.

Though elected, Leguia was by nature an autocrat. He imposed a new constitution on the country in 1920, then ignored its prohibition on consecutive terms by getting himself reelected in 1924 and 1929. Under his eleven-year rule he cultivated Peru's commercial and industrial elites, rather than the old agrarian aristocracy. He expected lavish public works to legitimize his high-handed methods, but the 1929 economic crash upset all his plans. As Leguia's popularity plunged, the old aristocracy convinced Colonel Luis Sánchez Cerro, commander of the Arequipa garrison, to pronounce against the government. Other military contingents joined in to remove the president in a smooth, bloodless coup. Sánchez Cerro entered Lima to a hero's welcome and installed himself in the Presidential Palace. Politically, Peru had come full circle.

Two-Party Oligarchies: Colombia and Uruguay

Colombia

Colombia and Uruguay are unique in Latin America for having two traditional parties that dominate politics and trace their origins back to the early postindependence years. In both countries the parties are more than just personalist vehicles for ambitious *caudillos*. Although they lack coherent, structured ideologies, they nevertheless are institutionalized in the sense that their followers, through generations of struggle, have developed loyalties to party labels and symbols. Certain historical events, dates, and persons act as rallying points, while inherited memories of injustices at the hands of the opposing party and desire for revenge add to a sense of cohesion.

In nineteenth-century Colombia, the Conservatives and Liberals drew support from the same upper and upper-middle classes. Many of the early leaders were drawn from the aristocratic families of Bogotá and Popayán, but in time new faces appeared from other regions and from the professional and mercantile strata. Even so, the politicians were a small, relatively closed group whose relationship to the urban and rural masses was essentially patronal. Although the Liberals were originally for universal suffrage, and incorporated it into their 1853 and 1858 constitutions, they reversed themselves when writing the 1863 constitution because they had discovered in the meantime that the Catholic clergy had more influence than they over the lower classes.[6]

Despite party rhetoric and the almost constant violence, the two parties were not ideologically distinct. David Bushnell once concluded that "one often needs a magnifying glass and an aptitude for refined hair-splitting to distinguish between the programs of the Liberal and Conservative parties." They originated in a quarrel between Bolívar and his vice president, Francisco de Paula Santander, over the former's attempt to make himself dictator for life. After Bolívar's exile those factional lines soon became blurred. By midcentury both parties had come to favor a constitutional, republican form of government with the classic tripartite division of powers. The Conservatives may have preferred a stronger president, but they still wanted his powers limited by the constitution. Moreover, both parties favored classical liberalism, with its belief in free enterprise and limited government—as opposed to the Positivism that characterized contemporary Mexico, Guatemala, and Venezuela. Finally, both parties were for individual liberties, although the Conservatives drew the line at religious freedom.

There is where the two parties divided uncompromisingly. Liberals saw the Catholic Church as a medieval force holding back progress and thought it was necessary to break the power of the Church by taking away its wealth and privileges. Conservatives, on the contrary, thought that religion was the necessary foundation for social order and decent behavior. They feared that without the common bond of Catholicism, community life in Colombia would disintegrate. In sum, both parties were liberal, except that the Liberals wished to separate church and state, while the Conservatives wanted the church and state to reinforce each other.

This may seem in retrospect like a small difference, but, as we have seen, it was enough to generate a constant climate of violence in the form of military revolts and attempted coups. Despite that, however, the level of violence was seldom enough to keep a president from finishing his term. Because of strong party loyalties, even a weak president could rally enough support to suppress a rebellion. The few instances where an incumbent was ousted are traceable to factional divisions that kept a party from closing ranks. The same was true with elections. Factions within the same party might compete heatedly for office, but only when those factions became too polarized was the party that was out of power able to supplant the current officeholders.

It was a Liberal split, beginning in the 1870s, that allowed the Conservatives to establish a political hegemony that lasted until 1930, when the Great Depression brought a complete upheaval to the political system. The split occurred when Rafael Nuñez, formerly a Liberal of the radical wing, became disgusted with the country's constant disorder and moved to the far right. Treated as a traitor by the radical Liberals, he formed his own National Party and struck an alliance with the Conservatives that won him the presidency in 1880. He turned over the office two years later and waited out another two-year term, as required by the constitution, after which he was reelected in 1884. This time the radical Liberals revolted but were crushed with Conservative help. When the fighting was over, Nuñez excoriated the Liberals as the cause of Colombia's endemic instability and announced that their liberal 1863 constitution was "dead." Again with the Conservatives' help, he wrote a new one in 1886 that abolished federalism, which had encouraged *caudillismo*, and replaced it with a unitary state in which the Interior Ministry would appoint state governors, and the governors would name the local *jefes políticos*. Nuñez also strengthened the presidency at the national level and increased the term from two years to six. This constitution, though often amended, remained in effect until 1991.

Nuñez was elected to a third term in 1892 but died in office two years later. After his death the Conservatives absorbed his National Party and consolidated their hold on power. The Liberals continued to revolt, however. The century ended with Colombia's most serious civil war up to that time, the War of a Thousand Days (1899–1903), which cost an estimated 100,000 lives, or about 2 percent of the population. Although the Conservatives won, so much property was destroyed and such a climate of uncertainty was created that Colombia paid dearly in terms of lost investment and lack of economic development.

Conservative rule ran into increasing difficulties during the 1920s. Despite official repression, a labor movement emerged in the cities that demanded reforms. Out in the countryside, a shortage of land led to clashes between Liberal and Conservative peasants. Finally, the decade closed with the onset of the Great Depression, whose disruptive effects on the economy helped bring the Liberals back to power in 1934. The new president, Alfonso López Pumarejo, embarked on an ambitious reform program that included land redistribution, import-substituting industrialization, the encouragement of labor unions, and the creation of a modern welfare state. He soon found most of his projects blocked by a coalition of "moderate" Liberals and diehard Conservatives. After stepping down in 1938, as required by the constitution, he returned to office in 1942, only to resign three years later under relentless pressure from his opponents.

The "moderate" Liberals and Conservatives then formed a "national union" coalition that brought Conservative Mariano Ospina Pérez to the presidency in 1946. However, renewed squabbling between the parties caused the Liberals to withdraw from the cabinet in March 1948. Meanwhile, the reformist wing of the Liberal Party found another popular leader in Jorge Gaitán. His assassination, a month after the Liberals left the government, touched off several days of rioting in Bogotá. This *bogotazo* led to another round of interparty warfare that would last almost twenty years and cost at least 200,000 lives.

Ospina Pérez tried to restore calm by forming another national union government, but it was short lived. The Liberals, having won a majority in Congress, tried to impeach him. He fought back by dissolving Congress, declaring a state of siege, and engineering the election of the Conservatives' most reactionary figure, Laureano Gómez, to succeed him. Gómez, an admirer of the Inquisition and the Spanish Falange, welcomed the new civil war as an opportunity to finally settle scores with the Liberals. "La Violencia" continued to escalate until June 1953, when the army, disgusted at being used to repress fellow citizens for partisan purposes, overthrew Gómez and put its leading general, Gustavo Rojas Pinilla, in power.

Rojas Pinilla's dictatorship was reformist. He appealed to "the little man" by increasing taxes on rich landowners and businessmen to pay for public works, social welfare programs, and easy credit for small entrepreneurs and farmers. When he nationalized the oil industry and the airlines, he went too far for the country's elites, who were thoroughly alarmed. Liberal and Conservative leaders put aside their old quarrels and closed ranks against "the demagogic tyrant." In July 1956 they met in Benidorm, Spain, to forge the National Front, which, after ousting Rojas Pinilla, would (1) divide equally all legislative seats, both at the national and local levels, between the two parties; (2) divide equally all cabinet and subcabinet posts, and seats on the Supreme Court; and (3) rotate the presidency between the two parties. The pact would remain in force until 1974.

The army, respecting Colombia's long tradition of civilian rule, removed Rojas Pinilla from power in May 1957 and turned power over to the National Front. For the next sixteen years this elite arrangement monopolized political power. No other parties could be legally recognized, although Rojas Pinilla returned from exile in 1958 and formed a "movement" known as the National Popular Alliance (ANAPO). Especially in the cities, the lower and lower-middle classes rallied around him. In the 1970 presidential race he garnered 39 percent of the vote, according to the official tally. (Rojas claimed that he was denied a victory through fraud.) ANAPO was essentially a personalist vehicle, however, and Rojas's declining health eventually caused it to fade away.

After the National Front dissolved in 1974 its two parties settled down to more peaceful competition, but only because they both were faced by new and even more threatening challenges. During their long monopoly of power they had excluded other political alternatives. Moreover, they had put an end to reformism. "Political elites failed to incorporate new groups into the system or to diminish structural unemployment," conclude one pair of observers, "and consequently guerrilla movements, drug trafficking, and an underground economy flourished."[7] Linked to the Communist Party, and battlehardened from the period of "La Violencia," groups like the Armed Forces of the Colombian Revolution (FARC) and the Army of National Liberation (ELN) controlled large territories in Colombia's remote interior. They constituted de facto governments, distributing land to peasants, selling protection to drug dealers, and raising money through kidnapping and extortion. In the absence of any protection from the legal authorities, landowners in nearby regions formed paramilitary "death squads" to strike back at the guerrillas. Thus, Colombia's long history of violence and lawlessness continued into the twenty-first century: the product of oligarchic rule behind a democratic facade.

Uruguay

Uruguay's two traditional parties, the Blancos ("Whites," or National Party) and the Colorados ("Reds"), trace their roots back to civil wars that wracked the country in its first decades after independence.[8] The Blancos had their main strength in the rural interior, where they raised their armies from the great landowning *caudillos* and their gaucho clientele. The Colorados were based mainly in the port city of Montevideo, an important commercial center. Each party had support from outside. Argentina's gaucho dictator, Juan Manuel de Rosas, had a natural affinity for the Blancos, especially since many of his Unitary opponents had taken refuge in Montevideo. Brazil, Argentina's rival for power in the La Plata region, backed the Colorados. From 1843 to 1852 the Blancos' chief, Manuel Oribe, aided by Rosas, laid siege to Montevideo. The city resisted heroically, its Colorado forces supplemented by Brazil and by romantic foreign legionnaires led by Giuseppe Garibaldi. Furthermore, Great Britain and France, who were intent on ending Rosas's control of access to the La Plata–Paraná river system, kept the city's inhabitants provisioned. Rosas's fall from power in 1852 ended the siege and tilted the political balance toward the Colorados and their main foreign backer, Brazil. Revolts and counterrevolts continued for another decade, and Brazil often intervened on the Colorado side. The Blancos then turned to Paraguay for support, but the Paraguayan War that erupted in 1865 and ended with the defeat and death of Francisco Solano López in 1870 gave the Colorados a permanent advantage. Every government from 1865 to 1958 was headed by a Colorado: a ninety-three-year hegemony.

Similar to other Latin American republics of that time, the Colorados' hegemony rested upon a military base. From 1876 to 1890 three Colorado military officers—Colonel Lorenzo Latorre, Colonel Máximo Santos, and Colonel Máximo Tajes—controlled the presidency. But the Colorados' strength was bolstered by other important factors too. In the same period the country's population more than doubled, and Montevideo's tripled. In 1870 about one out of five Uruguayans lived in the capital; by the turn of the century more than one in three did. The city had expanded far beyond its old colonial walls. It was now the terminus of a railway network that fanned out into the interior, bringing agricultural and pastoral products to its busy port. Its streets were lit by gas lamps, its houses were serviced by running water and a modern sewage system, and its downtown was an imposing cluster of banks, stores, and office buildings. The railroads, banks, and utilities were built by foreign capital; but parallel to this, and important for the political future, was a large influx of European immigrants. Uruguay, with its great expanses of fertile land and its well-situated port, had long attracted foreign settlers. As early as the 1860s some 25 percent of the population was foreign born. By the end of the century that number had risen to 30 percent—and in Montevideo it was about 42 percent. Commercial shops and services as well as small manufacturing establishments were largely in the hands of this new urban-immigrant bourgeoisie. About two-thirds of the urban working class was foreign born as well.

The rural areas were becoming transformed too. In 1888 there were about 3,900 owners of rural property, of whom an estimated 3,000 were immigrants. The railroad had opened up opportunities to produce for export, and those immigrants showed the way by introducing sheep raising for wool. By the end of the century wool was Uruguay's leading export. The cattle industry also improved with the importation of European breeds and better varieties of pasturage. Modern stock-raising methods included the fencing in of ranchland, which doomed the free-roaming gaucho. In place of the traditional rural *caudillo* and his gaucho band there now appeared the agrarian capitalist, often a medium-sized sheep raiser, who belonged to the newly founded Agrarian Society (1871) and scowled on revolutions as being bad for business.

Since nearly everyone had a stake in order and stability, the Blancos and Colorados reached a deal in 1872 that became known as "co-participation." Under its terms, the majority Colorados agreed to give the Blancos a free hand in four of Uruguay's thirteen departments (the equivalent of states or provinces). That meant that the Blancos would have guaranteed representation in the Senate and Chamber of Deputies. Co-participation brought a generation of peace and liberal reform. A system of free, secular public schools was created, local industry expanded behind protective tariff walls, and civilians finally took over from the military in 1890. It was far from being a perfect system, however. The Colorados' civilian presidents were in many ways as authoritarian as the colonels had been. They restricted the suffrage, handpicked the *jefes políticos*, and even tried to cheat on the co-participation deal by reducing the Blancos to only three departments. That touched off a revolt in 1897 that ended with boundaries being redrawn to create nineteen new departments, of which six would be reserved for the

Blancos. The Blancos also were guaranteed one-third of the seats in Congress if they managed to get one-fourth of the total vote.

Co-participation took on a different form after the 1903 election of José Batlle y Ordóñez to the presidency. Batlle was opposed to deals that would make elections meaningless by giving Blancos a free hand in certain departments. He favored instead a system of open elections with proportional representation. The Blancos, knowing of Batlle's intention to extend the suffrage, feared his popularity and felt betrayed. Another revolt in 1904 lasted nine bloody, destructive months and ended in a complete Colorado victory. Twice president (1903–1907 and 1911–1915), Batlle would dominate his country's political life until his death in 1929 and carry out a peaceful revolution. He instituted universal male suffrage, nationalized big foreign enterprises, protected small domestic industries through tariffs, improved working conditions, encouraged public education, created a modern social welfare system, and completely separated church and state.

Batlle's great concerns were to maintain peace with the Blancos and to prevent any return to dictatorship by diluting the executive power. To achieve this, the Colorados called a constitutional convention in 1918 and worked out a deal beforehand with the Blancos by which the executive branch would be divided between a president, who would supervise the ministries of foreign affairs, defense, and the interior, and a nine-man body called the National Council of Administration, which would be in charge of the ministries dealing with education, finance, economic development, and health. Six of the Council's members would be from the majority party and three would come from the minority. All males over eighteen could vote (women first voted in 1934), registration was obligatory, voting would be secret, and congressional seats would be allocated according to proportional representation. These reforms increased the electorate from 46,000 when Batlle was first elected to over 188,000 in 1919; but they also restored co-participation. Furthermore, they split both parties, for not everyone approved of the new constitution. The constitution even encouraged factionalism by setting up an extreme form of proportional representation in which not only the parties, but also the factions within the parties, would be represented according to their electoral strength.

This system lasted until 1933, when it was clear that the divided executive was too cumbersome to deal with the crisis of the Great Depression. President Gabriel Terra, an anti-Batlle Colorado, made a new deal with Luis Alberto de Herrera, the main Blanco leader, that allowed him to assume dictatorial powers. Both parties were afraid that because of the Depression, Great Britain, the county's chief trading partner, would stop importing wool and meat from Uruguay in order to preserve its market for Commonwealth members. Since the *batllista* wing of the Colorado Party had long been antagonistic to foreign capital, Uruguay's rural and mercantile interests wanted to eliminate the National Council of Administration as a way of getting the *batllistas* out of the government. As expected, the British Foreign Office was so pleased by the coup that Uruguay was allowed to keep its access to the British market, albeit at a reduced level.

A new constitution promulgated in 1934 gave the Colorados and Blancos equal representation in the Senate. In addition, Terra included the Blancos in his cabinet and gave them representation on the boards of all state-owned companies. Ironically, it was Terra's picked successor, his brother-in-law and chief of police General Alfredo Baldomir, who ended this latest form of co-participation in February 1942. Support for the Allies' cause was widespread in Uruguay, yet many Blanco leaders were displaying strong pro-fascist sympathies. Baldomir proclaimed a state of siege, dismissed the Blancos from their government posts, dissolved Congress, and appointed a council of state to draft a new constitution. The new document, which restored the presidential system and democratic guarantees, was approved in November 1942.

One-Party Oligarchies: Argentina and Brazil

Argentina
The overthrow of Juan Manuel de Rosas in 1852 was followed by a convention attended by all of the Argentine provinces for the purpose of drafting a new constitution. The interior provinces still demanded a federal structure of government but abandoned their old insistence upon internal trade barriers. They would accept the city of Buenos Aires as the country's logical capital but wanted it converted into a federal district so that its port revenues would be shared by everyone. The *porteños* (residents of the city and province of Buenos Aires), however, rejected any loss of control over the port or the income it received from taxing imports and exports. By the time that the convention produced the constitution of 1853, Buenos Aires had withdrawn and refused to ratify the document. Thus, from 1853 to 1862 Argentina had two parallel governments: one in Paraná, the capital of General Urquiza's home state of Entre Ríos, and a second in Buenos Aires. A series of clashes between the two governments' armies—one led by Urquiza and the other by General Bartolomé Mitre—ended in 1862 with a compromise: Buenos Aires accepted the 1853 constitution but kept control of the port. Mitre became Argentina's first president under a united government.[9]

Bartolomé Mitre's career is, in many important respects, central to the story of Argentina's development in the second half of the nineteenth century. Born in 1821 to a *porteño* family, in 1837, at the early age of sixteen, he was forced into exile by Rosas for participating in a "suspicious" circle of intellectuals called the Asociación de Mayo. The group had been formed by a young poet and novelist, Esteban Echeverría, who recently had returned from studying in Paris. Although its purpose was ostensibly to study Argentina's independence movement, it really met to revive the liberal ideas of the Unitaries. Once in exile, its members scattered. Juan Bautista Alberdi, whose writings on law would someday influence the 1853 constitution, went to France. Domingo Sarmiento, whose famous polemical work, *Facundo, or Civilization versus Barbarism*, would become the classic indictment of the crude, savage conditions in rural Argentina that made possible tyrants like Rosas, went to Chile. Echeverría and Mitre went to Uruguay. There Echeverría published his progressive ideas in a work called *Dogma Socialista*. Unfortunately, he did not live to see Rosas overthrown. Mitre became a journalist and a soldier in the Colorados' army. After serving as an artillery officer during the siege of Montevideo he visited Bolivia to help establish a military academy. From there he went to Chile, joined Sarmiento, and worked as a journalist. When Urquiza rose up against Rosas, Mitre hurried back to join the fight. He quarreled with Urquiza (and Alberdi) afterward, however, over the issue of federalizing the city of Buenos Aires. After defeating Urquiza in 1861, Mitre united Argentina on Buenos Aires' terms.

The 1853 constitution, patterned closely upon the U.S. Constitution, contained the classic liberal separation of powers with checks and balances. The president was to be chosen by an electoral college every six years. In order to discourage one-man rule, he could not immediately succeed himself. There was to be a bicameral congress with the upper house, or Senate, based on equal representation of the provinces and chosen by the provincial legislatures for nine-year terms. The lower house, or Chamber of Deputies, was directly elected for four years, but voting was restricted by income and literacy requirements. There was a supreme court, consisting of five justices who served for life. A bill of rights guaranteed the freedom of speech, the press, religion, and assembly. Private property was inviolate. The federal system gave more power to the national government than was the case in the United States, for the federal authorities had the right to intervene in a province in the event of an internal disturbance, gross financial mismanagement, or electoral fraud.

As president, Mitre frequently used the power to intervene in provinces to put down uprisings by provincial *caudillos* who resisted the constitution's centralizing influence. He also put an end to Francisco Solano López's expansionist intrigues by joining Brazil in the war against Paraguay. During his presidency, Congress also adopted new commercial, civil, and penal codes; reorganized the judiciary; and approved a nationwide system of free, compulsory, secular public schools.

In 1868 Mitre turned over the presidency to Domingo Sarmiento, who continued his progressive work. Sarmiento increased the number of public schools, which proved to be a good investment in social overhead capital, as literacy increased from 22 percent in 1869 to 65 percent in 1914. He also carried the war against Paraguay to its conclusion, in 1870; and he eliminated the last of the provincial *caudillos*, Ricardo López Jordán of Entre Ríos, in 1874.

Bartolomé Mitre expected to return to office in 1874, but he and Sarmiento quarreled in the meantime. To his surprise, Sarmiento had been meeting with leaders from the provinces who agreed to back his education minister, Nicolás Avellaneda, instead. Avellaneda also won the support of a *porteño* rival of Mitre's: Adolfo Alsina, leader of the Autonomist Party. A fusion of the two groups resulted in a nationwide political machine, the National Autonomist Party (PAN). When Avellaneda won, an outraged Mitre charged the government with fraud and raised a revolt. The *porteños* were divided, however, and the revolt was quickly smashed by General Julio A. Roca, head of the federal forces. Mitre, who had previously been elected to the Senate, was stripped of his seat and also of his military rank—although Avellaneda eventually restored the latter to him.

The 1880 election was in many ways a repeat of 1874, but this time General Roca headed the PAN ticket while Carlos Tejedor, Buenos Aires' governor, refused to accept defeat and raised the provincial militia. Once again, Mitre was on the losing side. The federal army, better equipped and better trained, made short work of the revolt. Mitre negotiated the *porteños'* surrender, after which General Roca triumphantly proclaimed the city of Buenos Aires to be a federal district.

This final consolidation of the Argentine Republic accelerated a process of rapid economic and demographic growth that was to change in many ways the whole character of the nation. Argentina's first official census was held in 1869. From then until the third census, in 1914, the country did indeed undergo a substantial process of modernization. The total population rose from 1.74 million to 7.89 million, and much of that was due to European immigration. There had been only about 210,000 foreign residents in 1869, or a little more than 12 percent of the country's population; by 1914 they numbered around 2.4 million, or slightly over 30 percent. Urbanization had triumphed too by 1914. Whereas nearly two-thirds of the population was classified as rural in 1869, by 1914 that figure had fallen to less than 43 percent. Buenos Aires had grown from 230,000 inhabitants to over 2 million, of which about half were foreign born—about 80 percent from Spain and Italy and the remainder from France, Germany, Switzerland, Great Britain, and Ireland.

Immigrants made up 47 percent of the economically active population in 1914: two-thirds of all factory owners, three-fourths of all merchants, over half of all industrial and commercial workers (white- and blue-collar), and just under half of all practitioners of the liberal professions. Their numbers were much less in the countryside, where *estancieros* continued to monopolize the best land on the pampa, but even there foreigners had an impact as colonists, small farmers, tenants, managers, and overseers. They introduced sheep raising, showed the *estancieros* how to improve their cattle and pasturage, and began the growing of temperate-climate grains such as wheat and corn, which eventually surpassed meat and wool as Argentina's leading exports. Indeed, by 1914 Argentina ranked eighth in the world in the value of its exports, and tenth in the value of its imports, making Buenos Aires one of the world's busiest ports. As the result of agricultural diversification and the introduction of industry, Argentina's per capita income quintupled between 1886 and 1914. Its per capita gold reserves were greater than those of Great Britain or the United States.

Economic and social change created pressure for political reform. The old "Generation of 1837," to which Mitre, Sarmiento, and Alberdi belonged, had succeeded in bringing about an urbanized, Europeanized, commercialized, and rapidly industrializing Argentina. However, the "Generation of 1880," which General Roca personified, was ambivalent about the results. The new Argentine upper class luxuriated in the great wealth that material progress created, but it also felt less secure in its privileges. Anarchist, syndicalist, and Marxist socialist ideas, imported from Europe, encouraged the workers to class warfare—to make demands, and strike, and even question the sanctity of private property! Sheltering itself in its rural estates, its mansions in town, its exclusive clubs and *barrios*, Argentina's plutocracy fought back with the police, the army, and harsh laws for deporting immigrant "agitators."

Equally disturbing was the rise of a new political party, the Civic Union (Unión Cívica), which appealed to the middle classes by calling for universal suffrage. Bartolomé Mitre was among its founders, a "traitor to his class," as was Leandro Alem, a Buenos Aires ward boss whose father had been a member of Rosas's Mazorca (and who was lynched after Rosas's fall). Other members—and "class traitors"—were Alem's nephew, Hipólito Yrigoyen, a wealthy *estanciero* and member of the Rural Society; Aristóbulo del Valle; Juan B. Justo, who would later found the Argentine Socialist Party; and Lisandro de la Torre, a reformer from the province of Santa Fe. They had been brought together in 1889 to protest the corruption and financial mismanagement of the administration of Miguel Juárez Celman, General Roca's brother-in-law and handpicked successor.

The Civic Union received a major boost the following year when the long-expected financial crisis forced Argentina to suspend payment on its foreign debts and brought on an economic depression. Prodded by Alem and Yrigoyen, the Civic Union tried to take advantage of the crisis by launching a revolt. Fortunately for him, Mitre was out of the country when the revolt occurred, because it failed. Nevertheless, it did succeed in forcing General Roca to remove Juárez Celman from office and replace him with Vice President Carlos Pellegrini. Pellegrini, a capable financier, quickly reached an agreement with Argentina's creditors and began a series of reforms that restored order to the economy.

Undeterred by its initial defeat, the Civic Union prepared to contest the 1892 election, with Mitre at the head of the ticket. Then, to their dismay, the reformers discovered that Mitre, thinking to reach a compromise that would gather all of Argentina's elite under one broad political umbrella, made a deal with Roca to run as PAN's candidate. Immediately, Alem and Yrigoyen repudiated him and broke away to form the new *Radical* Civic Union (Unión Cívica Radical, or UCR). Mitre then withdrew from the race and PAN found a new candidate, Luis Sáenz Peña. After PAN rolled up its usual fraudulent victory, the Radicals (as the new party of Alem and Yrigoyen was called) tried a second revolt the following year. It too was crushed.

Nevertheless, the Radical Civic Union gained in strength.[10] After a power struggle between the more moderate Alem and the "intransigent" Yrigoyen, the Radicals came under the latter's determined leadership. Yrigoyen announced that the party henceforth refused to participate in fraudulent elections and would instead prepare for a popular revolution. Yrigoyen had charisma, although in retrospect it is difficult to understand why. He was not a good orator and seldom spoke in public. He was solitary, taciturn, and austere. Yet he created a mystique about himself as a man of deep convictions and great concern for the common people. His platform consisted of vague clichés, but somehow he conveyed the feeling that radicalism was a crusade, a "cause"—a kind of religious movement that demanded "faith" from his followers, his "apostolate." At the same time, he was a "meticulous organizer who created a disciplined, loyal party."[11] He brooked no opposition to his personal control of the UCR. Many thought that he drove his uncle, Leandro Alem, to suicide, after ousting him as head of the party. Juan B. Justo and Lisandro de la Torre quit the UCR to found their own parties, after clashing with Yrigoyen. When dealing with those outside of radicalism Yrigoyen made a simple but rigid distinction: those who followed him were "the People" and those who didn't were "the anti-Nation."

Argentine conservatives became alarmed at the prospect of a real revolution. Radical Party clubs were proliferating, and the urban middle and working classes were becoming more threatening. A third revolt, in 1905, involved many of the junior army officers. A split in PAN between General Roca and Pellegrini weakened the machine's grip on power and led to the election in 1910 of a conservative reformer, Roque Sáenz Peña. Two years later the president pushed through Congress an electoral law that enfranchised all male citizens over eighteen and all immigrants who completed their military service in Argentina. Voting would be secret and compulsory. Minority representation was guaranteed in each province's congressional bloc. With the electorate thus expanded Yrigoyen won the presidency in 1916. As he rode to the Casa Rosada (Argentina's presidential palace), a cheering crowd unhitched the horses from his carriage and pulled him there themselves.

Yet, Yrigoyen was soon to disappoint many of his original supporters. He made no attempt at land reform: after all, he and his cabinet ministers were members of the Rural Society, the wealthy estancieros' pressure group. Also, after sympathizing with striking railway and maritime workers early in his administration Yrigoyen was unnerved by a violent strike in January 1919 by the anarchist metallurgical workers' union. It became too much for the police to control, and the army had to be called in to crush it—which it did, mercilessly. Late in the following year the army was used to smash a strike by dockworkers and ranch hands in Patagonia. It restored order, but only by using mass arrests, torture, and mass executions. Not surprisingly, the Radicals lost the working classes to the Socialist Party, the anarchists, and, later, to the Communists and Peronists.

There were other ways in which Yrigoyen continued the practices of his conservative predecessors. Government spending almost doubled, and its borrowing increased eightfold. Under PAN, much of this went to patronage, but much also went to finance infrastructural improvements; under Yrigoyen spending on public works actually decreased as a percentage of the budget, so that more could be spent on patronage and government salaries. Like the conservatives, too, Yrigoyen used the power of federal intervention in the provinces to overturn election results and remove opposition politicians from office. But he did it more frequently than any previous administration had and usually didn't bother to get congressional approval, as required by the constitution. He preferred to act through executive decrees. Only in the area of university reform, where he supported demands to professionalize the faculty, update the curriculum, and provide student representation in campus government at the various state universities, did Yrigoyen live up to his progressive image.

Yrigoyen's authoritarian style eventually split his party. After turning over the presidency to his fellow Radical, Marcelo T. Alvear, in 1922 he insisted on running the government from party headquarters. When Alvear resisted, Yrigoyen rallied a majority of the Radicals in Congress to thwart his proposals. Those who still backed the president broke away to form a separate anti-*personalista* radical movement; nevertheless, Yrigoyen came back in 1928 to win the presidential election with nearly 60 percent of the vote, while his followers gained majorities in both houses of Congress.

Conservatives, Anti-Personalistas, and Socialists now feared that Yrigoyen would turn into a populist dictator. Meanwhile, the army harbored grievances against him for playing favorites and using political criteria in military promotions and assignments. The collapse of Argentina's economy in 1929 gave Yrigoyen's enemies their opportunity to stop him. The old man was seventy-six and growing senile. As the government drifted helplessly in the economic crisis, Yrigoyen's popularity plummeted. Finally, in September 1930 General José Félix Uriburu took control of the government by a coup.

But how to put the masses back in their place and keep them there? Uriburu favored a corporate state, like Mussolini's fascist Italy. Only a small fraction of the military and a handful of extreme right-wing intellectuals supported him, however. There was much stronger backing for General Agustín P. Justo, who simply intended to restore the old oligarchy to power, behind the facade of a carefully controlled democracy. In 1932 Justo gently eased Uriburu out of power and formed a government composed of the main anti-Yrigoyen parties: Conservatives, Anti-Personalistas, and Independent Socialists. For the next eleven years this coalition, known as the "Concordancia," rigged elections to ensure that the Yrigoyen Radicals would be a minority in Congress and the provincial governments. When fraud proved insufficient, force was applied. Though the Concordancia did a good job of steering Argentina through the Depression years, and even fostering—somewhat inadvertently—industrialization, it was never popular. Yet, when the pendulum finally swung back to popular government it would not be the Radicals who would benefit, but a new mass movement fashioned by Argentina's second great charismatic leader: Juan Perón.

Brazil

After overthrowing the monarchy, Marshal Deodoro da Fonseca soon fell out with his fellow conspirators. His autocratic personality clashed with Congress, which he finally dissolved in November 1891. The Republicans, who had not revolted against the emperor only to submit to a dictator, rose in revolt. When the navy joined them Deodoro resigned in favor of his more popular vice president, General Floriano Peixoto. The one accomplishment in the marshal's two years in power was a new constitution that set up a federal republic.[12]

The constitution of 1891 was patterned after the U.S. Constitution. It provided for the separation of powers and checks and balances between the three classic branches of government, and it adopted the principle of federalism in defining the relationship between the central government and the states. Brazilian federalism gave much more power to the states, however. States could raise their own armies (militias), which, in the case of larger states, were often the equal of the federal army. States could also tax interstate commerce and contract foreign loans without seeking permission from the federal government. Since there was almost no federal civil service, federal law had to be applied by state bureaucrats. Such extreme decentralization reflected the influence of classical liberal ideas on the constitutional convention, as opposed to those of Positivism. Positivism's only lasting influence on the convention was in the adoption of the national flag. On a green background a yellow diamond surrounds a blue globe that is encircled by a band, on which are written the words "*Ordem e Progreso*" ("Order and Progress").

Even if Positivism failed to shape the governmental structure it still had lingering influence in the military's continued devotion to scientific and technical training and in its tacit assumption that, like the emperor, it possessed the right to intervene if the political system fell out of balance. Although the "moderating power" appeared nowhere in the constitution it existed informally in the General Staff Headquarters. The military brought the republic into being, and it eventually would bring it to an end.

Economic and social change needed no technocratic elite to guide it. Throughout the First Republic's history Brazil enjoyed an economic boom, thanks to rising exports of coffee, cacao, rubber, and meat. Coffee was king, and by 1910 Brazil was furnishing three-fourths of the world's total supply. Production more than tripled as more and more land was cultivated. Profits from coffee helped to finance the expansion of the railway, telephone, and telegraph systems; new port facilities; and the growth of commercial and industrial enterprises in the cities. The population also rose, from about 14 million in 1890 to around 24 million by World War I. As in Argentina, much of the gain was due to European immigration, especially in the south. Many of those who came to work on the coffee *fazendas* eventually became planters themselves, while others migrated to the cities, where they formed a new middle stratum of merchants and manufacturers, or became skilled urban workers.

Three states accounted for most of Brazil's industrial and demographic growth: São Paulo, Minas Gerais, and Rio de Janeiro, in that order. Political power followed in the wake of economic power. The first three civilian presidents who followed General Peixoto were from São Paulo. They were then followed by a president from Minas Gerais and one from Rio de Janeiro. This power-sharing arrangement operated through a national political machine called the Republican Party, which was a coalition of state party machines. Each of the latter, in turn, rested upon local political bosses, the *coroneis* (colonels). A *coronel*, whether a *fazendeiro* (powerful landowner) or urban ward leader, controlled his district through the fact that the electorate was sharply limited by income and literacy requirements. The few eligible voters were usually linked to him by family ties, godfathership, or ties of economic dependency. With such restricted suffrage, a *coronel* who controlled a sizable local vote could hope to rise to the leadership of his state; and if his was one of the key states he might aspire to a federal cabinet post or even the presidency. These posts were allocated at meetings between top Republican Party state leaders. The biggest states won the top jobs, and middling states received most of the rest. So long as the big states agreed, which was most of the time, the Republican Party was unbeatable.

The 1910 elections are a good example of the machine at work. The Republican Party nominated Marshal Hermes da Fonseca, Deodoro's nephew, for president—a departure from normal practice in that (1) Hermes was a military man; and (2) he came from Rio Grande do Sul, a middle-rank state. This time, however, the official candidate was hotly opposed by a man whose honesty and personal prestige posed a real challenge. Ruy Barbosa, from the state of Bahia, had played a major role in writing the 1891 constitution and since then had distinguished himself as a diplomatic representative of Brazil. His platform consisted of a call for honest government and brilliant attacks on the corruption that had spread widely throughout the political system. Nonetheless, although he attracted large crowds wherever he spoke, Ruy Barbosa lost by a two-to-one margin, thanks to rigged registration lists, ballot stuffing, and curious counting techniques. So blatant was the electoral fraud that for the first time thoughtful Brazilians were shocked out of their complacency. It also should be noted that only 360,174 people voted, out of a population of around 22 million.

World War I accelerated the pace of economic and social change because, by disrupting the traditional trade pattern, it forced Brazil into import-substituting industrialization. The number of industrial establishments quadrupled, the amount of capital invested tripled, and the value of output quintupled. As before, most of this increase occurred in São Paulo and, to a lesser extent, in Minas Gerais and Rio de Janeiro. In societal terms, it meant an increase in the urban business class and a doubling in the size of the urban working class. There also was a rise in cultural nationalism, as writers and artists showed pride in Brazil's modernization. There was a bitter letdown after the war, however, when official policy swung back to free trade and many of the fledgling industries went under from foreign competition. Urban unemployment rose, resulting in strikes and, in 1922, the founding of the Brazilian Communist Party. Meanwhile, the urban middle classes focused the blame on the coffee barons.

The 1922 elections produced another rupture inside the Republican Party, with long-term consequences. Artur Bernardes, the governor of Minas Gerais, and Washington Luiz, the governor of São Paulo, had previously made a secret agreement to rotate the presidency between their two states. Bernardes would be the official candidate in 1922, and then Luís would run in 1926. When the deal was leaked, however, there were protests from Rio Grande do Sul, Rio de Janeiro, Bahia, and Pernambuco. This coalition of midlevel states decided to nominate a rival candidate, Nilo Peçanha, from Rio de Janeiro. While this was going on, the Military Club, led by Marshal Hermes da Fonseca, began quarreling with incumbent president Epitácio Pessoa about cutbacks in military spending. Bernardes jumped in on Pessoa's side, whereupon the Military Club endorsed Peçanha for president. The dispute eventually escalated to the point where President Pessoa ordered Marshal Hermes's arrest. As always, the Republican machine rolled up the necessary majority for its candidate, Bernardes, and ignored demands by Peçanha and the Military Club for a recount.

The senior officers grumbled but accepted the result; not so the junior officers, who tended to be from more middle-class backgrounds and more impatient for reform.[13] On 5 July 1922 a group of young officers revolted at the garrison located at Copacabana, Rio de Janeiro. Receiving no support from above, they surrendered after two days, except for a party of eighteen who dashed out on to the beach, firing at the surrounding government forces. All of them were killed. On the surface, the government had crushed a minor revolt, but underneath, the *tenentes* (lieutenants) who gave their lives became martyrs to other young reform-minded officers and civilians. The Copacabana revolt was, for them, a symbol of defiance against a corrupt order. Political dissidence spread to Rio Grande do Sul, where the Republican Party split into reformist and stand-pat factions. In São Paulo the opposition formed the Democratic Party to challenge the Republicans. In the north, dissident factions challenged the Republican machines in Pernambuco and Paraíba. Finally, on 5 July 1924—two years to the day after Copacabana—another group of young officers, supported by Democratic Party politicians, took control of the São Paulo garrison. For the next three weeks, until federal troops arrived, the city of São Paulo was in rebel hands. Then, instead of surrendering, 3,000 of the rebels escaped into the interior of the country. In October they were joined by another 2,000 rebels who had recently revolted in Rio Grande do Sul.

Now began a dramatic, three-year march by these rebel forces, led by Captain Luís Carlos Prestes, throughout the backlands of Brazil. Pursued by federal forces and local police, and attacked by gunmen hired by the *fazendeiros* who ran their remote estates like feudal barons, the "Prestes Column" covered 14,000 miles of territory, trying to instigate a social revolution. "They forded rivers, climbed mountains, and slashed their way through jungles, ravaging the countryside as they went, in a desperate effort to keep alive the flame of revolt, until finally, after two and a half years, with 800 ill-equipped, exhausted men left, Prestes sought asylum in Bolivian territory."[14] Though the "Long March" had failed, the *tenentes* had captured the attention and affection of the urban classes. Prestes, disillusioned by their failure to rouse the peasants of the interior to revolt, would eventually turn to Communism and become the party's leader. Another *tenente*, Miguel Costa, founded the Socialist Party. The majority of *tenentes*, however, became extreme nationalists, committed to an authoritarian, but non-Marxist, type of radical reform. Their opportunity would soon come.

The Old Republic crumbled under the economic blows of the Great Depression. The collapse of the world coffee market was devastating to this essentially monocultural economy. *Fazendeiro* bankruptcies led to a series of bank failures, while falling revenues at all levels of government meant the cancellation of public works projects and rapidly rising unemployment. Meanwhile, Washington Luiz, who had inherited the presidency from Bernardes as planned, violated the agreement to rotate the office between São Paulo and Minas Gerais. Instead of picking a *mineiro* to succeed him, he chose another *paulista*, Governor Júlio Prestes, to be the official candidate in 1930. The outraged *mineiros* were determined to oppose him, but they knew that by picking one of their own to run they would only make the contest a personal quarrel. To rally the other states they turned to the governor of Rio Grande do Sul, Getúlio Vargas, for their presidential candidate; and to balance the ticket they chose João Pessoa, from the northern state of Paraíba. This so-called Liberal Alliance attracted support from a great variety of reformist urban middle-class groups, junior army officers, and intellectuals. When the votes were counted, however, the Republican Party claimed its usual victory.

Vargas accused the government of fraud but seemed willing to accept defeat. His followers, however, were ready to revolt. When, a few months later, Pessoa was killed in a personal quarrel, the reformers rose all across Brazil to accuse the government of assassinating him. In Paraíba, Juarez Távora, a former *tenente*, began leading an armed column southward toward Rio de Janeiro. In Rio Grande do Sul, Lieutenent Colonel Pedro Aurélio de Goés Monteiro raised another column composed of soldiers, police, and civilians and began marching north toward São Paulo. A third rebel column, led by João Alberto, another *tenente*, began moving down from Minas Gerais. It grew in strength as it proceeded toward Rio de Janeiro as soldiers from the regular army joined the revolt. On 24 October 1930 top-ranking generals in Rio de Janeiro decided that the government's cause was hopeless; rather than be overwhelmed by the rebellion they chose instead to depose Washington Luiz and invite Vargas to assume the presidency.

Notes

1. Liliana de Riz, *Sociedad y política en Chile: de Portales a Pinochet* (Mexico: Universidad Nacional Autónoma de Mexico, 1979), 28–29. The translation is mine.

2. Federico Gil, *The Political System of Chile* (Boston: Houghton Mifflin, 1966), 48–50.

3. Gil, *Political System*, 53–55.

4. For this section on Peru, I have consulted mainly the following works: R. J. Owens, *Peru* (London: Oxford University Press, 1963); Arnold Payne, *The Peruvian Coup d'Etat of 1962: The Overthrow of Manuel Prado* (Washington: Institute for the Comparative Study of Political Systems, 1968); and James D. Rudolph, *Peru: The Evolution of a Crisis* (Westport, CT: Praeger, 1992).

5. Piérola was accused by the Civilistas of causing the assassination of their leader, Manuel Pardo, in 1878. Pardo had just been elected president of the Senate when he was shot by an army sergeant. Piérola's frequent inflammatory speeches against the victim were alleged to be the cause.

6. David Bushnell, "Politics and Violence in Nineteenth Century Colombia," in *Violence in Colombia*, ed. Charles Berquist, Ricardo Peñaranda, and Gonzalo Sánchez, 18 (Wilmington, DE: Scholarly Resources, 1992).

7. Harvey Kline and Vanessa Gray, "Colombia: Drugs, Guerrillas, Death Squads, and U.S. Aid," in *Latin American Politics and Development*, ed. Howard J. Wiarda and Harvey Kline, 209 (Boulder, CO: Westview, 2000). Other sources consulted for this

section are Robert H. Dix, *Colombia: The Political Dimensions of Change* (New Haven, CT: Yale University Press, 1967); Robert H. Dix, "Political Oppositions under the National Front," in *Politics of Compromise: Coalition Government in Colombia*, ed. R. Albert Berry, Ronald G. Hellman, and Mauricio Solaún, 131–80 (New Brunswick, NJ: Transaction, 1980); Mauricio Solaún, "Colombian Politics: Historical Characteristics and Problems," in Berry, Hellman, and Solaún, *Politics of Compromise*, 1–58; and Harvey F. Kline, "The National Front: Historical Perspective and Overview," in Berry, Hellman, and Solaún, *Politics of Compromise*, 59–86.

8. Main sources for this section on Uruguay are Javier Bonilla Saus, "Partidos políticos y formación del estado en Uruguay," *Cuadernos de CLAEH* 75, no. 1 (August 1996): 113–39; Gerardo Caetano, "Political Culture, Parties, and Electors in Uruguay: The Experience of the Second Constitution, 1919–1933," in *Political Culture, Social Movements, and Democratic Transitions in South America in the Twentieth Century*, ed. Fernando Devoto and Torcuato S. Di Tella, 209–43 (Milan: Fondazione Giangiacomo Feltrinelli, 1997); Henry Finch, "Uruguay since 1930," in *The Cambridge History of Latin America*, vol. 8, ed. Leslie Bethell, 195–232 (Cambridge: Cambridge University Press, 1991); Martin Henry John Finch, *A Political Economy of Uruguay since 1870* (New York: St. Martin's Press, 1981); Luis E. González, *Political Structures and Democracy in Uruguay* (Notre Dame, IN: University of Notre Dame Press, 1991); Martin Weinstein, *Uruguay: Democracy at the Crossroads* (Boulder, CO: Westview, 1988).

9. For this section I have drawn on the following works: Natalio R. Botana, *El orden conservador* (Buenos Aires: Editorial Sudamericana, 1977); Gino Germani, *Política y sociedad en una época de transición* (Buenos Aires: Editorial Paidos, 1962); José Luis Romero, *A History of Argentine Political Thought* (Stanford, CA: Stanford University Press, 1963); David Rock, *Argentina, 1516–1987* (Berkeley: University of California Press, 1987); James Scobie, *Argentina: A City and a Nation*, 2nd ed. (New York: Oxford University Press, 1971); Arthur P. Whitaker, *Argentina* (Englewood Cliffs, NJ: Prentice-Hall, 1964). The reader may also wish to consult Paul H. Lewis, *The Crisis of Argentine Capitalism* (Chapel Hill: University of North Carolina Press, 1990).

10. Mitre's "last hurrah" was his election to the Senate in 1894, where he remained until his retirement from public life in 1901, at the age of eighty. He died in 1906. In addition to his political career, Mitre gained fame as a historian with his biographies of General Manuel Belgrano and General José de San Martín.

11. Scobie, *Argentina*, 201.

12. My two main sources for late-nineteenth-century Brazil are José María Bello, *A History of Modern Brazil, 1889–1964* (Stanford, CA: Stanford University Press, 1966); and E. Bradford Burns, *A History of Brazil*, 2nd ed. (New York: Columbia University Press, 1980).

13. On the *tenente* revolts of 1922 and 1924, see Robert J. Alexander, "Brazilian Tenentismo," *Hispanic American Historical Review*, May 1956, 229–42; and John D. Wirth, "Tenentismo in the Brazilian Revolution of 1930," *Hispanic American Historical Review*, May 1964, 161–79.

14. Bello, *History of Modern Brazil*, 253.

CHAPTER FIVE

~

The Masses Enter Politics

The heyday of the Latin American liberal state, from 1870 to 1930, wedded export-led economic growth to elitist politics. Progress in urban services and material improvements in transportation and communications brought enormous benefits to a relatively small portion of the population. Political stability was another mixed blessing. If by the turn of the century the *caudillos* had largely disappeared, they had been replaced by either powerful dictators or exclusive oligarchies. In the countryside, liberalism left many people worse off. Small farmers and Indian communal holdings were under constant pressure from big producers of export crops: *latifundios* now converted into capitalist agribusinesses. They received no protection from the liberal state, which considered them anachronistic classes destined to be trampled under in the forward march of Progress.

Although those liberal dictatorships and oligarchies seemed firmly rooted at the time, their foundations were actually quite shaky. To begin with, progress in the cities created new social classes that demanded political participation and a more equitable distribution of the national income, while liberal dictatorships and oligarchies with their close connections to foreign capital were coming under fire from anarchists, socialists, and nationalists. That discontentment was echoed in the countryside, erupting occasionally in peasant revolts that required the military to restore order. In countries where mineral wealth contributed to export revenues, mining camps, with their archaic labor conditions, also became centers of social agitation and protest. Railway workers, traveling about the country, were often the carriers of new ideas about unionization and revolution.

The Mexican Revolution that overthrew Porfirio Díaz signaled a new era of mass politics for Latin America. It was a true social revolution, sweeping away all traditional institutions. Its violent upheavals, coming one after another for a whole generation, reverberated throughout Spanish America. Though it lacked an official ideology, there were some philosophical underpinnings that would begin to take form in the Mexican Constitution of 1917 and, eventually, become institutionalized in an official party of the revolution, especially as it was shaped by President Lázaro Cárdenas (1936–1940). Land reform, based on the proposition that land should belong to those who actually worked it, was one of those. Another was the idea that factory and mine workers should participate in management. Economic nationalism—a reaction to what was perceived as being excessive foreign influence over the economy—constituted a third underpinning. The assimilation of previously marginalized and exploited Indian populations into the national political mainstream was a fourth.

These concepts reverberated most powerfully in those Latin American countries whose social conditions resembled Mexico's. Peru and Bolivia were, like Mexico, "dual societies," divided into a handful of wealthy, traditional landowning families on the one hand and large masses of impoverished peasants, urban workers, and miners living in bleak company towns on the other. In both cases, a large part of the lower classes was Indian. The cities also contained a small but growing middle class of clerks, professionals, and small businessmen. Thus, Peru and Bolivia were divided socially and politically by both class and race. This volatile combination would eventually erupt, under the pressures of modernization, into revolution. Unlike Mexico, however, where the military gradually withdrew from politics as the revolution settled down and became institutionalized, in Peru and Bolivia the soldiers would become the governors, arbitrating as to what reforms were acceptable and how far they could go. In all three cases, however, radical and violent upheavals resulted in the destruction of the old order before giving way to another period of economic liberalism.

Mexico

The Course of Revolution
Francisco Madero was hailed as a hero when he entered Mexico City on 7 June 1911, but he soon showed his political ineptitude by surrounding himself with cynical relatives and flatterers. Some of the men around him had ties to the

old *porfiriato* and were secretly scheming to restore it. Although Madero was sincere in his belief in free elections and honest government, he showed little interest in land reform or the rights of workers. Discouraged, Emiliano Zapata and his armed peasants reverted to guerrilla warfare and began carrying out their own agrarian revolution. Meanwhile, Madero failed to see the plot that was forming against him. Chief among the conspirators was the American ambassador, Henry Lane Wilson, who was concerned to protect his countrymen's oil, mining, and ranching interests against the surge of Mexican nationalism that threatened them. In February 1913 he brought together two active rebels, Bernardo Reyes, the former political boss of northern Mexico, and Félix Díaz, the ex-dictator's nephew, with General Victoriano Huerta, whom Madero had chosen to command the army, despite warnings from friends and even his brother, Gustavo. Huerta, a corrupt, drunken libertine, nursed a grudge against Madero, besides holding him in contempt as a weakling and fool. He agreed that the revolution was a mistake, and a return to the old order was necessary. On February 18 Madero was made prisoner in a palace coup, and four days later he was shot by his guards. Huerta assumed the presidency.[1]

The counterrevolution was short lived. In the north, Pancho Villa led his cavalry against the government forces, vowing to revenge Madero. Emiliano Zapata, who never had laid down his arms, stepped up his campaign to wipe out the *hacendados* and redistribute the land. Venustiano Carranza, Madero's minister of war, raised a "constitutionalist army" and enlisted the aid of a brilliant general from Sonora, Álvaro Obregón. In July 1914 Huerta pocketed what he could from the treasury, fled to Veracruz, and took ship for exile.

The revolution now entered a radical phase. During the fight against Huerta, Carranza and Villa had quarreled. Meanwhile, Zapata rejected Carranza's orders to lay down his arms, now that the counterrevolution was defeated. The revolutionaries thus split into two warring camps: Carranza and Obregón on one side, Villa and Zapata on the other. The latter faction won the upper hand at first, forcing Carranza and Obregón to abandon Mexico City in December 1914. Zapata felt uncomfortable in the capital, however, and quickly returned home to carry on the agrarian revolution. By contrast, Villa and his men remained to enjoy the city's delights and debaucheries— until suddenly, on 29 January 1915, Obregón attacked. Villa's demoralized troops fled northward in confusion, with Obregón in hot pursuit. Villa quickly regrouped and struck back near the town of Celaya, but Obregón's men, carefully positioned in trenches, beat back repeated cavalry attacks. Villa retreated again, but before he could reach his home state of Chihuahua, Obregón's chief lieutenant, General Plutarco Elías Calles, decisively defeated him at Agua Prieta, eliminating him forever as a political factor.

With order more or less restored, Carranza called for a constitutional convention, to be held in the town of Querétaro. Although Zapata refused to attend, there were enough radical revolutionaries present that the final document, published in 1917, departed considerably from the 1857 constitution, especially in Article 27, which restricted private property rights. The state would own all subsoil wealth and claimed the right to regulate, and even expropriate, any private property that failed to serve a social function. Foreigners could own no property near the borders or coastlines; and in the event of a dispute with the state they would have no recourse to their governments but would have to accept the jurisdiction of Mexican courts. Industrial workers and miners, who had contributed armed "labor battalions" to the fight against General Huerta, were rewarded with Article 123, which recognized labor's right to unionize, strike, and bargain collectively. Workers were guaranteed an eight-hour day, old-age pensions, health and accident insurance, healthy working conditions, and living wages. The revolutionaries also renewed the old struggle against the Catholic Church. Articles 3, 5, and 130 abolished the Church's schools and religious orders, nationalized all of its property, limited the number of priests, and forbade public processions. Priests could not vote, hold office, wear clerical garb in public, or publicly criticize the government.

The new constitution served to split Zapata's movement in the south, for many of his followers saw no reason to continue antagonizing a government so clearly committed to reform. They perceived Zapata as an anarchist who opposed any sort of regime. As his movement dwindled, he took bloody revenge on such renegades until finally, in 1919, he was led into a fatal ambush. But President Carranza was also in trouble, for he opposed applying the more radical measures called for in the constitution. That led to a quarrel with General Obregón, and finally to an open break. Carranza refused to name Obregón as his successor when his term expired in 1920 because he suspected him of harboring dictatorial ambitions. He even attempted to have Obregón arrested, but the plot backfired. Obregón escaped from Mexico City, rallied his supporters, and seized the capital. Carranza was captured and shot while trying to flee.

Consolidation of the Revolution

After taking power Obregón began pacifying the country while also making progress toward social reform. Using the same tactics as Porfirio Díaz, he bought off the various *caudillos* and "generals" who had sprung up during the years of chaos by bringing them into the army and putting them on the government payroll. At the same time he alleviated the budgetary strain caused by such a huge increase in the officer corps by reducing drastically the number of enlisted men. Other *caudillos* were satisfied with governorships, congressional seats, or diplomatic posts. Those who would not be bought either were chased out of the country or found it expedient to disappear from public life.

Demands for social reform were temporarily satisfied by the distribution of some 2.8 million acres to small farmers. Most of this redistribution took place in the former *zapatista* areas in the south. Labor unions were encouraged and consolidated into a powerful nationwide organization called the Regional Confederation of Mexican Workers (CROM), which claimed over a million members. Workers' wages rose, but the biggest gains went to the new powerful union bosses, especially CROM's chief, Luis Morones, who used the threat of strikes to extort money from employers. Obregón's most lasting achievement, perhaps, was his support for public education. His brilliant education minister, José Vasconcelos, initiated a system of rural schools called *casas del pueblo*, which combined the functions of schoolhouse, agricultural extension division, and local civic center. Vasconcelos also encouraged the arts, including the commissioning of Diego Rivera, José Clemente Orozco, and David Siquieros to adorn public buildings with their murals. Finally, Obregón overcame a potential diplomatic crisis with the United States over the restriction of foreign property rights by agreeing to set up binational commissions to review individual complaints. Although he was criticized by Mexican nationalists for agreeing to this, he actually had conceded very little. Moreover, this detente with the United States proved to be timely because in 1924 his term ended and he had to pick a successor—which in this case was his top lieutenant, General Plutarco Elías Calles. With that, General Adolfo de la Huerta, who also had been considered a possibility, raised a revolt. It was quickly put down, thanks in part to U.S. military aid.

Plutarco Calles lacked Obregón's finesse in politics. He gradually slowed down the land redistribution program while simultaneously giving the corrupt CROM a freer hand. He also became embroiled in a quarrel with the Catholic Church over its criticism of the constitution. The quarrel soon turned violent, as Calles deported priests and encouraged his supporters to burn churches. That provoked a revolt by devout peasants known as the Cristeros because of their rallying cry: "Long live Christ the King!" Meanwhile, Calles also clashed with the foreign oil companies over their contracts and eventually found himself on the verge of a diplomatic break with the United States and Britain. Fortunately, the arrival in 1927 of a new American ambassador, Dwight Morrow, helped to improve the political climate. After gaining Calles's confidence, Morrow convinced him to call a truce in the conflict with the Church and to compromise with the oil companies by declaring that contracts written before 1917 would not be affected by the constitution's property clauses.

In 1928 Obregón announced that he would run again for the presidency, thus violating the constitution's ban on reelection. His contention that the constitution only forbade immediate reelection was an obvious sophistry, but he was popular nonetheless and succeeded in winning a second term. Two weeks later, however, he was assassinated while attending a victory banquet.

Although the assassin was a religious fanatic, Obregón's followers suspected Calles and Morones of having a hand in the murder, for they had opposed his reelection. With the country poised for another political explosion, Calles defused the situation by declaring that he would never seek the presidency again. Moreover, he promised to organize an official party that would embrace all factions within the revolution—labor, peasants, the military, and civil servants—and would regularize the procedures for presidential succession. The resulting National Revolutionary Party (PNR) was quickly assembled from the various state and local political machines headed by the revolution's *caudillos* and was financed by a kickback from the wages of every government employee. With such an immense war chest, the PNR was unbeatable, and Calles used it to run the country. Even though he himself never occupied the presidency, he was able to choose malleable stand-ins and dismiss them when they displeased him. In 1934, however, he made a mistake by choosing Lázaro Cárdenas, the former governor of Michoacán, to be his puppet president.

Radical Reform

Cárdenas had risen through the ranks of the revolutionary army from second lieutenant to general, serving under Obregón and Calles. Along the way he had been introduced to radical socialist ideas by some of the more politicized officers. As governor of Michoacán he had organized teachers, workers, peasants, and small shopkeepers into a mass organization called the Michoacán Revolutionary Labor Confederation and used them as "shock troops" against the local Cristeros. Although Cárdenas felt benevolently toward the lower classes, he was paternalistic rather than democratic. Teachers were expected to be missionaries of the new socialist ideology, and those who were not sufficiently militant were dismissed. State legislators and judges were supposed to carry out the governor's policies, not criticize or oppose.

As president, Cárdenas soon made it clear that he intended to be his own man. He began replacing pro-Calles military officers and cabinet ministers with men of his own choosing. He also expropriated and redistributed land at an unprecedented pace—more than twice as much as in all previous revolutionary administrations. To reform the labor movement, he switched the government's support to the General Confederation of Mexican Workers and Peasants (CGOCM), headed by Vicente Lombardo Toledano, a leftist labor leader who had broken with Morones. By the spring of 1935 Calles had become alarmed and let it be known that if Cárdenas did not mend his ways he would remove him from office. He was too late, however, for Cárdenas and Lombardo Toledano had organized the peasants and workers into "proletarian defense committees" whose mass power was a warning to the military and political fence straddlers that the president had popular support. When the showdown came it was Calles, Morones, and other cronies of theirs who were suddenly arrested and put on airplanes headed for California, with warnings not to return.

With Calles eliminated, Cárdenas was free to press ahead with his radical reforms. During his six years in office he redistributed more than 45 million acres of land to peasants, chiefly in the form of communal holdings called *ejidos*. Moreover, the peasants were urged to form leagues in order to protect their interests. Those leagues were then combined into the government-sponsored National Confederation of Peasants (CNC), which was created by detaching the peasants from Lombardo Toledano's CGOCM. By way of compensation, Cárdenas retained Lombardo Toledano as the head of a new official labor organization, the Mexican Workers' Confederation (CTM). Knowing that they enjoyed government support, the workers became very militant, and their strikes were almost always successful. In 1937 the railway workers' strike ended with Cárdenas expropriating the railroads and turning them over to the union to run as a cooperative. More spectacular still was his decree in March 1938 that expropriated the American and British oil companies, following a prolonged strike in which the foreign owners refused to obey a decision of the Mexican Supreme Court. It was the most popular act of his administration.

Cárdenas's care in organizing national peasant and labor federations was part of a larger plan to restructure the revolution's official party. Whereas Calles had based the PRN on state and local political bosses, Cárdenas intended to centralize power even more by switching to "functional representation." The new party structure represented four "sectors" of the revolution. There was a peasant sector, based on the CNC; a labor sector, based on the CTM; a popular sector, representing civil servants and teachers, which in 1943 would create its own mass organization, the National Confederation of Popular Organizations (CNOP); and a military sector. Each of the sector organizations reached down to the state and local levels, bypassing the old political bosses because now the peasants and workers would look to their sector leaders to protect their interests. In addition, the revolution's diverse elements would be forced to cooperate at election time by bargaining with one another over the creation of a common ticket. So many seats in Congress, so many governorships or mayorships, so many cabinet offices or diplomatic posts would be allocated in advance to each sector, after which the bargaining would begin. If, for instance, a CNC candidate were nominated for the governorship of a given state, then a CTM candidate might be picked for the Senate, a popular sector candidate for the Chamber of Deputies, and a military officer for the state legislature. Each sector would be expected to support the others' candidates, on the principle of reciprocity, and thereby ensure that the official party, now renamed the Mexican Revolutionary Party (PRM), would roll up its large majorities everywhere.

Although businessmen were not considered part of the revolutionary coalition, and therefore were not incorporated into the PRM, they nevertheless were required to join government-sponsored trade associations. Every firm capitalized at 500 pesos ($40) or more had to join either the National Confederation of Industrial Chambers (CONCAMIN) or the Confederation of National Chambers of Commerce (CONCANACO), depending on whether it was engaged primarily in production or sales. Each of the confederations was, in turn, divided into specialized chambers—about 50 in CONCAMIN and over 250 in CONCANACO. The exact placement of an individual firm in one of these confederations and its appropriate chamber would be decided by the Ministry of Economics. The Ministry of Economics also collected the membership dues for the chambers and confederations and reserved the right to remove officers who failed to fit their policies to "national needs." Ministry representatives attended all the national meetings.

In brief, Cárdenas created a corporative system for Mexico, in which the state organized all of the major economic groups into trade associations, through which it could control their behavior. This worked to the advantage of peasants and workers while Cárdenas was in office, because he used their mass organizations to mobilize for reform. But as the Mexican Revolution turned conservative under his successors, state control of the CNC and CTM made it easier to stifle protests while favoring the private enterprise sector and the middle classes.

The Mexican "Thermidor"

The initial step in this shift to the right came in 1943 when President Manuel Ávila Camacho, Cárdenas's successor, formed the CNOP to promote the interests of white-collar and professional people in the official party.

Originally based on the bureaucrats' Federation of Unions of Workers in the Service of the State (FSTSE), the CNOP gradually branched out to include small businessmen, small private farmers, teachers, cooperatives, the liberal professions, plus youth and women's associations. As it grew in size it also grew in influence, despite its heterogeneity. Another signal as to the revolution's rightward drift was Ávila Camacho's changing the official party's name to the Institutional Revolutionary Party (PRI) in 1945, as if to emphasize that the era of reform was over. He also abolished the military sector of the party, to keep the soldiers out of politics. Finally, Ávila Camacho made peace with the Catholic Church, even going so far as to admit publicly that he was "a believer."

Land reform slowed down after Cárdenas. Ávila Camacho redistributed only 16.5 million acres of land to peasants, as compared to Cárdenas's 45 million. The next president, Miguel Alemán, gave out only 13.5 million, and his successor, Adolfo Ruiz Cortines, redistributed only 7.7 million. Not only was the pace of reform slowed, but the form of land redistribution changed as well. Whereas Cárdenas preferred to encourage communal holdings (the *ejido*), his successors decided that private agriculture was more efficient. Thus, agrarian reform was gradually pushed to the bottom of the political agenda, leaving about 40 percent of all arable land in Mexico still in the hands of large private owners—who indeed account for most of the country's agricultural production. Although the CNC was designed to protect and extend the *ejido*, in practice the government was able to control the selection of leaders, meaning that party hacks rather than real peasants rose to the top.

Meanwhile, given the limited amount of land suitable for cultivation, post-Cárdenas administrations put increasing emphasis on industrialization as the solution to Mexico's poverty. To promote rapid industrialization, the government took a more pro-business approach, inviting businessmen to send representatives to government commissions studying economic policy and submitting to them proposed legislation for their opinions. At the same time, labor lost much of its influence. Like the CNC, the CTM lacked the capacity for independent action. Lombardo Toledano was ousted as leader in 1948, after which the organization officially repudiated Marxism as "an imported doctrine." When Lombardo Toledano then tried to revive his old CGOCM, he found that the new labor laws prohibited any activity by an organization that lacked official government recognition. Unauthorized strikes and picketing were quickly suppressed by the police. Moreover, workers participating in such strikes automatically lost their job security and could be replaced. Beaten in the labor field, Lombardo Toledano tried a run for the presidency in 1952 but was crushed by the PRI's juggernaut.

Corporatism thus proved to be serviceable to either the Left or the Right—which is not surprising since it historically has been used by a wide variety of political theorists, ranging from Catholic paternalists seeking to revive medieval guilds and Mediterranean Fascists like Mussolini on the Right, to revolutionary syndicalists and Guild Socialists on the Left. Although it was launched in Mexico by a man of the Left, it gradually evolved into a conservative mechanism for controlling the lower classes. That control mechanism was all the more efficient because it centralized power in the hands of the president, who during his six-year term was all but a dictator. His patronage powers were immense. As head of the official party he had the power to appoint and remove sector organization officials, which allowed him to exercise control over key pressure groups. He also acted as a referee between sector organizations, and between component parts of a single sector organization. His control over the sector organizations also gave him a grip over state and local governments, as well as over Congress, to a degree that even Porfirio Díaz never enjoyed. The only thing that kept this system from degenerating into a one-man tyranny was the principle, institutionalized after Obregón's assassination, that a president can serve only one term. No matter how popular or powerful he might be, once his six years were up he was forever ineligible to serve again. Although he had a dominant voice in selecting the PRI's official candidate for the next term, once his successor took office the old president surrendered all his powers. Oligarchic one-party rule thus substituted for dictatorship, just as revolutionary rhetoric created the illusion of a commitment to social reform. Much like George Orwell's *Animal Farm*, "revolutionary Mexico" more and more came to resemble the *porfiriato*.

Peru

In its early stages, as its land reform and labor legislation were sweeping away archaic systems of social stratification, the Mexican Revolution was an inspiration to other aspiring reformists throughout Latin America. One of its most important converts was a Peruvian student radical named Victor Raúl Haya de la Torre.[2]

Born in 1895, Haya came from the northern city of Trujillo. His family had once been wealthy, but they had been ruined by Peru's many revolutions, its war with Chile in 1879, and by competition from more efficient foreign agribusinesses. Only with the death of his father, who left him a small legacy, was Haya able to attend the University of San Marcos in Lima. In 1923 he became involved in violent student protests over President Augusto B.

Leguia's bizarre proposal to dedicate Peru to the Sacred Heart of Jesus. The students, joined by the city's workers, were finally crushed after a savage battle with the police. Their leaders, including Haya, were sent to prison. They then went on a hunger strike, which led to their deportation to Mexico. Thrilled by the revolution swirling around him, Haya formed his own revolutionary organization among the Peruvian student exiles: the American Popular Revolutionary Alliance, or APRA. When the *apristas*, as APRA's followers were called, finally returned to Peru in 1930, following Leguia's removal from power, they were determined to change their society as radically as the Mexican Revolution had done.

The young radicals immediately began proselytizing among the workers and peasants. They were far more successful in this than their rivals, the Communists, who mainly attracted intellectuals. The *apristas*, with their nationalistic and indigenous themes, won control of the sugar plantation workers and the textile workers and so became Peru's chief labor party. Like the Communist Party, APRA developed a cell system that allowed it to go underground in times of persecution. That was fortunate, because it soon clashed with General Sánchez Cerro's military government. When Sánchez Cerro scheduled elections for October 1931, Haya de la Torre declared his presidential candidacy. The *apristas* threw themselves into the contest with their usual fervor and Haya proved to be a dazzling speaker; however, when the votes were counted Sánchez Cerro was declared the winner. Naturally, APRA accused the government of fraud, but it was willing to abide by the result since it had elected twenty-seven deputies to Congress and was confident that it would soon increase that number. Then, on December 23, the government suddenly outlawed APRA, expelled its deputies from Congress, and put them under arrest. Haya and his executive committee went underground, but they were arrested on 5 March 1932. The next day Sánchez Cerro barely escaped assassination when a young APRA student shot and wounded him. The next blow came in July, when armed *apristas* took over Haya's hometown of Trujillo, seizing government, police, and army officials and locking them up in the local jail. When the army arrived to restore order it discovered that the *apristas*, who had fled, had murdered about sixty of the soldiers in their cells. Infuriated, the officers ordered a roundup of Trujillo's citizens, then took them out to the nearby pre-Incan ruins of Chan Chan and shot several hundred of them (some estimates range as high as 5,000 executed). APRA struck back the next year. On 30 April 1933 Sánchez Cerro was gunned down.

These events were fateful for Peru. Though it continued to be the country's largest party, and the principal representative of labor's interests, APRA remained outlawed for most of the following three decades. Apart from a few brief periods, the military would prohibit APRA either from participating in elections or, if it did participate, from occupying the presidency. General Oscar R. Benavides, Sánchez Cerro's successor, lifted the ban temporarily, but when an APRA-supported candidate won the 1936 elections he cancelled the results and extended his term for another three years. Then new elections, from which APRA was barred, brought a conservative civilian named Manuel Prado to power. Careful about provoking the military, Prado kept APRA outlawed until 1945, at which point he allowed them to field congressional candidates in the forthcoming elections.

Realizing that nominating Haya for president would almost certainly bring on a military coup, APRA contented itself with backing José Luis Bustamente, who was supposedly sympathetic to them. The *apristas* did well in the congressional races, however, so that when Bustamente won the presidency they were able to provide him with the majorities in the Senate and Chamber he needed to govern. The *apristas* demanded cabinet seats as the price for their support. They got three (Agriculture, Housing, and Public Works) but immediately clamored for more, whereupon an exasperated Bustamente accused them of wanting to turn him into the puppet of a one-party dictatorship and dismissed their ministers from the cabinet. As before, APRA was ready to respond to a setback with violence. In October 1948 its militants tried to take over Lima's port city of Callao but failed. Bustamente declared the party illegal, but already the armed forces were accusing him of having been "too soft" on the *apristas*. Three weeks after the Callao revolt the army removed him in favor of General Manuel Odría.

Odría systematically persecuted APRA for the next eight years. Haya de la Torre spent the first five of those in asylum at the Colombian Embassy before he was finally allowed to go into exile. Meanwhile, Odría tried to reduce APRA's hold on the labor unions by decreeing wage increases, creating jobs through public works programs, building public housing, and broadening the social security system. He was helped in this effort by a boom in exports, stimulated by the Korean War, that brought a spate of prosperity. The end of the war, however, burst the prosperity bubble. As his popularity plummeted, Odría scheduled elections for 1956—but APRA would not be allowed to participate.

APRA in Decline

The 1956 elections saw the emergence of a new party, Acción Popular (AP). Its leader was Fernando Belaúnde Terry, an architect from the bustling entrepreneurial city of Arequipa and currently dean of the Architecture School at San Marcos. AP appealed to the new middle class of modernizing, reformist intellectuals, professionals, and technocrats. As such, it posed a danger both to traditional upper-class interests, as reflected in the Conservative Party, and to APRA, which wanted to preserve its hold on the Left. Concerned that Belaúnde might win, the Conservative presidential nominee, Manuel Prado, struck a bargain with General Odria: in return for his official support, the Conservatives would make no attempt to investigate his government's financial dealings if they won. More shameful still was the deal reached between Prado and Haya de la Torre, by which APRA would pledge him its electoral support in return for a promise to legalize them afterward. Although the pact was intended to be secret its details were leaked to the public, disillusioning many *apristas*.

Prado won, thanks to *aprista* votes, and delivered on his promise to legalize APRA.

For the next six years Peru was governed by an unlikely coalition of Conservatives and *apristas* known as the "Convivencia." The APRA-controlled Confederation of Peruvian Workers (CTP) kept strikes to a minimum; APRA's chief newspaper, *La Tribuna*, backed the government's programs; and APRA's congressional bloc gave its votes to government bills, while sidetracking any initiatives proposed by Acción Popular. Although APRA's youth wing bolted the party in disgust, such cooperation with the Conservatives ensured that Haya de la Torre would be able to run for president in 1962.

The 1962 elections were a three-way race. This time General Odria represented the Right, while Haya and Belaúnde competed for the votes of the Left. In the final tally, Haya came in first with just under 33 percent of the vote, Belaúnde second with just over 32 percent, and Odria with a bit more than 28 percent. The remaining 6.5 percent was divided among four minor candidates. Since no candidate had received at least one-third of the total vote, Congress would determine the winner. Meanwhile, well-founded rumors were circulating that the army was considering a coup in order to prevent Haya from taking office. So, once again, APRA made a pact with the Right, this time to throw its congressional support to its former persecutor, General Odria, rather than see Belaúnde as president. For his part, Belaúnde was insisting that his razor-thin loss was due to the Prado government's rigging the election in favor of APRA. He demanded that the military intervene to cancel the results and prepare for new elections. The military agreed and acted accordingly.

New elections, held in June 1963, produced a Belaúnde victory, with 36 percent of the vote, to 34 percent for Haya, and 25 percent for Odria. However, APRA won more congressional seats than AP did. So, in collaboration with Odria's congressmen, the *apristas* were able to block all of Belaúnde's major legislation over the next five years. His land reform program was gutted by the opposition, and his ambitious public works programs ran into Congress's refusal to raise taxes to pay for them. As Belaúnde resorted to heavy foreign borrowing and monetary expansion as alternative means to fund them, his administration was increasingly plagued by budget deficits and mounting inflation. Factional squabbling in the government added to this scene of drift and disorder. Youthful radicals, impatient with the political stalemate and inspired by the Cuban Revolution, began organizing guerrilla bands in the mountains, eager to carry out their own version of land reform. The army was quick to suppress them, but even so a mood of alarm spread among the officers: unless long-overdue reforms were undertaken quickly, Peru might explode in a cataclysmic social revolution. As elections drew near, with the prospect of an *aprista* victory—now that AP was discredited— the armed forces decided to strike. On 18 October 1968 a coup replaced Belaúnde with a military junta committed to a radical reform agenda.

Military Radicalism
General Juan Velasco Alvarado, who led the October 18 coup, was from a modest, lower-middle-class provincial background. He had joined the army as a private and risen to the top by his own talents. Along the way, he had attended the Center for Advanced Military Studies, which had been instituted in 1950 to prepare officers to combat subversion. Its faculty was largely composed of civilians who were experts in economics, political science, public administration, anthropology, and sociology: disciplines deemed necessary for promoting effective civic action programs that would bring about a rapid improvement in the living standards of Peru's poorest populations and thus deprive Communists of fertile soil in which to plant their ideology. Ironically, most of the civilian "experts" were, if not actually Communists, at least positioned somewhere on the radical Left. Their message, which Velasco took to heart, was that reforms had to be deep and rapid. That would require rational central planning and firm supervision to make sure that reforms were carried out. Democracy, with its corrupt politicians and its pandering to special interests like the traditional oligarchy, foreign capital, or bureaucrats, was too inefficient to serve the purpose.

Velasco took over as president of the new government. The 1933 constitution was set aside in favor of a revolutionary statute of government, issued by the Supreme Revolutionary Junta, which was composed of the top commanders of the army, navy, and air force. The new Council of Presidential Advisers, composed of fifteen high-ranking officers, supplanted Congress. It would screen all of the decree-laws issued by the president and his cabinet.

Land reform topped the agenda. The Agrarian Reform Law of 1969 resembled those of the Mexican and Cuban revolutions in its scope. All holdings of more than 50 hectares (about 125 acres) on the coast, and over 30 hectares (75 acres) in the sierra, were expropriated, with compensation to be paid in long-term bonds. This affected almost 22 million acres, much of which had been held in the form of estates: agribusinesses producing export crops like sugar and cotton on the coast, and more traditional self-sufficient *latifundios* in the sierra. The former were converted into state farms, with management appointed by the government; the latter were converted into Indian cooperatives.

The 1970 Industrial Law was nearly as radical. The International Petroleum Company, a subsidiary of Standard Oil, was nationalized without any compensation—since the government claimed that it had evaded taxes for years. Foreign-owned mining companies, steel mills, transport services, and utilities furnishing gas, water, and electric power were seized as well. In their case, however, there was generous compensation. All of these were placed under a state holding company called "Indo-Peru." The government also took over foreign banks, in order to facilitate central planning and direct the flow of investment.

Domestic private industry was ordered to turn over 15 percent of profits every year to company employees, in the form of stock. The aim was to increase labor's share of company ownership until half of the board of directors was composed of workers. In the meantime, workers had a right to share in management decisions. In addition, it was almost impossible to fire a worker. After three months, job security was practically absolute.

To stimulate and channel popular support for its policies, the regime created SINAMOS, the National System of Social Mobilization. This umbrella organization controlled, in turn, various corporatist bodies. For labor, there was the Workers' Confederation of the Peruvian Revolution (CTRP), which tried to break APRA's grip on the unions. Although APRA had been outlawed again, its workplace cells enabled it to resist the onslaught so successfully that the government was forced to turn to the Communists for help. The peasants proved no easier to control. The National Agrarian Confederation (CNA), designed to represent peasants and Indian cooperatives, was riven by factions. The Indian cooperatives of the sierra clashed with the still-landless peasants who sought to seize part of their property. Workers on the coastal plantations, who had been highly paid by the foreign agribusinesses, resisted having their wages cut by the new state managers. Moreover, they already belonged to *aprista* unions and had no loyalty to the CNA. There were strikes, and even though troops were sent in to crush them, the workers eventually won out. In the end, the CNA was abolished. Similar problems occurred with SINAMOS's other component organizations for students and shantytown dwellers. Although the military claimed it wished to foster "popular participation," it soon became clear that it merely sought depoliticization through control from the top. SINAMOS's $95 million yearly budget, furnished by the Ministry of Public Works, accomplished very little, aside from creating more government jobs.

Indeed, none of the government's plans worked. Agrarian reform on the coastal plantations, which eventually resulted in worker management, failed to maintain the level of exports that the old agribusinesses had produced. As exports fell, Peru's balance of trade suffered. Up in the sierra, lack of financial and technical assistance for the cooperatives resulted in a drop in food production. For a population already living at bare subsistence levels, this meant starvation—and, in turn, a great migration of desperate people to the cities. Industry's failures were equally dramatic. Foreign capital avoided Peru, and domestic capital, faced with militant unionism and the prospect of worker control, also refused to invest. Instead, many small private entrepreneurs went into the underground economy, where they could evade the laws. The production and distribution of many commonly used items were handled through the "black market," which at one point was thought to compose about 60 percent of the country's GNP.

For the first four years the state was able to take up part of the investment slack, as a rise in world mineral prices gave it a steady source of revenue. Heavy borrowing from foreign bankers provided it with additional capital. That came to an end with the sudden upward spike in world oil prices in 1974. Then popular expectations, which had been raised so high by official propaganda, were suddenly dashed by the government's severe austerity measures. Press criticism of the regime was met by a sharp crackdown, in which all newspapers and magazines were put under state control. Meanwhile, in 1973 General Velasco suffered a stroke. Although he continued to act as president, he was no longer the skillful political tactician he once had been. He succumbed to a coup on 29 August 1975.

The military regime lasted another five years, during which it tried to repair the economy. Banks were denationalized, SINAMOS was shut down, the job security law was changed so that a worker had to be employed for three years—instead of three months—to qualify, and worker management schemes were scrapped in favor of profit sharing. The revolution had changed too many things permanently, however. The Peruvian upper class would never recover. Foreign investors shunned the country. The foreign debt remained a crushing burden. Domestic private industry, damaged and alienated, did most of its business in the underground economy. Lima was ringed by vast, sprawling shantytowns filled with recent migrants from the sierra who accounted for an estimated 60 percent of the city's population. The city center was choked with vagabonds and street vendors. Despite a stabilization agreement with the International Monetary Fund (IMF) and tough economic austerity programs, inflation remained high and unemployment rose to nearly half of the (potentially) economically active population. Angry protest demonstrations became so violent that the regime had to impose a state of emergency and suspend civil rights. Not until 1979, when rising world prices for Peru's food and mineral exports brought in abundant revenues, did the economic picture begin to brighten.

In the meantime, the military held elections in June 1978 for a constituent assembly, as a first step to restoring democracy. All parties, including APRA, were invited to participate—and indeed APRA won the most seats and was able to install Haya de la Torre as president of the assembly, but only because Fernando Belaúnde and his AP refused to present candidates. Belaúnde, still smarting from the 1968 coup, denounced the military's refusal to allow the assembly to convert itself into a legislative body. That made him so popular that he and his party easily outpaced their opponents in the 1980 general elections. Meanwhile, his chief rival, Haya, died in July 1979, two weeks after the new constitution was adopted, never having attained his long-sought goal of being Peru's president.

As Belaúnde soon learned, however, that goal was really not worth having under the wrong circumstances. In 1979, the year before he took office, the OPEC oil cartel suddenly limited the amount of oil available on the world market, thus driving up prices and disrupting economies around the globe. Belaúnde was saddled with an annualized rate of inflation of over 100 percent and had to take austerity measures to bring it down. Not only did that make him unpopular, but it opened up opportunities for well-placed bureaucrats to find ways for their friends and clients to evade the laws in return for bribes.

As the government floundered, a new guerrilla movement called "the Shining Path" (Sendero Luminoso) arose in the sierra. It had started in 1970 as a "discussion group" led by Professor Abimael Guzmán, who taught philosophy at the University of Huamanga, near the mountainous regional capital of Ayacucho. Guzmán was a Maoist maverick from the old Peruvian Communist Party (PCP), which many younger communists perceived as being too stodgy. The Shining Path carried over from the PCP the Marxist-Leninist idea of an elite vanguard party based on tight discipline, and of course the communist goal of the common ownership of all the means of production; but from Mao it borrowed the idea of guerrilla warfare, based on the support of peasants (rather than urban proletarians), as the proper route to power. What eventually made the Shining Path so formidable was its emphatic celebration of Peru's indigenous Inca traditions. For Peru, the communist utopia would involve a rejection of all foreign cultures, including the Spanish. Then Peru would turn its back on the world, make the self-sufficient Indian communal village the basis of everyday life, and restore Quechua as the lingua franca.

By 1980 the Shining Path had grown to about 500 active members, at which point Abimael Guzmán decided to begin the phase of armed struggle. That meant terrorist tactics: members undertook surprise nighttime raids on remote army or police outposts, killing the occupants and confiscating weapons and ammunition. By 1983 there were about 3,000 armed "combatants," and the scale of operations had increased to temporary takeovers of mountain towns and villages. Local inhabitants would be called out to the main square to hear an exhortation to join the movement and fight for social justice, after which there would be executions of the mayor, councilmen, or police chief—whichever authorities could be seized. Sometimes those might include technicians, engineers, teachers, or social workers sent out from the capital. Any foreigners, such as tourists, were certain to be killed, as were priests. Victims might also include uncooperative merchants, or even common villagers who expressed hostility toward the movement. The purpose was to create chaos and make the local people aware that the always remote and always hostile government could be challenged. Beyond that, the Shining Path hoped eventually to cut off food supplies from the countryside to Lima, for its ultimate goal was to destroy all urban life.

Belaúnde declared the region around Ayacucho an "emergency zone" and sent in the military. As the soldiers pursued the guerrillas, the latter blended in with the peasants. Some of the peasants were sympathizers, but others simply were afraid to turn over the guerrillas to the authorities because that was certain to bring swift reprisals. Caught between two ruthless foes, more than 7,000 peasants died in the developing civil war by 1985. Moreover, the military's attempts to encircle the Shining Path only spread the insurrection northward, beyond the Ayacucho region.

By the time Belaúnde's term ended, in 1985, the armed forces were ready to make peace with APRA as the last hope for rallying popular support against the Shining Path. The latter's numbers were estimated to be approaching 10,000 arms-bearing activists, with a great many more supporters and sympathizers ready to provide them with supplies, money, hideouts, and information. Both APRA and the military were concerned that either the

Shining Path or a new urban terrorist group—a youthful offshoot of APRA called the Tupac Amarú Movement—might successfully infiltrate the labor unions. With Haya de la Torre gone, the leadership of APRA had devolved upon Alan García, the son of a lifelong party activist and himself a former leader of the *aprista* youth. He swept to victory in the presidential elections of April 1985 with 53 percent of the vote in a multicandidate race.

Once in office, García was so inept that Peru's economy worsened considerably. He tried to make himself popular by moving far to the Left. He refused to pay on the foreign debt, whereupon the IMF and the World Bank cut off Peru from any more loans. He tried, unsuccessfully, to renationalize the banking system but succeeded only in frightening private capital and causing the GDP to fall by around 15 percent between 1987 and 1989. "Popular kitchens" were set up in shantytowns to provide subsidized food to the poor, but much of the foodstuffs disappeared into the black market. Inflation, which had been at an annualized rate of 100 percent when García took office, hit 1,000 percent in 1988 and passed the 2,500 percent mark in 1989. Despite periodic wage adjustments, real wages in 1989 were 60 percent below what they had been in 1985.

As García's popularity plummeted, the Shining Path's rose. The areas in the sierra under its control spread, and it was beginning to reach into the cities to make its power felt through the disruption of public services. Sabotage caused frequent blackouts. Transportation and sanitation facilities were disrupted. Schools and clinics had to be shut down; the postal services ceased to operate in some areas. García responded by ordering the killing of Shining Path prisoners, as a warning; and he even allowed the Ministry of the Interior to organize a "death squad," the Rodrigo Franco Command. In all, some 22,000 people are estimated to have been killed during his five-year term, without any effect at all in putting down the insurrection. The Shining Path looked more and more unbeatable.

Bolivia

In 1952 remote, mountainous, landlocked Bolivia erupted in a social revolution so profound in its consequences that it constituted not only a watershed event in that country's history, but also a more radical land reform than any seen in Latin America since the Mexican Revolution, and one not to be surpassed until the Cuban Revolution. As in Mexico (and unlike Cuba), this occurred in a society where a handful of political and economic elites dominated a large underclass of desperately poor, illiterate Indians who often spoke no Spanish and who toiled under unspeakable conditions on the *latifundios* or in the tin mines of the high *altiplano* (uplands). The elite landowning and mine-owning families were closely connected to other high-status power groups, such as the Catholic clergy, the military officer corps, and the upper strata of the legal profession. Nevertheless, the elite families had their petty personal disputes that divided them into political factions. Since those disputes never went deep enough to challenge the traditional social order, however, they had little effect on the majority of the population, which remained apathetic throughout most of Bolivia's history.[3]

That began to change with the Chaco War (1932–1935), in which Bolivia challenged Paraguay for control of a vast wasteland called the Chaco, where rumors said oil was to be found. The Indians were uprooted from their traditional villages and mining camps and sent off to fight—and die by the tens of thousands in the steamy jungle—in a war they couldn't understand. When Bolivia was decisively defeated by the Paraguayans, against all of the elites' confident expectations, those uprooted indigenous people returned from battle with very different attitudes. They were no longer apathetic; they were restless. Many of those who had worked in the mines came home to find no jobs waiting for them, for this was also the time of the Great Depression. With factories standing idle in the industrial world, the demand for Bolivia's chief export, tin, went into a sharp decline. Tin accounted for over 70 percent of the country's export earnings. With the collapse of tin on the world market, mines were shut down. Government revenues fell sharply too, spreading unemployment even further. Discontent spread throughout the society, even among the elites, who now blamed the army for drawing the country into war.

Much of the blame was deserved, for Bolivia's military leadership had not distinguished itself during the war. The officers hurled accusations against one another and tried to shift the blame to the tin companies and foreign bankers. Standard Oil was accused of fomenting the war, and so, waving the bloody shirt of wounded nationalism, one of the many short-lived post-Chaco military governments expropriated it. Social discontent and wounded national pride combined to make a volatile atmosphere in which several new parties appeared to challenge the traditional order. On the Left were the communists, divided into Stalinists (Partido de la Izquierda Revolucionaria, or PIR) and Trotskyists (Partido Obrero Revolucionario, or POR). Both parties were small, for their target group, the urban working class, was only beginning to emerge and was scattered among many small shops. The PIR was also successful in attracting many students. On the far Right were the Falange Socialista Boliviana (FSB) and the Movimiento Nacional Revolucionaria (MNR). The former was an imitation of the Spanish Falange. Like its model, it appealed chiefly to nationalistic middle- and upper-class students who wanted to combine Catholic corporatist ideas with a strong authoritarian government. The MNR, founded in 1941 by an economics professor named Victor Paz Estenssoro, also embraced the idea of corporatism but was more influenced by Mussolini's corporate state than by Catholic social encyclicals. Although Paz came from a distinguished conservative family from the southern town of Tarija, his experiences in the Chaco War made him sympathetic to Bolivia's indigenous soldiers. Those sympathies were strengthened after the war when he worked as an economist for the Patiño Mining Company, one of Bolivia's largest, and saw how badly treated the miners were. He soon quit, ran for Congress as a reformer, and supported the brief and doomed reformist government of Lieutenant Colonel Germán Busch (1937–1939). A real war hero, Busch stirred up hopes in the lower classes with a series of attempted reforms, including a progressive labor code and greater regulation of the mining companies by the state. Due to systematic sabotage by the landowning and mining elites, none of his projects bore fruit, however, and Busch finally committed suicide. Soon afterward, a new president, General Enrique Peñaranda, named Paz to be his economics minister.

During 1941 Paz founded the MNR, whose initial manifesto proclaimed it to be both patriotic and socialist: a multiclass alliance of labor, peasants, and middle-class nationalists. This was in keeping with the odd combination of men who joined Paz in founding the party: Hernán Siles Suazo, the son of a former president, and Walter Guevara Arze were former fellow travelers of the Trotskyist POR; on the other hand, the journalists who turned out the MNR's newspaper, La Calle, were anti-Semitic admirers of Nazi Germany, while Paz himself thought that Fascist Italy had found the right solution to the problem of class warfare.

The outbreak of World War II sharpened ideological divisions in Bolivia. Traditional elites, including General Peñaranda, favored the Anglo-Saxon powers, since most of Bolivia's trade was with them. Also, after Hitler's attack on the Soviet Union, the Stalinist PIR switched from neutrality to the Allied cause. By contrast, the Bolivian Falange loudly supported the Axis. The MNR, too, favored the Axis cause. Because the Patiño Mining Company's smelters were located in Liverpool, England, instead of in Bolivia, nationalists accused the country's elites of collaborating with Anglo-Saxon imperialism to keep Bolivia subservient. Bowing to American and British pressure, Peñaranda dismissed Paz from his government as a "Nazi sympathizer" because of the MNR's pro-Axis position. That turned out to be to the MNR's advantage, for it now could throw itself into the task of organizing the

miners to strike for better wages, hours, and working conditions. Its chief rival for labor's support, the PIR, hesitated to do the same for fear that any disruption of production might endanger the Soviet Union. When Peñaranda
sent in soldiers to shoot down striking workers at the Patiño mines in Catavi,
the PIR was silent—but the MNR excoriated the government. With that,
Juan Lechín, head of the National Federation of Bolivian Miners (FSTMB),
who up to then had been a Trotskyist, became another powerful recruit. The
MNR also opened up contacts with a secret lodge, Razón de Patria
(RADEPA), that had formed among the army's junior officers, many of
whom had served on the front lines in the Chaco War and viewed their senior officers with contempt. RADEPA's leader was Major Gualberto Villarroel.
Like Paz, he perceived Nazi Germany and Fascist Italy as models of rapid national development without class conflict.

On 20 December 1943, just a day before the anniversary of the Catavi
massacre, Villarroel overthrew the Peñaranda government. The MNR,
backed by thousands of miners' votes, became the new government's mass
base of support—although the MNR had to give up cabinet positions temporarily in order for Villarroel to receive diplomatic recognition from the
United States. For the next three years the government struggled against a
formidable coalition that ranged from the communist PIR on the Left to
traditional conservatives, the Falange, and the U.S. Embassy on the Right.
Although Villarroel didn't accomplish any radical reforms, he gave legal
recognition to Lechín's FSTMB. The workers' new militancy alarmed the
mine owners, whose newspapers began attacking the government bitterly.
The government lashed back, closing down the opposition press and ban-
ning public protests. The opposition parties then banded together as the
Anti-Fascist Democratic Front, whose increasingly violent clashes with the
authorities finally climaxed, on 21 July 1946, in an invasion of the Presidential Palace. Villarroel was shot, dragged out to the balcony, and thrown
down to the street, where a mob seized his body and hung it from a lamp-
post in the plaza across the way. Paz Estenssoro fled to Argentina, where
the friendly government of Juan Perón gave him asylum. The other MNR
leaders went underground.

The Revolution
Villarroel's ouster was followed by a return to conservative civilian rule. The
armed forces were purged of all supposedly revolutionary elements, but the
conservative restoration was never stable. The Anti-Fascist Democratic
Front quickly broke up, as the government also turned on its former communist allies, the PIR. Despite the repression, however, a revolutionary coali-

tion was forming underground. The PIR, rebaptized as the Bolivian Communist Party (PCB), continued to control many of the urban labor unions, including the railway workers. The MNR, through Juan Lechín, remained strong among the miners. Both the MNR and PCB were able to avoid being uprooted by creating large networks of secret workplace cells, and in late 1950 they agreed to coordinate their efforts to overthrow the government. Although Paz Estenssoro was still an exile in Buenos Aires, the MNR was very capably led by Hernán Siles and Juan Lechín.

In early 1951 the outgoing president, Mamerto Urriolagoitia, called for a political truce and legalized the MNR in time for it to participate in the May congressional elections. When the results showed a huge upsurge of popular support for the MNR, however, he cancelled the results and turned over the government to a military dictator, General Hugo Ballivián. But military defeat, politics, and frequent purges had left the armed forces fragmented and demoralized, so when the long-planned insurrection exploded in La Paz, on 9 April 1952, the army's high command was paralyzed. Armed peasants and miners joined the workers in the capital to take over the city. There was some resistance from the police and the cadets at the Colegio Militar, but the regular army conscripts refused to fight. After three days and nights of skirmishing, the revolution triumphed.

Paz Estenssoro, the MNR's undisputed leader, hurried back from Argentina to form a government. Hernán Siles would be the new vice president, and Walter Guevara Arze the minister of foreign affairs. Juan Lechín was in charge of the MNR's official labor confederation, the Central Obrera Boliviana (COB), and also served as minister of mines. The new government's proclaimed goals were (1) universal suffrage, with votes for the previously excluded Indians; (2) land reform, involving the elimination of the *latifundio* and the redistribution of land to peasant families; (3) nationalization of the three largest tin mining companies, with labor's participation in the new management; and (4) the dissolution of the armed forces. All of these would be achieved, except the last—and that would prove to be a fatal error.

Having learned from the past, Paz insisted that the revolution cultivate good relations with the United States. Accordingly, the MNR emphasized its anti-communist, pro-Western position in the Cold War and turned against its former collaborators in the PCB. At the same time, it cracked down hard on its right-wing rival, the Falange. The latter had refused to participate in the revolution and had even tried to alert General Ballivián to the growing conspiracy. Now it had to go underground. In consolidating its hold on power, the MNR forced the traditional parties to dissolve as well. Opposition newspapers were closed and the jails were filled with suspected opponents. Eventually, detention camps were set up in remote jungle areas to hold political dissidents.

The first several months of the revolution saw the government basking in popularity as it made good on most of its promises. Even before the 1953 Agrarian Reform Law, peasants had begun seizing the big estates and parceling them out among themselves. The best the government could do was to recognize the fait accompli and issue titles to the squatters. The MNR also organized "syndicates" to help the Indian peasant communities with local administration, credit, and marketing. Given the revolution's limited resources, however, such help was necessarily meager. The "syndicates" soon became all but autonomous local governments, each with its own militia and "chief." Nationalizing the tin mines also proved to be a mixed blessing, because Paz and Lechín were soon at odds over whether they should be run by the workers (Lechín) or by the state (Paz). As a compromise, the mines were put under a state holding company called the Mining Corporation of Bolivia (COMIBOL), but workers were included in the management.

Paz and Lechín also quarreled over what to do about the military. Immediately following the revolution the armed forces had been disarmed and confined to barracks. Lechín wanted to replace the army altogether with worker and peasant militias; Paz wanted to keep a downsized army as a counterweight to the workers and peasants, whose militancy might carry the revolution too far. Once again there was a compromise, in which Paz received most of what he wanted. The senior army officers were purged and their replacements were encouraged to join the MNR. These new officers were then sent as "advisers" to train the worker militias (the local peasant militias were temporarily left alone). As the worker militias became better trained they were, bit by bit, appended to regular army units and eventually absorbed altogether.

In 1956 Paz turned over the presidency to Hernán Siles Suazo. By then Bolivia was being lashed by runaway inflation that would soon tear apart the revolutionary leadership. The effects were felt mainly by the urban population, for the peasants were self-sufficient and the miners had their subsidized commissaries. Before leaving office, Paz signed a stabilization agreement with the IMF that required the government to balance its budget by raising taxes and cutting out subsidies to workers. Price controls were abolished, but wages were frozen. Siles, the new president, kept to the agreement and finally brought inflation under control by pegging the local currency to the dollar and making it freely convertible. The Left felt betrayed, however. When Lechín threatened to mobilize the COB, Siles called on the peasant militias to defend the revolution. Although this tactic was successful, the price was to grant the local peasant leaders even more autonomy from La Paz. Even so, peasant support made it possible for Siles to survive.

Paz, who returned to power in 1960, began his second term by trying to patch up the quarrel with labor. He had made Lechín his running mate and vice president. Nevertheless, the alliance was strained by the need to maintain the austerity program. Like Siles, Paz was forced to turn to the peasant militias, but by now the peasant leaders were resembling the old nineteenth-century *caudillos*. Some of them refused to recognize the central government's authority altogether, whereupon Paz turned to the army to suppress them. Thus, the MNR, which once had been a vehicle for uniting social classes, now began to play upon class divisions to keep itself in power.

Indeed, the MNR by 1960 had dropped its old corporatist ideology in favor of a more conventional capitalist approach to development. Although COMIBOL was retained, its workforce was sharply cut back as the tin mines became depleted. Meanwhile, Paz opened up Santa Cruz Province, Bolivia's empty eastern lowlands, to peasant colonization and foreign oil exploration. Lechín bitterly opposed all of these policies. Finally, in desperation, he broke with the MNR altogether and formed his own Revolutionary Party of the Nationalist Left (PRIN), in preparation for the upcoming 1964 elections. Great was his indignation, then, when Paz broke an unwritten rule and announced his candidacy for immediate reelection. The MNR split again, for this time even Siles refused to support him.

To hold things together, Paz turned to the army and chose General René Barrientos as his running mate. The military, meanwhile, had been extending its own power base in the public. Under both Paz and Siles soldiers had been used for civic action programs in many local communities, building roads, schools, bridges, and clinics. At other times they had been used to suppress, and even supplant, local peasant *caudillos*. When the Falange took over Santa Cruz in late 1958 and proclaimed its independence, Paz sent in the army to back up the local peasant militia. Continued Falangist violence finally made him declare the province a "military zone" and place Barrientos in charge. After pacifying Santa Cruz, Barrientos was sent to his native province of Cochabamba with orders to suppress the peasant militias that were threatening to join Lechín in a revolt. The general not only restored order quickly, but with his charismatic personality and his fluency in Quechua he quickly won over a personal following among the peasants, whom he organized into an MNR province-wide militia.

Paz's reelection was a pyrrhic victory, because by now he had alienated all of his former colleagues in the MNR and reduced his party to fragments, while simultaneously making himself completely dependent on the army to stay in power. Soon after the votes were counted, he had the MNR's security police, Control Político, round up the top labor and peasant leaders while army units took control of the mining camps. With the labor and peasant bases destroyed, there was no more institutional resistance to an army takeover, but there was also no popular foundation for a civilian government—a dangerous situation in the officers' eyes, especially with the Cuban Revolution trying to spread its influence throughout Latin America.

The army, meanwhile, had been politicized, first by the MNR cells that had been placed in all the units, and second by American advisers sent down after the Cuban Revolution to teach the officers counterinsurgency doctrine and tactics. Barrientos himself had received special training in the U.S. Canal Zone. With his political bases secured in the key provinces of Santa Cruz and Cochabamba, he seemed to his fellow officers to be the logical man to give Bolivia a fresh start. Accordingly, after consulting with the army's commander in chief, General Alfredo Ovando, Barrientos overthrew Paz in November 1964 and made himself dictator. The revolution was over, the MNR had ceased to exist, and the army was back in control.

Notes

1. On the Mexican Revolution and its conservative aftermath, I have mainly used the following works: Charles C. Cumberland, *Mexico: The Struggle for Modernity* (New York: Oxford University Press, 1968); Roger D. Hansen, *The Politics of Mexican Development* (Baltimore: Johns Hopkins University Press, 1971); Enrique Krauze, *Mexico: Biography of Power* (New York: Harper-Collins, 1997); Edwin Lieuwin, *Mexican Militarism* (Albuquerque: University of New Mexico Press, 1968); Colin MacLachlan and William H. Beezley, *El Gran Pueblo: A History of Greater Mexico* (Englewood Cliffs, NJ: Prentice-Hall, 1994); and Raymond Vernon, *The Dilemma of Mexico's Development* (Cambridge, MA: Harvard University Press, 1963).

2. For the section on Peru, *aprismo*, the military regime of General Juan Velasco Alvarado, and the origins of the Shining Path (Sendero Luminoso) movement, I have drawn especially on the following sources: Grant Hilliker, *The Politics of Reform in Peru* (Baltimore: Johns Hopkins University Press, 1971); Harry Kantor, *The Ideology and Program of the Peruvian Aprista Movement* (Washington: Saville 1966); Arnold Payne, *The Peruvian Coup d'Etat of 1962: The Overthrow of Manuel Prado* (Washington: Institute for the Comparative Study of Political Systems, 1968); George D. E. Phillip, *The Rise and Fall of the Peruvian Military Radicals, 1968–1976* (London: Athlone, 1978); and James D. Rudolph, *Peru: The Evolution of a Crisis* (Westport, CT: Praeger, 1992).

3. On the Bolivian Revolution, I have consulted mainly James M. Malloy, *Bolivia: The Uncompleted Revolution* (Pittsburgh: University of Pittsburgh Press, 1970); Christopher Mitchell, *The Legacy of Populism in Bolivia: From the MNR to Military Rule* (New York: Praeger, 1977); Lawrence Whitehead, "Bolivia since 1930," in *Cambridge History of Latin America*, vol. 8, ed. Leslie Bethell, 509–83 (Cambridge: Cambridge University Press, 1991); and Cornelius H. Zondag, "Bolivia's 1952 Revolution: Initial Impact and U.S. Involvement," in *Modern Day Bolivia*, ed. Jerry R. Ladman, 27–39 (Tempe: Center for Latin American Studies, Arizona State University, 1982).

CHAPTER SIX

~

Corporatism

Corporatism is a concept whose roots go back to medieval times, when many political philosophers and jurists analogized society to a human body (corpus) composed of many interrelated parts, arranged in a hierarchy of functions according to their importance for sustaining life.[1] According to such theories, society was composed of groups, each of which had a function that contributed to the welfare of the whole. Rights were related to function, as attested to by ecclesiastical and military *fueros* (privileges). Similarly, the medieval idea of contract, which apportioned rights and obligations between lords and vassals, derived from their interrelated functions. A group's importance in the social hierarchy was related to its function, not its numerical size.

This corporatist idea went into temporary eclipse after the French and American revolutions, with their belief in the principle of one man, one vote; but when revived as a nineteenth-century ideology, corporatism offered a third way between liberal capitalism and collectivistic socialism. Since "rights" could be justified only by the performance of a social function, corporatism differed from liberal capitalism by rejecting individualism. Rights were not inherent in the individual person; they belonged to the social group assigned to each function. Corporatism would also differ from socialism by rejecting both statism and, in most cases, egalitarianism. Groups should be self-regulating so long as they carried out their functions properly, and inequality was part of the natural order of things.

Catholic social theorists in France, Austria, Italy, and Spain began to revive corporatism toward the end of the nineteenth century. Eventually, with

129

the papal encyclicals *Rerum Novarum* (1891) and *Quadragesimo Anno* (1931), Catholic corporatism took on a modern shape. Catholics were encouraged to form trade associations to represent labor, capital, farmers, and liberal professions. These would then coordinate their interests through a parliament based on functional (i.e., group) representation. A sense of Christian brotherhood, promoted by the faith, would facilitate cooperation. A corollary, known as the principle of subsidiarity, held that decision making should take place at the lowest possible level, depending on the issue.

These ideas would eventually become embodied in the Austrian Constitution of 1934, under the rule of the Christian Social Party; and in the 1933 constitution of Doctor Antonio de Oliveira Salazar's "Estado Novo" in Portugal. They also formed part of the core doctrine of the Bavarian People's Party of Weimar Germany, the Popular Party of pre-Mussolini Italy, Charles Maurras's Action Française, and the Spanish Falange. What these right-wing groups and regimes had in common was a desire to adapt the hierarchical, but paternalistic, order of the medieval world to modern conditions—and also restore the authority of the Church and the nobility. Not surprisingly, this kind of corporatism appealed to many Latin American conservatives looking for new institutions on which to base their traditional monopoly of power.

The political Left produced its own form of corporatism: revolutionary syndicalism.[2] Rather than seeking cooperation along class lines, syndicalists agreed with Marxists that all of the means of production should be owned in common. The syndicalists were an urban offshoot of anarchism, however, and so they rejected Marxism's belief in state economic planning and control. Like the anarchists, they viewed the state—any state—as a repressive institution and predicted (correctly, it seems) that Marxism would only result in a brutal dictatorship. To avoid that, the labor unions had to take over the factories, shops, and farms. Every economic field would have its own union (syndicate), organized at the local, provincial, and national level. Not only would these be institutions of combat against the capitalist system, but after the revolution they would each organize their own branch of production. A syndicalist parliament would then coordinate the whole economy. Syndicalism became a powerful force in the labor movements of France, Spain, Italy, and Portugal, until it was superseded by communism after the Bolshevik Revolution. In Great Britain a nonviolent form of syndicalism called Guild Socialism was for many years a powerful current within the Labour Party. Thanks to the influence of anarchist and syndicalist labor leaders in Mexico, syndicalism would have an impact on the Mexican Revolution, as it became institutionalized in a single party based on functional representation under Lázaro Cárdenas. It may also have influenced Josip Broz Tito's version of communism in Yugoslavia, in which workers' councils controlled decision making in state-owned enterprises, through the election of management boards. In addition, the 1953 Yugoslav Constitution provided for one chamber of the bicameral parliament, the Producers' Council, to be elected by corporatist bodies. The leftist Peruvian military regime of General Juan Velasco Alvarado also used corporatist forms to mobilize the poorer classes, while at the same time controlling and channeling their activities.

Italian Fascism, which produced the most famous corporate state in the 1930s, owed much to both of these strains of corporatism, while adding some distinct features of its own. Benito Mussolini came out of the radical, syndicalist wing of the Italian Socialist Party. When he broke with the Socialists, many of his syndicalist followers joined his new Fascist Party.[3] Fascism differed from syndicalism in that it embraced the idea of forming compulsory guilds, or syndicates, for both employers and labor. These would be organized in every important area of the economy. Fascism differed from Catholic corporatism by assigning the state the role of final arbiter, in the event that employer and labor syndicates failed to agree. Indeed, in practice the state went so far as to control the elections for syndical leaders, so as to avoid disputes. The integration of labor and employer syndicates in decision making in any given field constituted a "corporation." Corporations, in turn, were supervised by the Ministry of Corporations and so became conveyer belts for the transmission of official policy in their respective economic areas.

Fascist corporatism became a model for the young Victor Paz Estenssoro, although he quickly abandoned it after coming to power. Getúlio Vargas's "Estado Novo" in Brazil constitutes a better example of an attempt to apply a corporate state structure to a backward economy. Unlike Mussolini, however, Vargas made no attempt to build up a totalitarian party. Fascist corporatism exerted a more direct influence on Argentina's Juan Perón, who in fact was proud to claim Mussolini's Italy and even Hitler's Germany as models. Perón went far in constructing not only a corporatist system for Argentina, but also a hierarchically organized mass party that marginalized all opposition. Thus, the Peronist system will serve as the most philosophically complete example of Fascist corporatism ever applied in Latin America.

Brazil

Brazil's nineteenth-century liberals subscribed to David Ricardo's "Law of Comparative Advantage." Extending Adam Smith's argument that specialization increased the total amount of goods available for exchange, and thus provided "the wealth of nations," Ricardo held that each nation should specialize in producing those goods for which it had a natural advantage and trade them for other things. Comparative advantage, married to free trade, would raise the living standards of all nations. In Brazil's case, as elsewhere in Latin America, this meant exporting primary products and importing finished goods from western Europe and North America. Given the extraordinary pace of material progress and commercial expansion between 1870 and 1910, this formula's success seemed self-evident. Liberalism gradually hardened into an ideology.

World War I was a bump in the road, to be sure. Although it created a greater demand for Brazil's exports, it cut off the supply of finished products because the industrial countries were focused on war production, not foreign commerce. Nevertheless, local demand for manufactured goods remained high. Some of those products, such as clothing or pharmaceuticals, were necessities; others might be luxuries—such as cigarettes or scotch whiskey—but were highly desired anyway. Local manufacturing expanded to fill the vacuum. Increased sales of exports meant there was plenty of capital to loan out to anyone who wanted to start a new factory or enlarge an existing one. Thus, the industrial middle class grew in size, and so—even more—did the industrial working class, for the inability to import machinery meant that factories had to depend on labor-intensive methods. Once the war was over, however, world commerce returned to its "normal" state. Why protect Brazilian manufacturers against renewed competition from abroad? After all, foreign goods were usually better made, and often cheaper. The war period seemed to be a mere temporary deviation, although nationalists argued that it proved the folly of neglecting one's own industry.

Liberals in the Republican Party ignored the nationalists during the long Indian summer of the 1920s, when peace and prosperity seemed guaranteed. Then came the stock market crash of 1929, which again severely disrupted the Brazilian economy. This time, however, it was the Latin American economies' exports that suffered, due to sharply falling demand in Europe and North America. The industrial countries needed to sell their finished goods in order to revive their idle factories, but the primary producers lacked the foreign exchange to buy. Once again there was a vacuum that local manufacturing was called upon to fill, but now the lesson had been rubbed in—a country cannot rely on others to supply its industrial necessities: it must have its own manufacturing base. Economic nationalism, or import-substituting industrialization, thus replaced economic liberalism as the dominant ideology.

Getúlio Vargas presided over this important transition in Brazil.[4] Indeed, his presidency, from 1930 to 1945, was a watershed in Brazil's history. It was a period of unprecedented industrial development. Manufacturing production increased almost eightfold; investment—partly private, partly state—increased by 1,000 percent; and both the number of factories and the number of industrial workers doubled. It was also the period in which Brazil changed from being a mainly rural to a mainly urban society. The collapse of export agriculture combined with the rise of manufacturing to create a mass migration to the cities. Rio de Janeiro's population increased by an estimated 50 percent, while São Paulo's doubled. The Vargas era also put an end to the extreme decentralization of the political system. During most of the period the states and major cities were under the rule of federal interventors. The federal bureaucracy grew and became more professional, while the old state political machines were dismantled. Finally, this era also saw the irreversible rise of big government. Its first task was to promote industrialization, by protecting domestic industry from foreign competition and providing easy credit. Where private industry was unwilling or unable to invest heavily, or in crucial areas such as steel or energy, the state would take the lead. The state would also encourage domestic private investment by undertaking various infrastructural projects. Big government's second task was to ensure social justice by encouraging labor to unionize (under government supervision) and providing it with decent wages and working conditions, pensions, and insurance. The state also undertook to decrease illiteracy and provide children with at least a primary education. Under Vargas the number of schools and enrollments both tripled.

There was little about Vargas's early career that presaged all this. Like many young men of the upper class, he believed in Positivism and modernization. But he also had spent his apprenticeship in the Republican Party of Rio Grande do Sul and showed all the signs of a typical machine politician. His father had been a general and a cattle rancher in São Borja, a district in the far northwest corner of the state, on the Uruguay River. Vargas's early education was at a military academy, but in his twenties he switched to law. Shortly after earning his degree he became an assistant district attorney in the state capital of Porto Alegre and became active in the state Republican Party, faithfully serving its boss, Antônio Borges de Medeiros. With Borges's backing, Vargas spent two terms in the state legislature. Then, because of his early military training, he was made a lieutenant colonel in the militia and was sent to put down a rebellion by a dissident faction of the state party machine. Rather than fight, however, he got himself elected to the Federal Chamber of Deputies, where he came to be known as a financial expert. He supported Washington Luiz for president in 1926 and was rewarded with an appointment to the cabinet as minister of finance. A year later, however, he resigned to run for governor of Rio Grande do Sul and was elected. As governor, from 1927 to 1930, he showed an enthusiasm for funding internal improvements: new roads, new schools, the creation of a state mortgage bank and a state agricultural credit bank. And as a presidential candidate in 1930 he projected the same enthusiasm for public works. But nothing prepared the public for what was to come after he came to power. As a deputy and cabinet minister he had been known as a believer in balanced budgets. And he had not applauded the two *tenente* revolts. On the contrary, he had expressed his satisfaction when the rebels were finally driven into exile. Many of those men came back in 1930 to lead the revolt that brought him into power, and to help him administer the country immediately afterward.

The Vargas era falls into four phases. The first phase, lasting from 1930 to 1934, is that of the Provisional Government, under which Vargas assumed temporary dictatorial powers. Congress was closed, as were the state legislatures and municipal councils. Federal interventors, most of them young, inexperienced *tenentes*, replaced the old state governors and municipal mayors. There was no definite plan of action, for the 1930 uprising had attracted a broad spectrum of support, ranging from liberal constitutionalists who simply wanted a more honest and open version of the old republic, to the nationalistic *tenentes* who aimed at more serious social reform and saw in the dictatorship an efficient means for brushing aside all opposition. At first Vargas seemed to side with the *tenentes*, giving them a free hand to dismantle the old state and local political machines and punish corruption. The government helped urban workers to unionize and also encouraged the forming of parallel employers' associations as the first steps toward a corporatist system. Vargas began cooling off toward the *tenentes*, however, when they formed the "3 de Outubre Club," as a kind of unofficial regime party. Such an organization threatened his maneuverability, and he was well aware that the *tenentes'* loyalty to him was not deep. On 9 July 1932 the liberal constitutionalists in São Paulo rose in revolt, demanding a new democratic constitution and the holding of free elections. It was a formidable challenge because the state militia was large and well equipped, but after a two-month siege federal troops, assisted by militias from Minas Gerais and Rio Grande do Sul, managed to suppress it. Once the rebels surrendered, however, Vargas was conciliatory. Anxious to divest himself of the *tenentes*, he agreed to most of São Paulo's demands. Elections for a constitutional convention were held in May 1933 and by mid-July of 1934 the convention produced a document that satisfied nearly everyone. For the liberal constitutionalists, there were guarantees of free elections and an impartial judiciary; for the *tenentes* there were provisions extending the government's power to foment economic development, protect labor, and provide for social welfare for the poor; for the old-guard politicians, the federal system was restored. All that Vargas asked for himself was that the Constituent Assembly be allowed to elect the country's next president for the 1934–1938 term and that he be allowed to stand as a candidate. On 16 July 1934 the Assembly ratified its new constitution, without a referendum, and the next day it chose Vargas to be Brazil's president.

Phase 2 of the Vargas era covers the years 1934 to 1937, during which he governed as a constitutional president. The *tenentes* no longer had a role to play in the government, although they remained politically active in other ways. Many were attracted to a Brazilian fascist movement called Integralism. Led by a São Paulo journalist named Plinio Salgado who sported a Hitleresque moustache and called for a corporate state similar to Mussolini's, the Integralists dressed in green shirts and jackboots, adopted the Greek *sigma* as their symbol in place of the swastika or fasces, and gave the fascist salute. Like other fascists, they organized in military formations and, secretly armed and trained by the military, they carried on street battles with the Communists. Their slogan was "God, Country, and Family." For them, the Vargas government was merely a pale precursor to the coming fascist revolution.

The Great Depression of the 1930s also stimulated the spread of communism. The Communist Party was fortunate in having the very prestigious and capable leadership of Luís Carlos Prestes, who succeeded in making great inroads into the labor movement and among the army's junior officers. However, the Communists got carried away by their initial successes, giving Vargas the opportunity he needed to increase his presidential powers. In July 1935 Prestes gave a passionate speech that called for the workers to rise up and seize the state. A frightened Congress then voted Vargas emergency powers to deal with the threat, which he used to outlaw their front organization, the National Liberation Alliance. The Communists then retaliated in November by using junior officers and noncommissioned officers to take over the military bases in Recife and Natal. In the latter case, senior officers were murdered as they slept. The revolts were quickly smashed, and Vargas's gestapo-trained police systematically uprooted most of the Communist Party's activists. Even so, a frightened Congress kept extending Vargas's emergency powers.

Thus, as Vargas's term neared its end and presidential candidates aspiring to succeed him already had begun campaigning, he was able to seize upon a wholly fabricated Communist plot called "the Cohen Plan" to suddenly call off the elections and assume dictatorial powers. Taking Salazar's Portugal as his model, he called his new regime the "Estado Novo" (the New State).

Congress was dissolved, the press was censored, and all political organizations were banned. The Integralists, who had collaborated with army intelligence in inventing "the Cohen Plan," expected to be the nucleus of the Estado Novo, but instead Vargas ordered them to disband as well. When they revolted, he had their leaders arrested and exiled to Portugal.

The Estado Novo was the third phase of the Vargas era. Like Salazar's Portugal and Mussolini's Italy, it was officially—according to its 1939 constitution—a "corporate state."[5] All workers and all employers, outside of the agricultural sector, had to join officially sanctioned trade associations, or "syndicates." Only one labor and one employers' syndicate was permitted for any given area of the economy. Local syndicates in a particular economic field would combine to form state-level federations, and state-level federations would then combine to form a national-level federation. For example, textile workers in various cities in São Paulo would form their local syndicates, which then would create the São Paulo Federation of Textile Workers. That, in turn, would join other state-level federations of textile workers to establish the National Textile Workers' Federation. Finally, the textile workers would combine with a similar hierarchy of steel, chemical, food and beverage processing, and other industrial workers to form a peak organization called the National Confederation of Industrial Workers. Besides that confederation, there was the National Confederation of Commercial Workers, which represented workers in branches of the economy such as insurance and banking, wholesale and retail sales, and services. There was also the National Confederation of Land Transport Workers, for railway workers and bus and streetcar drivers.

At every level, the textile workers' syndicates and federations would be paralleled by government-sanctioned textile employers' syndicates and federations—and so on throughout each economic field. Labor and employers' syndicates or federations, when meeting together to establish policies about wages, hours, work rules, and productivity, were called "corporations." Unlike Catholic social theory, in which corporations were supposed to be self-governing and encouraged by subsidiarity to keep decision making localized, Brazilian corporatism was designed to harness capital and labor to a national government program of rapid industrialization.

Therefore, government-imposed compulsory arbitration substituted for the free collective bargaining of more open political systems. The Ministry of Labor could intervene in a recalcitrant labor or employer organization, remove its elected officers, and appoint other leaders who were more willing to conform to the ministry's policies. No strikes or lockouts were permitted. All workers and employers had to pay an *imposto sindical* (dues), which the Ministry of Labor collected monthly and held in an account from which it would disburse operating funds to the federal, state, and local branches, according to a formula.

The 1939 constitution also changed the system of representation for Congress. Instead of deputies being elected on the basis of one man, one vote, they would be elected by syndicates. This was never put into practice, however, because Vargas never called Congress back into session. Nor did he ever revive the political parties, not even so far as to create an official party of the regime. Brazil's Estado Novo was a no-party state, rather than a typical fascist one-party state.

Meanwhile, import-substituting industrialization allowed Vargas to assemble an impressively broad coalition of supporters because it offered something to every important interest group. Labor was a main pillar of support, enjoying for the first time ever a panoply of social welfare benefits: old-age pensions, health and accident insurance, job security, higher wages, an eight-hour day, annual paid vacations, and year-end bonuses. So what if its unions were run by government-appointed *pelegos* (time servers)? In many cases those workers had never been unionized before and therefore couldn't regret the loss of liberties they never had. And they clearly were living better now. Private industry was contented too. Import substitution meant tariff protection from competing foreign goods, plenty of easy loans and other subsidies, and a tame labor movement that never went on strike. The military, long a supporter of industrialization, was behind the regime, satisfied that Vargas had discovered the formula for class cooperation and national economic self-sufficiency. The old *fazendeiro* elite, while not enthusiastic, was bought off by government price supports for its crops, mainly through official purchases of the surpluses. Agriculture also was exempted from the labor laws. Finally, the urban middle class found many new employment opportunities through the growth of government. The rise of the welfare state and the spread of the government's regulatory powers created thousands of new white-collar jobs.

World War II and the Japanese attack on Pearl Harbor posed a dilemma for the Estado Novo. The United States was eager to line up support in Latin America and, in the particular case of Brazil, to acquire air bases on the easternmost part of the bulge that would facilitate transporting troops to Africa. The Brazilian military was divided, with many of the nationalist officers secretly sympathizing with the Axis. In the end, promises of massive lend-lease military aid made Vargas decide in favor of the pro-American faction, and even agree later on to send a Brazilian expeditionary force (FEB) of some 25,000 men to fight in the Italian campaign. The nationalist military faction was assuaged by the knowledge that Brazil would be strengthened in its rivalry with Argentina, because the latter's refusal to break with the Axis deprived it of any U.S. aid.

Not only did the FEB distinguish itself in Italy, but its participation in the war against fascism made the officers question their support for a quasi-fascist regime back home. On returning to Brazil they used their prestige among fellow officers to pressure Vargas for liberal reforms. Indeed, Brazilians in general were celebrating the Allies' victory and were caught up in the surge of enthusiasm for democracy. Vargas was forced to schedule elections for December 1945. Certain shifts in his administration aroused suspicions that he was preparing another coup, however, so the army removed him from office in a bloodless coup on October 29.

Phase 4 of the Vargas era is the story of his surprising return to the presidency and his ultimate disgrace and death. It begins with the scramble for power that attended the establishment of democracy in 1945. The first political coalition to form, the National Democratic Union (UDN), consisted of all those who had not benefited from the Estado Novo: small businessmen, democratic reformers, laissez-faire liberals, and remnants of the pre-Vargas state political machines. Opposing them were Vargas-appointed state and municipal interventors and their hangers-on, who were concerned to preserve *getulismo* without Getúlio by combining to form an incumbents' party, the Social Democratic Party (PSD). São Paulo's interventor, Adhemar de Barros, insisted on creating a separate, personal vehicle, however, which he called the Social Progressive Party (PSP). Then there was the enormous trade union and social welfare bureaucracy, whose Brazilian Labor Party (PTB) stood somewhat to the left of the other three. Finally, there was the Communist Party, which received 10 percent of the national vote in the first democratic elections for Congress. To the chagrin of those who had hoped to see an end to *getulismo*, the PSD ticket won in 1945, behind the candidacy of General Eurico Dutra, Vargas's former war minister.

Meanwhile, Vargas began plotting his comeback. He was still popular, as was shown by his being elected senator from two different states and federal deputy from seven others (the constitution did not require residency to qualify as a candidate). He accepted the PSD's senate seat from his home state, Rio Grande do Sul, and although he attended the sessions infrequently he cultivated the image of a democratic politician. He kept up his contacts with former cronies in the PSD and PSP, while simultaneously making populist speeches at PTB rallies. The Communist Party, declared illegal by Dutra in 1947, lent its support to Vargas too. As the official PTB candidate for president in 1950, with a PSP man as his running mate and a portion of the PSD supporting him, Getúlio easily outdistanced his rivals and returned to power.

His triumph was short lived, because inflation—which would worsen during his administration—was already beginning to create tensions. The expansion of consumer goods industries under the Estado Novo had not freed Brazil from its dependence on foreign imports, for those industries now required continued inputs of machinery, parts, and fuels, all of which had to be imported. Those imports were far more costly than Brazil's agricultural exports, which resulted in unfavorable trade balances. Moreover, during the 1930s industry, not agriculture, had attracted most private and government investment. Agricultural methods were backward and production was stagnant—all the more so because many agricultural workers had moved to the cities and were not replaced by machinery. This created a dual problem: not only was agriculture unable to pay for the cost of capital goods imports, but it was unable to adequately supply Brazil's own burgeoning urban population. Rising food prices were part of the problem of inflation; an inadequate supply of housing for the urban newcomers, which drove up rents, was another. Yet another inflationary factor was the high cost of inefficiently produced domestic consumer goods. When Dutra tried to hold the cost of those goods down by permitting competing foreign goods to enter, the outcry from local industry was so great that he backed off. Besides, Brazil's foreign exchange reserves were already being depleted by the unfavorable trade balances, and they would be reduced even more by Dutra's decision to purchase outright the foreign-owned railroads and port facilities.

Vargas was a politician, not an economist, and his base of support lay chiefly in the urban working class. From an objective viewpoint the situation may have called for cutbacks in spending on subsidies to local industry, lower tariffs, a smaller government payroll, a wage freeze, higher interest rates, and currency devaluation, but then Getúlio would have lost his political base. Instead, he took the populist route and blamed foreign capitalists and international bankers for Brazil's problems. To placate the unions, he brought his young protégé, João ("Jango") Goulart, into his cabinet as labor minister. Goulart, who had succeeded Vargas as head of the PTB, sought to solidify the workers' backing for the government by decreeing a 100 percent wage increase. That would push industrial wages higher than many army officers' salaries. The military, which only a year earlier had forced Vargas to dismiss his war minister for being too far to the left, now demanded Goulart's removal as well. It was no idle demand, either. Coup rumors were rife. Reluctantly, Getúlio gave in, in February 1954. His own fall was only a few months away.

The anti-*getulista* UDN continued to hammer at Vargas's mishandling of the economy. One of its most talented journalists, Carlos Lacerda, was also publishing shocking revelations of corruption emanating from the Presidential Palace in Rio de Janeiro's *Tribuna da Impensa*. On August 5 Lacerda was the target of a gangland-style machine gun attack as he was walking along the street with an air force officer. Although Lacerda escaped with a minor wound, the officer was killed. Immediately the armed forces took charge of the investigation and soon traced the authorship of the crime to the president's bodyguard. On August 24 they presented Vargas with an ultimatum: he must either resign or be deposed. At the end of his rope, and saddened by revelations that his son was involved in the network of graft, he locked the door to his bedroom and put a bullet through his heart with a .32 revolver. A suicide note, found beside the body, blamed a sinister cabal of "international economic and financial groups" allied with certain local interests that conspired against the people.

The shock of Vargas's suicide and the emotional tenor of his final note overturned all the work that his enemies had done to discredit him. Riots broke out all over Brazil, with mobs attacking opposition newspapers and radio stations, U.S. companies and bankers, and American consulates. *Getulismo* suddenly found new vigor. Juscelino Kubitschek, the candidate of the right-wing *getulista* PSD, won the presidency the following year, and his vice president was "Jango" Goulart, leader of the left-wing *getulista* PTB. For the next five years this *getulista* government spent lavishly to maintain its popularity, even building an entirely new capital city, Brasília, in the hinterland. Then followed a brief hiatus, when the anti-*getulistas* found a charismatic presidential candidate in the erratic, unpredictable Jânio Quadros. When Quadros took office, however, he found himself facing a 60 percent inflation rate, due to Kubitschek's heavy spending. He then asked for, and was denied, extraordinary powers from Congress to make massive cuts in the government budget—whereupon he suddenly resigned, after only seven months in office. Goulart, who had been reelected vice president on a separate ticket, now took over—to the military's horror—and promised to carry on the *getulista* tradition.

Argentina

At the beginning of June 1943, the Second World War was reaching a turning point. On the Russian front in Europe, German armies were in retreat after their disastrous defeat at Stalingrad a few months earlier. In North Africa, British and American forces had just captured Tunis, putting an end to the fighting in that theater of war. They were now preparing to invade Sicily and were carrying out bombing raids on Italian cities. Mussolini would fall from power in July. Out in the Pacific, American forces had recently won a crucial victory over the Japanese at Guadalcanal and were now preparing to press their advantage in New Guinea, the Philippines, and the Solomon Islands. The Axis was not yet beaten, but an Allied victory was all but certain. At this moment in history, on 4 June 1943, the Argentine army pulled off its second major coup of the twentieth century in order to install a pro-Axis regime.

The Concordancia coalition government, under President Ramón Castillo, had kept Argentina on a neutral course during the war's early phases, but his picked successor, Robustiano Patrón Costas, wanted Argentina to abandon neutrality and join the Allies. Like most upper-class *estancieros* with commercial ties to England, he was pro-British. Indeed, Patrón Costas was the quintessential Argentine oligarch. As the political boss of Salta Province, in the extreme northwest, he owned extensive estates where peasants labored under feudal conditions. He also had lucrative connections with Standard Oil, which exploited oil deposits in Salta's lowlands. He was a senator and a prominent figure in the Conservative Party. In short, Patrón Costas belonged to the old, traditional Argentine "Right" and symbolized everything that the new, nationalistic "Right" despised. The nationalists had made a grab for power in 1930, behind General Uriburu, but had been quickly shunted aside by the Concordancia. For the next ten years they worked assiduously to recover power by forming discussion groups and publishing magazines that praised the work of regimes like Mussolini's Italy, Franco's Spain, Salazar's Portugal, and Hitler's Germany. In a Spanish-speaking country like Argentina, where large numbers of Germans and Italians lived, their propaganda had effect. They had many supporters in the Catholic clergy, which favored Franco's side in the Spanish Civil War, and they also found recruits among junior and midlevel army officers who admired the militarism of Mussolini and Hitler. The examples of European and Japanese fascism also brought home the lesson that modern military power rested upon industry. The old Right of the Concordancia wanted to keep Argentina agricultural; the new Right was for industrializing. Thus, the army's support for the Concordancia began to erode. Patrón Costas's rigged electoral victory and the prospect of another six years of traditional rule were the last straws. The army officers who staged the June 4 coup removed President Castillo from office, cancelled the election results, and proclaimed a military dictatorship.

The core of this military conspiracy was a secret lodge called the Group of United Officers (GOU), whose leader was Colonel Juan Domingo Perón. Unlike most Argentine officers, Perón had a common touch that made him popular with ordinary soldiers and noncoms. He had grown up in the Patagonian interior, where he had learned from the gauchos how to ride and shoot. Perón was no lower-class upstart, however. His grandfather had been a prominent physician and professor of exact sciences at the University of Buenos Aires, but he died relatively early in life and left no fortune. By contrast, Perón's father was a mediocrity who washed out of medical school, moved to the small provincial town of Lobos, where he failed in business, and wound up managing a sheep ranch for some relatives in Patagonia. Along the way he fostered two illegitimate sons by a half-Indian girl, whom he later had the decency to marry and take with him to the south. Perón, the second son, had a lively intelligence reminiscent of his grandfather's. Fortunately for him, his grandmother recognized this and brought him to Buenos Aires to make certain that he received a good primary and high school education. Perón would have preferred to become a doctor, but the family couldn't afford to send him to medical school. Instead, at the age of fifteen he passed the entrance examinations for the Military Academy and began an army career.

Three years later, Perón was commissioned as a second lieutenant, graduating just above the middle of his class. Taller than most Argentines, and powerfully built, he excelled at sports, especially boxing and fencing. This would serve him well as a young officer posted to provincial garrisons, for he won popularity with the soldiers by organizing boxing contests to relieve the boredom. His superiors recognized Perón's talent for dealing with subordinates and assigned him to the army's School for Noncommissioned Officers. Once again he was extremely popular with the men beneath him and even undertook to write a manual of hygiene and comportment to help them improve themselves. That earned him an appointment to the Superior War School, a crucial hurdle in the career of a junior officer. He made the most of this opportunity by spending extra hours in the school library, with the result that he graduated near the top of his class. He also had become engaged to a schoolteacher named Aurelia Tizón. They were married in January 1929, just a few weeks before Perón graduated.

After graduation, Perón was promoted to captain and assigned to General Staff Headquarters, which he discovered to be a hotbed of conspiracy against the government of President Yrigoyen. In mid-1930 he was approached about joining a coup plot, to be led by General Uriburu. He agreed to attend some meetings and for awhile acted as the plotters' officer in charge of operations. But although he had enormous respect for Uriburu, he became convinced that the scheme would fail. He finally pulled out at the last moment and sided with the faction supporting General Justo instead.

That was a misstep, for Uriburu did indeed succeed in his plans, and Perón was punished by being posted to a distant garrison on the Bolivian frontier. Influential friends in the Justo faction had him returned to Buenos Aires in a few months, however, and even secured his promotion to major. In the meantime, a new Perón was beginning to emerge: the military scholar and intellectual. He already had published in 1928 a monograph on German strategy on the Russian front in World War I. He followed that up with a second volume, which drew some theoretical generalizations from the data. Now he was at work on a two-volume study of the Russo-Japanese War. His superiors were sufficiently impressed to secure him a teaching appointment at the Superior War School.

Perón would remain at the Superior War School until February 1939, except for a two-year stint as a military attaché in Chile, from 1936 to 1938, where he acted as a (not very skillful) spy. While at the school he wrote several more works, on topics ranging from military history to the geography and strategic importance of Patagonia; but the most important book for understanding Perón's evolving political thoughts is his *Apuntes de historia militar* (Notes on Military History), published in 1932. Chapter 3, "Preparations for War," lays out a well-structured view of the world.[6] Wars are inevitable because man's nature is conflictual; therefore, nation-states have to be ready to fight, or else resign themselves to being subjugated. Moreover, modern warfare requires industry, so nations that have a large industrial capacity are advantaged. That, in turn, means that the state must be able to direct the process of industrialization so as to maximize a country's ability to fight. Not only the armed forces but natural resources, capital, labor, trade, and research must be mobilized for defense and kept in a constant state of preparedness, for it is never certain when war may break out.

The political implications of total mobilization were the militarization of society, in which all citizens would be organized like an army with a chain of command. In such an army, Perón argued, leadership is the crucial element. Industry, natural resources, troops, and arms all contribute to national power, but to be effective they must be handled and coordinated by a skillful leader. In the hands of a defeatist or a coward, they are useless. Twelve years later, when he was minister of war under the military government that came to power in 1943, Perón further elaborated on his thesis.[7] A nation had to be unified, just as an army, in order to mobilize effectively. To avoid internal conflicts a government must regulate the social, intellectual, and moral life of a country—not just economic matters. Intellectuals, educators, the press, and the cinema must be harnessed to counter "cosmopolitanism" and instill a sense of national solidarity. With respect to the economy, government policies should have a popular character so as to enlist the masses in the national project.

In March 1938 Perón was promoted to lieutenant colonel. His reputation was on the rise among his fellow officers, but just at that moment Aurelia was diagnosed with cancer. Although she underwent surgery, she died in September. Perón went into a depression, so to shake him out of it his friends in the War Ministry dispatched him in February 1939 as a military attaché to Italy, with orders to study mountain warfare with Mussolini's Alpine troops. The assignment was really open ended, for Perón was quite free to travel about once he finished his training. Fascist Italy captivated him. It was for him a living laboratory for all the ideas he had expressed in *Apuntes*. He read the 1926 Fascist Law of Syndical Corporations, the 1927 Fascist Labor Code, and the 1934 Constitution of the Corporate State, down to their minute details. He claimed to have attended university classes in Turin and Milan on Fascist organizational theory and principles, and to have had a personal interview with Mussolini. "Italian fascism achieved effective participation for popular organizations in the nation's life," he concluded. "I saw the resurgence of corporative institutions and I studied them in depth. . . . I began to see that evolution leads us, if not to corporations or guilds—because you can't go back to the Middle Ages—at least to a formula in which the people might have active participation."[8]

His travels also took him to Nazi Germany, where similar things were happening: "an organized state that aimed at a perfectly organized community and also a perfectly organized people." Germany impressed him as "an enormous machine that functioned with marvelous perfection, and where nothing—not even a tiny screw—was missing. Its organization was something formidable. . . . I studied this social and political phenomenon a great deal. They had there a great crucible where they were forging something new."[9] For Perón, Fascism and National Socialism offered a "third way" between the twin extremes of selfish, plutocratic capitalism and the statist anthill society of communism. This third way was superior to both because, he concluded, its organization by groups—syndicates and corporations—retained a true, natural pluralism.

On his return to Argentina, in January 1941, Perón's European experiences put him in great demand among nationalist clubs as a speaker. Within the army, he soon gathered around himself a group of pro-Axis officers that called itself the Group of United Officers. The GOU's nominal head was General Edelmiro Farrell, who was conspiring with the war minister, General Pedro Ramírez, to overthrow the Concordancia. After the June 1943 coup Ramírez would become president of Argentina, Farrell would be appointed war minister, and Perón would be named undersecretary of war. From that position Perón could control military promotions and assignments, which enabled him to put his own men into key positions. When Farrell ousted Ramírez in February 1944 and took over as president, Perón became his vice president and also minister of war. But while he was consolidating his position in the army, Perón was also building a mass base in the Argentine labor movement.[10]

Labor had never been a powerful political force in Argentina. Persecution of unions under Yrigoyen, Uriburu, and the Concordancia had kept most workers from organizing. Out of approximately 4.5 million nonagricultural workers, only about 470,000 were in unions, and those were divided along ideological lines into Communists, Socialists, and Radicals. Wages were depressed by the enormous migration of rural people into the cities during the 1930s, as the agricultural depression pushed them off the land and the hope of jobs lured them to the urban areas. Most were unskilled laborers who were unable to find steady work and were forced into squalid, makeshift shantytowns that spread out from the cities' outskirts. The fortunate few who did get factory jobs were poorly paid, worked long hours, and labored under unhealthy—and often dangerous—conditions. They had no vacations, no pensions, and no health or accident insurance. The old established unions, often led by European immigrants, made little attempt to incorporate these rural migrants, who reacted against such foreign ideas as Marxism or anarchism. The migrants were dismissed as ignorant bumpkins. The measure of Perón's political genius was that he recognized the potential of this neglected mass of new urban workers.

As the new military government was being formed, following the June 1943 coup, Perón requested and received the seemingly unimportant post of secretary of labor and social welfare. In previous governments this job did little more than collect statistics on strikes, factory conditions, and workers' living standards. Occasionally it succeeded in convincing Congress to pass laws to limit the labor day or provide workers' insurance, but such laws were seldom enforced. Perón, however, had the Labor Secretariat raised to cabinet status, after which he began a vigorous campaign—backed by all the power of an authoritarian regime—to enforce all the labor laws on the books. There would be an eight-hour day, clean and healthy factory conditions, accident and health insurance, annual paid vacations, and compulsory contributions by employers and workers to pension funds. Going further, he not only insisted on the workers' right to form unions but launched a drive to unionize all previously unorganized workers, even rural labor. In November 1944 he began a purge of the Communists and forced all unions to join a single national confederation: the General Confederation of Workers (CGT). By the beginning of October 1945 he felt strong enough to issue a decree-law, through President Farrell, establishing the Law of Professional Associations, based on Mussolini's labor code.

The new law's provisions were similar to those adopted by the Estado Novo in Brazil. Government recognition was required for a union to legally exist, and only one union per field could receive it. The Labor Secretariat would collect all dues and control the bank accounts. No strikes or lockouts were permitted. If union officials were deemed not to be acting in the unions'—or the nation's—interests, the government could remove them and appoint new officials. Labor contracts would result from industry-wide bargaining involving workers, employers, and the government, the latter having the final voice in drawing up the agreement. Finally, there would be a system of labor courts to iron out specific grievances.

Clearly, the Law of Professional Associations would give Perón the power to bring the entire labor movement under his control, giving him a mass base from which to pursue his obvious political ambitions. As vice president, he already was only a heartbeat away from the pinnacle of power. Suddenly alarmed, his military colleagues forced Farrell to dismiss him from all his positions and place him under arrest to ensure that he would be unable to mount any resistance. All their plans were upset, however, when, on October 17, a spontaneous mass rally of workers and their families filled the Plaza de Mayo in front of the presidential palace, and all the streets leading into it. Faced with hundreds of thousands of people chanting, "We want Perón!" the military caved in, brought Perón out of arrest, and placed him on the balcony in front of the jubilant crowd. Elections were promised for January, and Perón would be a candidate.

Two coalitions contested the elections. Perón's was composed of the hastily formed Partido Laborista, representing the unions; a group of young, nationalistic Renovationist Radicals; and right-wing Catholic nationalists. The opposing Democratic Union was an even more motley assortment, combining the Radical, Socialist, Conservative, and Communist parties, with open support from the U.S. Embassy. In what was broadly acknowledged as a fair contest, Perón won the presidency by a wide margin. Moreover, his supporters gained majorities in both houses of Congress, won every one of the gubernatorial races, and claimed majorities in all but one of the provincial legislatures.

Given such a clear mandate, Perón might easily have governed democratically. That suited neither his temperament nor his plans, however.[11] Soon after taking office he ordered the various components of his coalition to merge into a single party, which became known as the Peronist Party. Some of the union leaders, thinking to convert the Partido Laborista into something equivalent to the British Labour Party, resisted this loss of their autonomy. They were hounded out of their unions, arrested on trumped-up charges, and sent to jail in Patagonia. The resulting party was based on the principle of "verticality," meaning that orders flowed down from the top (Perón), through his handpicked Supreme Council, and were then carried out by provincial, municipal, neighborhood, and workplace organizations. Parallel to the party, as part of the broader Peronist Movement, was the CGT, or "labor wing." A feminist wing, the Partido Peronista Feminista, constituted the third pillar of the movement after women were awarded the suffrage in 1947. Perón's wife, Eva, was its president.

While Perón was organizing his movement into an invincible political army he also was busy eliminating any effective opposition. All of the judges sitting on the Supreme Court were impeached as soon as Congress met after the 1946 elections. The lower courts were not purged until 1949, when a new Peronist constitution went into force, giving Perón the excuse that judicial appointments made under the old system were legally terminated. Disciplined Peronist majorities in Congress steamrollered the opposition parties and even made it a crime to publicly criticize Perón, Evita, the cabinet, the top military officers, or official policy. Under the law of *desacato* (disrespect), a senator or deputy could be stripped of his immunity and prosecuted. The 1949 constitution further increased executive powers by allowing the immediate reelection of the president for an indefinite number of terms, greatly expanding the president's power to legislate through decree-laws, and exempting cabinet ministers from congressional questioning.

Opposition parties were allowed to exist, but Peronists took care to prevent them from ever becoming a majority. Some newspapers, like the Socialist *Vanguardia*, were destroyed by Peronist thugs; others were bought up; others, like the conservative *La Prensa*, were simply seized on the pretext that they had violated some law. By 1954 there was only one independent newspaper in Argentina, *La Nación*, which was very circumspect in how it reported the news. All of the radio stations were state owned, and when television was introduced in the 1950s it too was under state ownership. Thus, although elections were still held, opposition parties had no access to the media. Printing establishments were afraid to print their propaganda, and rallies were often broken up by Peronist bullies. Nor could opposition parties form electoral coalitions; each had to run separately. If a candidate's campaign speeches hammered too hard at the authorities, he could be jailed for "disrespect," as was Ricardo Balbín, the Radicals' presidential nominee in

1952. Hanging over every prominent opposition figure's head was the fear of brutal reprisals by Perón's storm-trooper organization, the National Liberating Alliance (ALN), composed of about 1,000 well-armed men who did the regime's dirty work, ranging from beating up opponents to burning and sacking opposition party offices, or even murder. Equally sinister was the Special Section of the Federal Police, where arrested opponents were routinely tortured with electric cattle prods, and sometimes made to "disappear."

Perón was not simply interested in exercising power for its own sake, however. Power enabled him to put his long-maturing ideas into actual practice.[12] He bragged that he would put Mussolini's corporate state into practice, without committing Mussolini's mistakes. The "nation in arms," or, as he preferred to call it, the "organized society," became his goal. Officially, the regime's ideology became known as *Justicialismo*, a concept difficult to translate precisely into English but that can be summarized by the *Trés Banderas* ("three flags") that flew from its ramparts: national power, economic sovereignty, and social justice. These would be achieved through the state's organizing all employers, workers, and professional people into syndicates, federations, and confederations and coordinating their activities. Labor already was organized through the CGT; now Perón began to pressure employers to follow suit. They resisted, however, so that it was not until 1953 that farmers, ranchers, industrialists, and merchants were forced into the General Economic Confederation (CGE), which encompassed separate branches for agriculture, industry, and commerce. Also in 1953, professionals such as doctors, lawyers, engineers, architects, and teachers were herded into the General Confederation of Professionals (CGP). Earlier, Perón had met opposition from the universities by closing down all student and professorial associations and forcing their members to join the General University Confederation (CGU). Even high school students were captured by the regime through its official Union of Secondary School Students (UES).

The middle classes were forced into conformity by the spread of the state's economic power. Perón had inherited from previous governments a state oil company and various German- and Italian-owned businesses that had been expropriated in the last months of World War II, when Argentina finally broke with the Axis. To these he added railroads, port facilities, subways, and telephone and utilities companies formerly under U.S., British, or French ownership, paid for with wartime credits that Argentina had built up from its sales of food and raw materials to the Allies. Indeed, Argentina's postwar prosperity enabled Perón to launch new state enterprises in the areas of natural gas, a merchant marine, and airlines. On top of that, he nationalized the Central Bank, which previously had been a joint enterprise with local private capital. In this way, the state not only owned the "commanding heights" of Argentina's industrializing economy, but it could also control the flow of credit. An industrial bank was set up to target those industries the state particularly wished to promote. Meanwhile, the army was building its own industrial combine, Fabricaciones Militares, to produce weapons and explosives, so that it might be self-sufficient in the event of war. The navy and air force had similar, though less ambitious, programs.

The "renewable resources" needed to keep financing this plan to turn Argentina into an industrial and military power were to come from a state monopoly for the export of agricultural products: the Argentine Institute for Production and Trade (IAPI). IAPI would function as the sole purchaser of agricultural goods from Argentine farmers and ranchers, for which it would pay prices substantially below those offered in the world market. Then it would act as the sole exporter of Argentine foodstuffs, hoping to drive up prices on the world market and pocket the profits. Since Argentina was a major world producer of meat and grains, and since the war's destruction of European agriculture created a food shortage in the immediate postwar period, Perón was confident that the world would have to pay Argentina, in dollars, in order to eat. The scheme went awry for two main reasons, however. First, the United States, with its much more efficient agriculture, was able to supply Europe with food through the Marshall Plan. Second, Argentine agriculturalists, reacting to IAPI's low prices, cut back on production. The drop in supply meant that the state could not export large amounts and simultaneously satisfy domestic demand. If it chose to export, domestic shortages would drive up prices and undermine working-class support for the regime. If it chose to supply the domestic market, the industrialization program would stall for lack of investment.

In fact, industry was stagnating anyway. The spread of import-substituting industry during the 1930s had not freed Argentina from its dependence on industrial imports; rather, it had changed the nature of such imports. Import-substituting industrialization had begun with consumer goods industries, such as food and beverages, textiles, clothing and leather goods, or small appliances. However, consumer goods industries require constant inputs of capital goods, such as machinery, motors and engines, and heavy vehicles; and intermediate goods such as steel sheets and tubes, aluminum, rubber, and industrial chemicals. Those were more expensive than consumer goods and also required heavier capital expenditure to produce and a higher level of technology. Although Perón had plans to build such heavy industries, Argentina in the early 1950s was incapable of satisfying those needs by itself. Those goods had to be imported, but to do so Argentina had to earn the foreign exchange by exporting—and there lay the bottleneck that frustrated all of Perón's economic schemes.

Even worse, after the initial flush of popularity he enjoyed from nationalizing the foreign railways and utilities, Perón discovered the heavy expense of maintaining them. Their former owners, realizing that the emotional nationalism of the times would eventually result in their expropriation, had neglected to invest in new equipment. Thus, the state took over factories and plants that were often dilapidated and in need of large inputs of capital to keep them running. Unable to earn enough money from exports, the government began printing paper money to cover its debts, which only fueled inflation.

Labor was another problem. The unions, confident of government backing, drove up wages far beyond productivity, which indeed was falling. That too was inflationary. When Perón tried to limit wage increases, workers responded by not showing up for work, since job security was almost total. Often their absenteeism was the result of their having a second job, in order to keep up with the rising cost of living. Productivity suffered all the more, and inflation continued to rise.

By the time of Perón's reelection, in 1952, the regime was showing signs of decay. In the early days of his government he had attracted some original thinkers, but they had been weeded out by Eva Perón, who distrusted people who were too independent. In her ghostwritten autobiography, La razón de mi vida (The Reason for My Life), she propagated the cult of Perón as the infallible leader. Dismissing Justicialismo and its corporatist doctrine, she asserted that "the people surrender themselves more easily to a man than to an idea. It is easier for them to love a man than to love a doctrine, because the people are all heart."[13] A talented rabblerousing speaker, she reduced Peronism to simple, popular slogans like "My life for Perón!" These were incorporated into grade school textbooks, where children learned to read by learning such passages as Perón ama a los niños. (Perón loves children.) Mi papá. Mi mamá. Perón. Evita. Inevitably, a cult grew up around Evita too. For many poor people she was an angel of mercy, with her Social Aid Foundation that built clinics, orphanages, and old-age homes, besides distributing food, clothes, medicine, and sometimes plain cash to the needy. Funded by "voluntary contributions" from businesses and unions, a fifth of the proceeds from the national lottery, and special grants-in-aid from Congress, the foundation indeed did a lot of good, charitable work. It also funneled an estimated $700 million into numbered accounts overseas, under Evita's name. Nonetheless, when she died of cancer in 1952, shortly after Perón's inauguration for a second term, she was sincerely mourned by Argentina's poorest classes, and she retains even today something of the status of a secular saint.

By the time of her death, however, the regime had begun to display totalitarian tendencies. The Peronist cult, the indoctrination and mobilization of youth, the political police and the National Liberating Alliance, the control of the media, and Perón's determination to perpetuate himself in power deeply disturbed the Catholic Church and the army: two institutions that originally had supported him. His reelection campaign had provoked a barracks revolt in 1951, which, though quickly suppressed, prompted Perón to crack down even harder on whatever civil liberties remained. Indoctrination courses on Peronism were required in the Military Academy, and sergeants were encouraged to join the Peronist Party and keep a watchful eye on their officers. Meanwhile, the Church not only distanced itself from the regime but even began to organize parallel youth, women's, and labor groups to counter Peronism's influence. An angry Perón finally lashed out against the clergy in a fiery speech in November 1954, followed by mass rallies of the party faithful. The Church organized its own street processions in response, and soon the conflict escalated into open war, with priests being expelled from the country or attacked by Peronist bullies. In June 1955 the pope finally excommunicated Perón. On the sixteenth of that month the navy air force revolted, supported by armed civilians from the Radical Party. The revolt failed, and it was followed by the sacking and burning of downtown churches, including the National Cathedral and the Archbishop's Palace, by the National Liberating Alliance.

Perón's struggle with the Church provided his enemies with a common rallying point. Businessmen, landowners, and military officers were often devout, or at least nominal, Catholics. Even the traditionally anticlerical Radicals rediscovered their latent faith. Finally, on September 16, a retired general named Eduardo Lonardi raised a revolt in the Córdoba garrison. Although he was soon supported by other units, Perón's forces were greater and threatened to close in on him from all sides. Then the navy joined the revolt and threatened to bombard Buenos Aires unless Perón resigned. At that point his generals, whose morale had been declining for a long time, informed him that he had to go. After packing a few suitcases with clothes and money, Perón was driven to a Paraguayan gunboat anchored in the harbor, where he was given diplomatic asylum and finally, after much wrangling, was allowed to leave the country.

For the next four years Perón became a rootless exile, first in Paraguay, then in Panama, Venezuela, and Trujillo's Dominican Republic, before finally securing an invitation from General Francisco Franco to settle in Spain.[14] In Panama he picked up a nightclub dancer, María Estela ("Isabel") Martínez, who would later become his third wife. He also began to reestablish contact with some of his principal followers, both in exile and underground in Argentina. Bit by bit the shattered Peronist Movement began to regain life. Though proscribed by the Argentine authorities, a clandestine terrorist organization spread throughout the working-class barrios and gained ground daily within the trade unions. Argentina's moribund economy, though really a legacy of Perón, was blamed on his successors. Attempts to control inflation through austerity measures played into the hands of Peronist propagandists, who contrasted labor's falling real incomes with the glory days of the past. Attempts by the military to outlaw and uproot the movement only sharpened the workers' feelings of class solidarity.

Meanwhile, civilian politicians, knowing that the Peronists could not put up candidates for elections, tried to capture the lower-class vote with extravagant promises. Throughout it all Perón kept the reins of the movement tightly in his hands through emissaries constantly shuttling back and forth between Madrid and Buenos Aires, bringing him information and transmitting his orders. As the economy continued to worsen the movement continued to grow, until no government—civilian or military—could govern effectively. One president after another succumbed to coups, and as they did, the military became increasingly unpopular. Violence, much of it growing out of the underground Peronist resistance, reached unprecedented levels by 1971, whereupon the military government of General Alejandro Lanusse opened negotiations with Perón as the only man capable of restoring order to Argentina. Two years later Perón was back in the Casa Rosada, ready to resume his project of "the organized society."

Notes

1. Medieval theorists who used the organismic analogy include John of Salisbury, Marsiglio of Padua, and Nicolas of Cusa: writers in the twelfth, fourteenth, and fifteenth centuries, respectively. In *The Statesman's Book*, for example, Salisbury compares the clergy to the soul; the prince to the head; the senate or upper chamber to the heart; judges and provincial governors to the eyes, ears, and tongue; soldiers and government officers to the hands; tax collectors and financial officers to the stomach and intestines; and farmers to the feet. For a thorough discussion of medieval corporatist theory, see Otto von Gierke, *Natural Law and the Theory of Society* (Boston: Beacon, 1957); and Anthony Black, *Guilds and Civil Society in European Political Thought from the Twelfth Century to the Present* (Ithaca, NY: Cornell University Press,

1984). For the development of Catholic social corporatism in Europe, see Matthew H. Elbow, *French Corporative Theory, 1789–1948* (New York: Octagon, 1966); Joseph N. Moody, ed., *Church and Society: Catholic Social and Political Thought and Movements, 1789–1950* (New York: Arts Incorporated, 1953); Michael P. Fogarty, *Christian Democracy in Western Europe, 1820–1953* (London: Routledge & Kegan Paul, 1957); Alfred Diamant, *Austrian Catholics and the First Republic* (Princeton, NJ: Princeton University Press, 1960); Ralph H. Bowen, *German Theories of the Corporative State* (New York: McGraw-Hill, 1947); and Joaquin Azpiazu, *The Corporative State* (St. Louis: B. Herder, 1951).

2. F. F. Ridley, *Revolutionary Syndicalism in France* (Cambridge: Cambridge University Press, 1970); M. Tuñon de Lara, *El movimiento obrero en la historia de España* (Madrid: Taurus Ediciones, 1972); G. D. H. Cole, *Guild Socialism Restated* (London: Leonard Parsons, 1921).

3. David D. Roberts, *The Syndicalist Tradition and Italian Fascism* (Chapel Hill: University of North Carolina Press, 1979); A. James Gregor, *The Ideology of Fascism* (New York: Free Press, 1969).

4. For the career of Getúlio Vargas I have consulted mainly the following sources: John W. F. Dulles, *Vargas of Brazil: A Political Biography* (Austin: University of Texas Press, 1967); Robert M. Levine, *Father of the Poor? Vargas and His Era* (Cambridge: Cambridge University Press, 1998); Robert M. Levine, *The Vargas Regime: The Critical Years, 1934–1938* (New York: Columbia University Press, 1970); and Thomas E. Skidmore, *Politics in Brazil, 1930–1964* (New York: Oxford University Press, 1967).

5. On Vargas's corporatist scheme, see especially Kenneth Paul Erickson, *The Brazilian Corporative State and Working Class Politics* (Berkeley: University of California Press, 1977).

6. Juan Domingo Perón, *Apuntes de historia militar: Parte teorética* (Buenos Aires: Círculo Militar, 1934).

7. Juan Domingo Perón, "Significado de la defensa nacional desde el punto de vista militar," published as a preface to the 1982 edition of his *Apuntes de historia militar* (Buenos Aires: Editorial Volver, 1982), v–xxxii. The speech was given at the University of La Plata on 10 June 1944, at the inauguration of a chair in national defense studies.

8. Juan Domingo Perón, *Yo, Juan Domingo Perón: Relato biográfico*, ed. Torcuato Luca de Tena, Luis Calvo, and Esteban Peicovich (Barcelona: Editorial Planeta, 1976), 28–29. See also Enrique Pavón Pereyra, *Perón, preparación de una vida para el mando, 1895–1942* (Buenos Aires: Ediciones Espiño, 1953).

9. Perón, *Yo, Juan Domingo Perón*, 28.

10. Perón's relationship to the labor movement was crucial to his political career. Two books in particular are important for tracing and understanding this relationship: David Tamarin, *The Argentine Labor Movement, 1930–1945: A Study in the Origins of Peronism* (Albuquerque: University of New Mexico Press, 1985); and Daniel James, *Resistance and Integration: Peronism and the Argentine Working Class, 1945–1976* (Cambridge: Cambridge University Press, 1988).

11. On the authoritarian politics of the Peronist government, see Robert J. Alexander, *The Peron Era* (New York: Columbia University Press, 1951); and George Blanksten, *Peron's Argentina* (New York: Russell & Russell, 1953).

12. For Perón's economic and organizational policies, see Paul H. Lewis, *The Crisis of Argentine Capitalism* (Chapel Hill: University of North Carolina Press, 1990).

13. Eva Perón, La razón de mi vida, 17th ed. (Buenos Aires: Ediciones Peuser, 1953), 14–16.

14. The best general biography of Perón is Joseph Page, *Perón: A Biography* (New York: Random House, 1983). Page does a good job of following Perón's political moves in exile.

CHAPTER SEVEN

~

Tyranny and Succession

The Dominican Republic under Trujillo

Background to Tyranny

Rafael Leónidas Trujillo ruled the Dominican Republic from his "election" to the presidency on 16 May 1930 until his assassination on 30 May 1961. Sometimes he ruled directly as head of state; at other times he preferred to act through a puppet president—always retaining, however, control of the military. Throughout his thirty-one years in power he systematically constructed one of the most terrifying tyrannies that Latin America has ever seen. He himself was an imposing figure: fairly tall for a Dominican, with an aloof manner and the air of a man accustomed to command. His athletic figure was always well groomed and decked out in expensively tailored—sometimes flamboyant—uniforms that dripped with dozens of medals and decorations. But if Trujillo sometimes looked like a comic-opera Latin dictator, there was, nevertheless, nothing funny about him. He had a forceful and dominating personality, a good memory, and a command of details. He thoroughly controlled the people under him through a combination of methods that included economic pressure, exile, murder, and the ubiquitous presence of spies and informers. Even his closest associates were afraid of him, for their wealth and power depended entirely on his whim. Outside of his immediate family Trujillo had no permanent loyalties. He was suspicious of everyone and would frequently turn on those around him, humiliating them publicly and even sending them to prison and ruin. He was a shrewd judge of men, and an excellent organizer and administrator. He was in his office before dawn and often stayed at his desk until late in the evening, and even then he would sometimes take work home. Being dictator of the Dominican Republic was, for Trujillo, a full-time, day and night job.

The Dominican Republic occupies the eastern two-thirds of Hispaniola, the second-largest island, after Cuba, in the Greater Antilles. The hundred or so families that constitute the Dominican Republic's upper class claim to be pure white descendants of Spaniards. Their wealth, derived from plantations growing sugar, tobacco, cacao, and rice, allow them to lord it over an impoverished peasantry of blacks (about 20 percent of the population) and mulattos (about 70 percent), for the indigenous Indian communities were wiped out during the early colonial years and had to be replaced by imported African slaves. This elite also views French-speaking Haiti, which occupies the western third of the island, with great loathing. Haiti's independence movement (1791–1804) resulted in the slaughter of the whites and mulattos, resulting in a population more thoroughly black than the Dominican Republic's. Furthermore, Haiti's population is almost double that of the Dominican Republic, causing an intense population pressure on the land that led to two invasions during the nineteenth century. Indeed, Haiti ruled the whole island from 1822 to 1844.

Trujillo's family came from the small town of San Cristóbal, on the southern coast, about nine miles west of the capital, Santo Domingo. Born in 1891, he was the third of eleven children. His father was a small-time merchant and part-time cattle rustler. His mother was descended from Haitians. The smattering of primary education that Trujillo received came from his Haitian maternal grandmother, Luisa Chevalier. The Trujillo boys were unruly and sexually precocious, often in trouble with the law. As a teenager, Rafael was rumored to be rustling cattle. He also was convicted of forging a check but was let off. When he was about twenty-one he joined a gang of toughs attached to a *caudillo* named Horacio Vásquez. When they were not fighting with rival gangs during political campaigns they engaged in petty holdups. By his midtwenties, however, Rafael Trujillo began to settle down. He married his first wife (two more would follow as he climbed the ladder of power) and found a job as a telegraph operator, and then as a private policeman at a sugar plantation. The real turning point in his life, however, came in 1918, when he joined the National Guard, a constabulary being formed by United States marines.[1]

The marines had been sent by President Woodrow Wilson to take over the Dominican Republic's government in 1916, to put an end to the country's endemic anarchy and financial irresponsibility. It was not the first time that the Dominican Republic had been occupied by a foreign power other than Haiti. After gaining its independence in 1844, it had fallen into such political chaos that its liberator, General Pedro Santana, actually convinced Spain to reestablish its colonial rule. Although that lasted only a few years (1861–1865), a decade later another Dominican government petitioned the United States to take it over. A treaty was even signed to that effect but was never ratified by the U.S. Senate. Even so, the United States continued to evince an interest in acquiring a naval base in the Dominican Republic, because of its strategic location at the entrance to the Caribbean. When, in 1905, European creditors threatened to occupy the country to collect the enormous debts that improvident Dominican governments had accumulated, President Theodore Roosevelt sent in the marines to forestall that. The United States took over the collection of the customs revenues and paid off the debts. The marines were withdrawn in 1907, but only after the Dominicans agreed to allow the American president to appoint a receiver general to permanently manage the customs house.

Uncontrolled violence returned during the political campaign of 1912, bringing the marines back once more as "observers" to supervise the elections. After they left, in 1913, anarchy broke out again, prompting Wilson to occupy the country on a more long-term basis, with the intention of creating a nonpartisan police force that would maintain order. The Dominican elites refused to have anything to do with the National Guard, however, so there was a shortage of qualified officers. Thus, the marines did not enquire into twenty-seven-year-old Rafael Leónidas Trujillo's shady past when he applied for officer training. Though not of the elite, he was clearly above the peasant class, well spoken, neat, and energetic. He adapted well to military life and graduated in January 1919 with a second lieutenant's commission. His American instructors considered him to be one of the best officers in the service.

Trujillo moved up quickly through the officer ranks. By the time the marines left, in 1924, he had attained the rank of major and was made commander of the Dominican Republic's northern region. In the meantime, his old *caudillo*, Horacio Vásquez, had also been prospering in his political career and was elected president just before the marines withdrew. Vásquez viewed Trujillo as his protégé and so boosted his career even further, promoting him to colonel. In 1928 the National Guard was renamed the National Army, and Trujillo, now a brigadier general, was brought to Santo Domingo and appointed the army's chief of staff. From that position he was able to influence all promotions and assignments and thus turn the army into his personal vehicle. Despite his power, however, Trujillo was snubbed when he applied to join the elite social clubs. Even a second marriage, to a woman of a good family, could not compensate for his humble lower-middle-class origins. So the army, whose officers were from backgrounds similar to his own, became the center of his world.

In February 1930, with elections scheduled, President Vásquez, though old and in poor health, tried to extend his term of office. That provoked a revolt by Rafael Estrella Ureña, who headed a coalition of opposition parties. Vásquez looked to Trujillo for support, but the latter turned against him and sent him into exile. Then Trujillo informed Estrella Ureña that the rebels would be allowed to enter the capital only if they first laid down their weapons. After that, Trujillo's army had a monopoly of force. New elections were scheduled for May, and Trujillo was now a candidate. Estrella Ureña was offered the position of vice president on the Trujillo ticket. The elections were a farce: soldiers beat up all opposition candidates and forced them to withdraw from the race. Nearly half of the voters stayed away from the polls too. Thus began the Trujillo era.

The Benefactor

Trujillo's first administration (1930–1934) was devoted to consolidating his power. Both the Senate and the Chamber of Deputies were packed with members of his Patriotic Citizens' Coalition. His older brother, Virgilio, became minister of the interior, and thus head of the regular police. Then, in September, came the first major test of Trujillo's leadership. The country was hit by a powerful hurricane that devastated Santo Domingo. Of the 10,000 or so buildings in the capital, only some 400—mostly in the old colonial quarter—were left standing. More than 2,000 people were dead and another 2,500 were so severely injured as to need hospitalization. Neighboring countries sent aid, while the Red Cross rushed in to help; but it was chiefly Trujillo himself who, with an amazing show of energy and resourcefulness, organized the rescue and temporary housing of victims, the setting up of emergency clinics, the provision of blood, medicine, and food, and the maintenance of order. It was an impressive display of organizational skill that won him praise from every quarter and was a first step toward building his reputation as the country's indispensable leader.

Still, there were dissidents. Two army plots were crushed between 1931 and 1934, one of which implicated Vice President Estrella Ureña, who had to leave the country suddenly, taking his family. The Patriotic Citizens' Coalition was dissolved too, in favor of a new official party, the Dominican Party. Trujillo headed it, with the title of director. Many of the old Coalition supporters were frozen out of the new party and lost their congressional seats, to be replaced by Trujillo's relatives and friends. No other parties were permitted, and it quickly became necessary to be a Dominican Party member in good standing in order to get a government job. Those who did find government jobs were required to kick back 10 percent of their salary to the party, to help provide welfare for the poor and help finance public works. A new constitution, ratified in 1934, formalized what already was an enormous increase in presidential power. One major change was to dissolve provincial governments and replace them with new governors appointed by the president. These were often army officers.

Not surprisingly, Trujillo was elected unopposed for a second term. This was followed by more opposition conspiracies, all of which were nipped in the bud by the regime's efficient intelligence services. After each failed conspiracy there were purges in the Dominican Party. By the end of his second term Trujillo had consolidated his grip on the country to such an extent that Congress and the courts were reduced to rubber stamps. All legislation originated in the Presidential Palace, and Congress simply ratified it. The average debate on any given bill, including the annual budget, lasted no more than ten minutes.[2]

About half of all spending went to the armed forces, which Trujillo, as "supreme chief," maintained under his personal command. Much of the money went to purchase the latest in military equipment. The army, which was the largest branch, was strategically placed throughout the country, guarding all the roads and airstrips, and checking the documents of all travelers. Its efficient intelligence service operated a spy network that probed into every village and barrio, while its military attachés overseas were assigned the task of keeping political exiles under surveillance. For the most part, the military was professional, although Trujillo also had a weakness for placing his relatives in top commands. These men usually abused their positions by engaging in graft and extortion, while corrupting the officers around them. Such corruption was tolerated, but it also was noted and recorded in the event that an officer became too powerful and had to be demoted.

Trujillo's principal method for maintaining his personal control of the political system was to continually shuffle his chief subordinates. Cabinet members, congressmen, judges, and military chiefs were rotated every few months. As head of the Dominican Party, Trujillo had to approve every candidate's nomination to the official ticket, and all nominees had to file with him signed but undated resignation letters, allowing him to dismiss them whenever he decided it was time for a turnover. Few senators or deputies ever finished their terms. Moreover, the victim was usually dismissed without being informed beforehand; one day when he showed up to take his accustomed seat in Congress he would be told that he no longer was a member. In the meantime, his seat would be occupied by a new person sent by Trujillo and approved by a unanimous vote of the chamber. A similar procedure kept the military under control. In addition to frequent unannounced visits by corps of inspectors, commands were shifted frequently, and sometimes officers were switched to strictly political tasks, such as local government posts, or perhaps diplomatic or cabinet-level positions. Others were assigned to the police. Still others were ousted from the ranks altogether and disgraced. Jesús Galíndez, an exile who once worked in Trujillo's government, reported, "Trujillo's strategy toward the Army is the same that he uses for the state civil administration. That is, to not permit any general, even those he trusts the most, to remain in a command whose organization might allow him to gather around himself a group of personally loyal subordinates who might one day become a threat to Trujillo himself and succumb to the temptation of rebellion."[3]

In addition to this policy of "musical chairs," Trujillo kept the military under control by providing officers with high pay and special privileges, such as allowing them to engage in corruption. The armed services were also taught to view themselves as an elite of merit. They were, after all, one of the few avenues of upward social mobility for poor boys. Trujillo encouraged them to look down on the rest of society, even the old aristocratic families.

As with Congress and the military, so with cabinet officials and the judiciary. Trujillo had a free hand in naming and dismissing ministers and secretaries; and in creating, dissolving, or merging cabinet departments. There also was constant turnover in the Supreme Court and lower courts. Turnover, at any point in the regime, might be followed by a promotion for the individual involved, or a new but lateral assignment, or simply a hiatus in one's public career. But it also might involve humiliation and punishment. Trujillo often took cruel pleasure in publicly degrading those whom he had raised to great heights. Sometimes humiliation was followed by prison, where torture was routine and daily conditions were gruesome. Political prisoners, especially, were denied visits from their families or any medical attention. Thus, no one was secure around Trujillo—and no one could refuse to serve him, either. He was surrounded by terrified sycophants.

Naturally, those sycophants constantly tried to win the favor of their leader by showering him with honors. In 1936 they engineered a plebiscite that changed the name of the capital from Santo Domingo to Ciudad Trujillo. Congress also bestowed on him the title of "Benefactor of the Fatherland," after which Trujillo insisted on being addressed as "Benefactor." The University of Santo Domingo awarded him an honorary doctorate and professorship in political economy.

In addition to spies, censorship of the mail, and wiretapping, all news outlets were under Trujillo's control. He owned *El Caribe*, the capital's leading newspaper, and took pleasure in writing a column called Foro Público ("Public Forum"), which published his "letters to the editor" under various pseudonyms. Everyone knew that the letters were written by Trujillo himself, and so they were read with keen interest because they contained signals of what was to come: who was on the rise and who was about to fall. The only radio station—and later, the only television station—was owned by one of the dictator's brothers.

The Trujillo family's business interests ranged far beyond the world of journalism, too. In 1938 it was estimated that the dictator and his relatives owned about 40 percent of the Dominican economy and that their combined fortune was around $500 million. They had extensive landholdings, some of which had been confiscated from opponents, and the rest purchased at bargain prices from former owners who could not refuse an offer. They enjoyed monopolies in the sale of salt, tobacco products, and milk. Their meatpacking plants had most of the domestic and export market; they owned the lottery; and they had significant investments in banks, insurance, the domestic airlines, shipping, beer, edible oils, fruit juice, furniture, and construction materials. Exporters of rice, sugar, and cacao had to take them in as partners, as did importers of automobiles, machinery, and appliances. Otherwise they could not get licenses to stay in business. In brief, there was scarcely any corner of the Dominican economy that was free from the Trujillo family's web of interests, which gave the regime enormous economic pressure it could bring to bear on any dissident. In one ironic passage, Galíndez observes, "The Trujillo dictatorship is not so bloody as the exiles claim. But the Trujillo style is more notable for another, less bloody, type of domination: hunger—the certainty that it is not possible to earn a living without actively supporting the regime—is more efficient. Trujillo prefers to force an old enemy to collaborate: to humiliate him rather than eliminate him violently, which might later rebound against the regime." And Robert Crassweller concludes that "signs of an evolution toward a truly authoritarian government were becoming apparent" by the late 1930s. The absence of any utopian ideology meant that Trujillo's kind of totalitarian state would lack the dynamism of Stalin's or Hitler's, but he was more than just a typical *caudillo*: his regime used twentieth-century techniques of science and propaganda to keep the population under control.[4]

In 1937, near the end of his second administration, Trujillo decided to take drastic action against the thousands of Haitians living illegally on the Dominican side of the border. Some of these were squatters; others were working without documentation on plantations. What mattered to most Dominicans, and above all to Trujillo, was that the despised Haitians were encroaching more and more on their territory. Accordingly, in October Trujillo sent in army units with orders to massacre the intruders, using machetes in order to make it look as though Dominican peasants had risen up spontaneously to do the job. His forces decapitated some 12,000 Haitians and threw their bodies into deep mountainous ravines. Despite all of Trujillo's precautions, however, news of the slaughter leaked out, and there were protests around the world. Even the United States, which had viewed Trujillo benignly because he had brought stability to a strategic country in the region and had respected foreign investments, began to distance itself. As his second term ran out, in 1938, Trujillo bowed to U.S. pressure and announced that he would not be a candidate for a third term. As his stand-in he chose an elderly judge, Jacinto Peynado, retaining for himself the armed forces command and inserting his younger brother Héctor into the cabinet as defense minister. When Peynado died in office, in 1940, his vice president, Manuel de Jesús Troncoso, succeeded him. Meanwhile, Trujillo, having secured the title of ambassador extraordinary, traveled through Europe and the United States. During his trips to the United States he managed to mend fences with the New Deal administration. Years of careful budgeting had allowed him to make regular payments on the Dominican Republic's foreign debts. Such financial responsibility was rewarded in 1940 when the American government signed a treaty with him, returning the management of the customs house to the Dominican Republic. It also earned Trujillo another official title: "Restorer of the Republic's Financial Independence." In the following year, after the Japanese attack on Pearl Harbor, the Dominican Republic's government was one of the first to pledge wartime allegiance to the United States. These actions paved the way for Trujillo to be elected for a third term, in 1942.

The war years and the early 1950s—which coincided with the Korean War—may be considered the high point of the Trujillo era. Exports of foodstuffs rose to unprecedented heights, bringing in enormous revenues. This made the Trujillos richer than ever, but much of the profits were plowed into public works. From an annual budget of less than $10 million before World War II, government spending rose to just under $30 million by 1945 and continued to rise until it hit a peak of $120 million in 1956. Roads, schools, hospitals and rural clinics, sanitation works, shipyards, and irrigation projects—there were improvements going on everywhere. Ciudad Trujillo became a showplace capital, with a new port, lots of attractive modern buildings, a sanitary water supply, clean paved streets, a national museum, and a symphony orchestra. There were even free breakfasts for public school children. Everyone had a job, except political dissidents, and amid the general prosperity there was a broad atmosphere of support for the regime. Trujillo took all the credit. "I have done it all by myself, all by myself," he told a visiting diplomat.[5]

Trujillo's fourth term, from 1947 to 1952, coincided with the onset of the Cold War. A brief period of liberalization just following World War II, during which opposition parties and free labor unions were allowed, came to an end in 1947 after Congress passed a series of anticommunist laws. Censorship returned, unions were forced to join a government-controlled confederation, and the armed forces were considerably strengthened by U.S. military aid.

Decay of the Regime

In 1952 Trujillo was approaching sixty-one years of age and beginning to think about his own mortality. His twenty-three-year-old son, Ramfis, was to be his intended successor, but there were worrisome problems regarding him. Pampered and indulged throughout his life, Ramfis had failed to develop any character. His father and his uncles were cruel, corrupt sexual libertines: hardly the proper models for a young boy. Everyone else around him was obsequious. He grew up willful, lazy, and undisciplined: a playboy devoted mainly to women and polo. His father sent him to the United States for military training, but he preferred to chase Hollywood actresses. He showed no interest in politics. In any case, he was still too young to assume the presidency, so his father, seeking to give his regime a slightly more liberal image, announced that he was turning over the presidency to his brother, Héctor. Rafael Leónidas would continued to run the country as commander of the armed forces.

The regime was beginning to run into trouble, mainly because conditions in the Caribbean were changing. In 1944 the dictatorship of Jorge Ubico fell in Guatemala, to be succeeded by the reformist government of Juan José Arévalo. In 1951 the Arévalo government gave way to an even more leftist administration under Jacobo Arbenz. Also in 1944, the dictatorship of Fulgencio Batista in Cuba held free elections and turned over power to Ramón Grau San Martín. He, in turn, was followed by another democrat, Carlos Prío Socarrás, in 1948. In 1946 Venezuela got its first taste of democracy with the election of Rómulo Gallegos, the choice of an *aprista*-type movement called Acción Democrática. In 1948 a revolution in Costa Rica, led by José Figueres, installed in power Otilio Ulate, who had been duly elected before but prevented from taking office by his opponents. Figueres himself was elected president in 1953. All of these new governments viewed Trujillo and similar dictators—such as Nicaragua's Anastasio Somoza—as enemies of democracy and deserving of elimination. Dominican exiles suddenly found support from many quarters. President Elie Lescot, in Haiti, gave them asylum, while the Prío Socarrás government in Cuba allowed them to train there for an invasion of the Dominican Republic. The United States put on pressure, however, forcing the exiles to shift their operations to Costa Rica, where, in collaboration with exiles from other countries, they formed the Caribbean Legion. The Legion's primary target was Somoza, but after a U.S.-negotiated truce between Costa Rica and Nicaragua it was forced to move to Guatemala. From there it attempted an invasion of the Dominican Republic in June 1949, which ended in disaster.

Caribbean international relations quieted down temporarily after that. In Cuba, Batista returned to power in 1952, overthrowing Prío Socarrás. Acción Democrática was ousted in Venezuela by General Marcos Pérez Jiménez, and Guatemala swung to the right when Carlos Castillo Armas seized power in 1954. But it was only a brief respite. Acción Democrática returned to power in 1958, under the dynamic leadership of Rómulo Betancourt; Fidel Castro forced Batista to flee Cuba in the first hours of January 1959; and in Costa Rica Figueres was still dedicated to eliminating the Trujillo and Somoza regimes. On 12 June 1959 Venezuela broke diplomatic relations with the Dominican Republic, and two days later Dominican exiles invaded from bases in Cuba.

As with previous attempts, this invasion also ended in failure. Trujillo's superior forces killed most of the exiles within hours of their landing; those who survived were quickly rounded up, and every one of them was executed. Nevertheless, the invasion had a severe psychological impact on the regime, for so many of the rebels were connected to leading Dominican families. Instead of intimidating the public, the severe repression that followed seemed to spur on the new "14th of June" underground movement. Every arrest and torture only increased the number of sympathizers. Moreover, Trujillo could no longer count on support from the United States as he had in the past.

The turning point in his relations with the United States could be traced back to the kidnapping and murder of an exile named Jesús Galíndez. A Basque refugee from the Spanish Civil War, Galíndez had gone to the Dominican Republic in 1939, taught in the Foreign Service School, and worked as a legal adviser to the Labor Department. He left in 1946, went to New York, became a U.S. citizen, and was teaching part-time while working on a doctorate at Columbia University. His dissertation topic was the Trujillo era, about which he had copious documentation. Word reached Trujillo about this, and so on the night of 12 March 1956 Galíndez was seized by Dominican agents, drugged, put aboard a private plane, and flown to Ciudad Trujillo. He was never seen again. It was not the first time that Trujillo had assassinated an exile, but Galíndez was different: he had influential friends and was a U.S. citizen. Moreover, the pilot who flew him to the Dominican Republic, Gerald Murphy, was a U.S. citizen too. When he also disappeared in the Dominican Republic, there was an outcry from his parents and from his girlfriend, a Pan American Airways stewardess, who had seen him in Ciudad Trujillo just a few days before and had been given some broad hints about his involvement in Galíndez's disappearance. The U.S. press seized on the scandal, and Congress began an investigation. In the end, a diplomatic break was avoided, partly because Trujillo spent lavishly on lobbyists and partly because of his strong anticommunist stance in the Cold War. But it was the beginning of a series of blunders that would eventually isolate him.

In a feverish attempt to surround himself with friendly neighbors, Trujillo involved himself in several clumsy assassination plots: one against Figueres, another against Ramón Villeda Morales, the reformist president of Honduras, and two attempts against Venezuela's Betancourt. The second attempt against Betancourt, in June 1960, nearly succeeded and indeed left the Venezuelan president's hands badly burned by an explosive. Venezuela then appealed to the Organization of American States (OAS), which in August 1960 imposed diplomatic and economic sanctions on the Dominican Republic. This time even the United States went along, for in its desire to isolate the Fidel Castro regime in Cuba it looked to democratic governments like those of Venezuela and Costa Rica as alternative models for Latin America. Trujillo had become a liability; unless the Dominican Republic reformed, it might produce another radical revolution like Cuba's.

The Catholic Church had begun to distance itself too. A new generation of Catholic priests, more liberal than their predecessors, issued a pastoral letter on 25 January 1960 condemning the lack of freedom and the inhumane treatment of political prisoners. Trujillo tried to adjust by making cosmetic changes. Héctor stepped down in August 1960, after the OAS sanctions, to be replaced as president by Joaquín Balaguer, a lawyer, diplomat, and scholar. He had served first as presidential secretary and then as vice president. He was honest, lived modestly, and provided a cleaner image for the regime. Still, economic sanctions soon caused general hardship. Tourism was in decline and there was a significant drop in export earnings. New investment dried up and loans were unavailable. Military aid was cut off too, forcing the regime to raise taxes on a wide variety of goods and activities in order to keep providing the armed forces with up-to-date equipment. Shortages of imported goods drove up the cost of living. As disaffection spread, various underground groups discussed schemes to assassinate the dictator. Finally, with the inauguration of the Kennedy administration in Washington, the CIA began to enter the picture, drawing together some of the plotters and providing them with weapons.

The assassination came on the evening of 30 May 1961, as Trujillo was being chauffeured along the coastal highway to one of his country houses west of the capital. Eight men ambushed the car, killing the dictator but leaving his driver wounded in a ditch. It was an amateurish job that left behind so many clues that the assassins and their immediate circle of supporters, some of whom were top-ranking army men, were quickly located and rounded up. Some were killed trying to resist arrest; others were taken into custody, tortured mercilessly, and then shot, after which their bodies were thrown to the sharks. Ramfis personally attended to the interrogations and executions. Trujillo's brothers, Héctor and José Arismendi, attempted a feeble plot in November to seize power, but the U.S. Caribbean fleet intervened to keep Balaguer in office. The Trujillo family then went into exile, taking with them the Benefactor's body, along with several millions of dollars.

The Somoza Dynasty in Nicaragua

Anastasio "Tacho" Somoza, who ruled Nicaragua from 1937 to 1956, was a political ally of Trujillo's. Like the Dominican "Benefactor," he was considered by progressive Latin Americans to be a right-wing tyrant: a "throwback" to an earlier era of personalist rule. The two dictators had much in common. Both came from modest middle-class backgrounds, both had knocked about in various occupations—often shady—before their rise to power, and both achieved power through successful careers in U.S.-trained constabulary forces. Upon rising to the top of those paramilitary organizations, both men took the final step to power by betraying a former mentor. Once in power, both Somoza and Trujillo found it prudent to turn over the presidency occasionally to trusted puppets, while maintaining control over the army. Over the course of their long rule they created vast economic empires within their respective countries that enriched them, their relatives, and their friends. Both were early morning risers who spent long hours at the office attending to government business. Exiles from both regimes found refuge in Arbenz's Guatemala and Figueres's Costa Rica and helped to form the ranks of the Caribbean Legion. Finally, both dictators eventually were assassinated.

But there are some important differences between Trujillo and Somoza as well. Nicaragua under "Tacho" Somoza never experienced the heavy atmosphere of terror that characterized Trujillo's Dominican Republic. Bernard

Diedrich, a journalist who knew both men, reported, "Unlike Dominican dictator Trujillo, Somoza killed only as a last resort. A spell in jail usually brought the enemy around." (Jail, however, often included a bit of electric shock torture, which helped to bring the enemy around.)[6] Tacho also was more accessible than Trujillo, who purposely distanced himself from those around him. Somoza spent hours every day with friends and petitioners who came to the Presidential Palace. He liked the give and take of an informal chat with the foreign press, especially when the conversation turned to sports. While in the United States he had become an avid baseball fan, and after he came to power he made that Nicaragua's national sport. He also liked boxing and in his youth had been a referee. In brief, there was a popular touch to Somoza that made him more like Perón than Trujillo. Crassweller describes an incident that occurred at a baseball game during Somoza's 1952 visit to Trujillo that illustrates the difference in their personalities:

> Trujillo was wearing a splendid uniform, topped by the bicorn hat with the long plumes; his guest was attired in a rather sober uniform. They were escorted to a special box some distance from the playing field. Before long, Somoza bounded up, found his way down to the front row alone, and flopped into an empty seat next to a very plain Dominican. In style, Tacho Somoza was essentially a man for a hammock, with a highball at hand and a neighbor's back to slap.[7]

Though forced to be allies because of their common enemies, neither dictator liked, or really respected, the other. Somoza left the Dominican Republic feeling insulted by Trujillo's self-important airs and his elaborate protocol. For Tacho, the Benefactor was a "fancy-dressed monkey." "Let's get out of here," he growled to his aides. "I can't stand this damn dictatorship."[8]

There was one other important difference between Trujillo and Somoza. The former was unable to groom his son, Ramfis, to succeed him. His death ended the Trujillo family's power over the Dominican Republic. Somoza, by contrast, left behind a family-based political machine that continued to rule Nicaragua through his two sons, Luis and Anastasio Jr. ("Tachito"), until the Sandinista revolution overthrew it in 1979.

The Rise to Power

Anastasio Sr. was born in 1896, in the little town of San Marcos. His father was a not-very-successful coffee farmer who nevertheless became a senator for the Conservative Party. When Tacho went off to school in the conservative city of Granada, his father put him under the guardianship of Diego

Manuel Chamorro, a former president and scion of a powerful Conservative family. Despite that, the strong-willed boy would later join the Liberals. Tacho also was sexually precocious. At the age of nineteen he impregnated one of the family's maids. So, to keep him from getting into more trouble, his father sent him to the United States, in 1916, under the care of an older relative living in Philadelphia. There Tacho studied bookkeeping and advertising at the Pierce Business School. After graduating, he stayed on to work for an advertising agency because, in the meantime, he had fallen in love with a Nicaraguan girl, Salvadora Debayle, who also was studying in Philadelphia. Her father, a famous surgeon back home, did not encourage the courtship because he considered Somoza to be socially inferior; but Salvadora was attracted to her attentive suitor. Shortly after they both returned to Nicaragua, in 1919, her father gave in and they were married.[9]

Dr. Debayle refused to support the newlyweds, however, and Tacho's family was going through one of its frequent financial crises, so he was forced to scramble to support his young wife. He tried opening a store. It failed. Then he opened an automobile agency. It failed too. He worked as a mechanic, a meter reader for the electric company, and even as an inspector of latrines for the Rockefeller Foundation's Sanitation Mission to Nicaragua. In desperation, he even turned to counterfeiting but was caught and had to rely on his old guardian, Diego Manuel Chamorro, to keep him from going to jail. Then he showed his ingratitude, in 1926, by joining a Liberal revolt led by General José María Moncada against President Emiliano Chamorro. He was soon captured; but Chamorro refused to take the young rebel seriously and pardoned him. Tacho spent a month as an exile in Costa Rica while the revolt went on. The United States Marines finally intervened in October 1926 to put an end to the fighting.

It was not the first time that the marines had occupied Nicaragua. Political turmoil and financial irresponsibility, plus Nicaragua's strategic location near the Panama Canal, had first brought them there in December 1910. Before they left the following year, the United States had taken over the customs house, the national bank, and the national railway system. The marines then departed but were sent back in 1912 after severe fighting broke out again. Most of them were then withdrawn after restoring order, but a small contingent remained in the country until 1925. Now that order had broken down again the marines were back, and they would turn Nicaragua into a U.S. protectorate until Franklin Roosevelt withdrew them in 1933.

Since Chamorro himself had come to power by a coup, the first step was to force his resignation in favor of a provisional president, Adolfo Díaz, but General Moncada refused to accept that and raised another revolt. President

Coolidge then sent down former defense secretary Henry Stimson to negotiate a settlement. That was a turning point in Tacho Somoza's career. As Moncada's aide-de-camp he smoothed the negotiations, and won Stimson's favor, with his fluent, colloquial English. He also charmed the American ambassador, Matthew Hanna, who came to view him as indispensable. When in 1927 the Americans began setting up a national guard to keep the peace in Nicaragua, Somoza was given a commission, although he had almost no military background.

U.S.-supervised elections in 1928 brought General Moncada to the presidency and paved the way for Somoza's rise through the officers' ranks. But one of the Liberal revolutionaries, Augusto César Sandino, refused to accept the American occupation. Calling Moncada a "traitor," he and his followers took to the mountains of northern Nicaragua and carried on a guerrilla war against the marines. Every attempt to trap him proved futile. After supervising another "clean" election, in 1932, the marines were happy to leave the following January. Meanwhile, Somoza was promoted to head the National Guard by the new president, Juan B. Sacasa, who just happened to be an uncle of Somoza's wife.

Sacasa, a Liberal, quickly sought a truce with Sandino. Somoza, however, saw in Sandino an inevitable rival for power and ordered his national guardsmen to continue hunting and killing the rebels. When Sandino arrived in Managua, on 21 February 1934, to sign a truce, national guardsmen kidnapped and murdered him. His demoralized followers soon gave up their struggle, leaving Somoza with the only organized armed force.

To prepare for the 1936 elections, Sacasa brought the two traditional parties together to agree on a common candidate. Somoza, however, refused to endorse their choice, Leonardo Argüello. He already had his national guardsmen busily organizing political clubs and arranging speaking engagements. Nicaragua was in the depths of the Depression, and people in the towns, where unemployment was high, were annoyed at the government's seeming lack of concern. Tacho adopted a populist style, promising that his administration would come to the aid of failing businesses, jobless workers, and poor peasants. It would be a "new deal": a sharp break with traditional politics. As the election approached, Somoza accused Sacasa of plotting to rig the results for Argüello. In mid-May, units of the National Guard declared themselves in revolt, whereupon Sacasa appealed for U.S. intervention. The Roosevelt administration refused to get involved, however, so Sacasa resigned on June 6. A provisional government, appointed by Congress, held the elections in November, but no one dared to oppose Anatasio Somoza. He was inaugurated in January 1937.[10]

Made in the USA

Having come to power by way of the U.S.-created National Guard, Tacho Somoza made good relations with the United States the touchstone of all his policies. The United States reciprocated his goodwill because, as Franklin D. Roosevelt put it, "He may be a son of a bitch, but he's *our* son of a bitch." When Somoza made a state visit in May 1939 FDR lavished him with attention and sent him back with a $2 million line of credit from the Export-Import Bank. World War II broke out soon afterward and Nicaragua's exports indeed boomed, bringing prosperity to the country and an immense fortune to the Somoza family, which controlled the issuance of export licenses, and also many of the export industries themselves. Somoza was quick to declare war on Germany and Italy, after which he personally took over most of their investments in Nicaragua. The United States, for its part, acquired airfields and a naval base that helped it to patrol the Caribbean. That, too, injected money into the Nicaraguan economy, as well as into the Somozas' bank accounts.

After two presidential terms, Somoza decided in 1947 to stay within the letter of the constitution and let a picked successor, Leonardo Argüello—the man he had originally cheated out of office—stand in for him. Like Trujillo, however, Somoza would continue to command the National Guard. Argüello had no intention of being a mere puppet, and it seems that he continued to nurse a grievance against Tacho, because the day after his inauguration, on May 1, he began shifting National Guard assignments in a way that would give him control. In the early morning hours of May 26 Argüello was awakened by his aides with the news that Somoza had seized the Presidential Palace and all of Managua's communications centers. The president had just enough time to get to the Mexican Embassy and ask for asylum.

Argüello's successor, Lacayo Sacasa, was so incompetent that Somoza removed him after only three days. Finally, he settled on his favorite uncle, Víctor Román y Reyes, the man who had paid for his education in the United States. He filled out the term, after which Tacho took back the presidency in 1951. Throughout this postwar period the Somozas continued to expand their web of economic interests, which involved farms, ranches, utilities, factories, and transportation. Like Trujillo's Dominican Republic, Nicaragua was turned into one big extortion racket, backed by the guns of the National Guard. Also, as with Trujillo, the United States was sometimes embarrassed by its protégé. After Argüello's ouster there was a temporary suspension of diplomatic relations. The onset of the Cold War and Somoza's outspoken anticommunism eventually brought about a reconciliation, however. In 1954 he gave the CIA the use of Managua's airport to facilitate Castillo Armas's overthrow of Jacobo Arbenz's leftist regime in Guatemala.

Feeling confident once more, Somoza had the constitution changed to allow his reelection in 1957, when his term would run out. He launched his last political campaign in September 1956. On the night of the twenty-first, as he celebrated his nomination by the regime's official party at a workingmen's club in León, a student of poetry named Rigoberto López Pérez quietly approached the head table and fired four bullets from a .38 revolver point-blank into Tacho's ample body. The dictator was mortally wounded and died a week later at an American hospital in the Canal Zone.

Fall of the Regime

Tacho Somoza's elder son, Luis Somoza Debayle, took over as interim president, while his younger son, Anastasio "Tachito" Somoza Debayle, assumed control of the National Guard. Luis, an engineer trained in the United States, had been presiding over Congress. Tachito was a military officer, trained at West Point. Luis was the more moderate of the two brothers. After his election to a full presidential term in 1957, he loosened up on censorship and restored the constitutional prohibition on immediate reelection, giving rise to hopes that Nicaragua might be on the path to democracy. First, however, Tachito opened this new period with a wave of persecution like that which Ramfis Trujillo had carried out in the Dominican Republic: political opponents were rounded up, imprisoned, and tortured.

Like their father, the Somoza brothers cultivated good relations with the United States. Nicaragua was one of the first countries to condemn the Cuban Revolution for spreading communist subversion, and in 1961 it allowed Cuban exiles to use military bases along its coast to launch their invasion of the Bay of Pigs. At home, Luis Somoza brought an era of prosperity to Nicaragua by having it join Guatemala, Honduras, and El Salvador to create the Central American Common Market. When he left the presidency in 1963 he turned it over to a close family friend, René Schick. Schick was a likable president who was accessible to the public and often gave petitioners money out of his own pocket; but the real power in Nicaragua was "Tachito" Somoza, who continued to head the National Guard. When Schick died suddenly, in 1966, his term was filled by Lorenzo Guerrero Gutierrez, a former police chief.

Many Nicaraguans were hoping for the return of Luis Somoza, but poor health kept him from running. Now it was Tachito's turn. Arrogant, imperious, and macho to the extreme, he was elected in a blitzkrieg campaign in which the National Guard was used to intimidate and arrest the candidates of an opposition front composed of Conservatives, dissident Liberals, and liberal Christians. As both president and National Guard commander, Tachito had no check on his power, especially when Luis died two months after the election. At the end of his term, in 1971, he changed the constitution to allow him to stay in power. There was opposition, but so far it was feeble. Pedro Joaquín Chamorro, editor of the Conservative newspaper, La Prensa, was a brave but constantly harassed critic. A guerrilla group calling themselves the Sandinista National Liberation Front (FSLN) was operating in the mountains, but so far it was failing to enlist much support from the apathetic peasants. Archbishop Miguel Obando y Bravo, reflecting the Catholic Church's new support for social reform, called for change, but with little effect. Tachito brushed off all criticism and bragged that he and his National Guard could handle any challenge. Then, on 23 December 1972, a massive earthquake hit Managua, killing over 10,000 and destroying most homes and commercial buildings.

In the aftermath, looters took advantage of the confusion to invade shops and homes. Instead of preserving order, national guardsmen joined them. Worse still, as relief aid poured in from the United States and international agencies, much of it went into the pockets of Somoza and his National Guard officers. Of some $32 million sent by the Nixon administration to help rebuild the capital, only half was ever accounted for. Items like medicines, blankets, clothes, and food were stolen by the National Guard and resold for profit. It was a scandal that transcended anything ever seen before in Nicaragua—and it was the beginning of the end for the Somoza regime. Although Tachito won reelection in 1974 through the usual brutal procedures, the Sandinista guerrillas were beginning to grow in strength. Two days after Christmas, FSLN guerrillas broke into a dinner party attended by several high-level regime officials and Somoza relatives. They demanded and received a million dollars in ransom money, the release of fourteen Sandinista prisoners, a manifesto of theirs read over the radio and printed in La Prensa, and a plane to fly them and the released prisoners to Cuba.

Humiliated, Tachito struck back with a stepped-up campaign of repression and torture. That only led to a broadening of the opposition movement, as businessmen, teachers, and clerics joined the opposition. Even the United States began withdrawing its support with the inauguration of President Carter in 1977. Carter called for Somoza to end his human rights abuses, but instead the dictator committed a dramatic blunder, on 10 January 1978, when La Prensa's editor, Pedro Joaquín Chamorro, was assassinated. Two weeks later a nationwide protest strike began that lasted ten days and paralyzed the economy. Surrounded on all sides by passionate opposition, and supported only by the indiscriminately violent National Guard, Tachito nevertheless insisted that he would stay in power until his term ended in 1981.

The Sandinistas got another boost in August 1978, when guerrillas captured the Congress building and took nearly 2,000 congressmen and other government officials hostage. This time Somoza had to pay half a million dollars in ransom, release sixty FSLN prisoners, and provide safe passage out of the country. The regime was humiliated, and even the National Guard's morale was affected. In May of the following year the FSLN launched its final offensive from Costa Rican soil, while inside Nicaragua guerrilla units began to gain ground against the demoralized National Guard. Seeing that the situation had turned definitively against him, Somoza resigned on July 17 and took a plane for Miami. Then, fearing that the United States would expel him, he sailed to the Bahamas. Finally, he accepted an offer of asylum from Paraguay's dictator, General Alfredo Stroessner.

The Sandinistas did not consider themselves safe so long as Somoza was alive, however, so in September 1980 their political police (the Fifth Directorate) sent a hit squad of hired Argentine guerrillas into Paraguay to kill him. On the morning of September 17, as Somoza's Mercedes-Benz headed toward downtown Asunción, it was stopped by a pickup truck that pulled in front. Three men with machine guns jumped from the truck and riddled Somoza, his financial adviser, and his chauffeur, while a man with a bazooka also opened fire on the car from the front porch of a house directly across the street. The demolished car rolled onto the sidewalk with its motor still running and its occupants literally blown to pieces.

Paraguay under Stroessner

Alfredo Stroessner was born on 3 November 1912 in Paraguay's southern port city of Encarnación. His father, Hugo, was a Bavarian immigrant who married into a local family of farmers and growers of *yerba mate*, the bitter green tea that is so popular in the lower part of South America. The family was poor but not impoverished. Hugo tried opening a small beer factory but eventually went out of business, after which he scraped together a living as a part-time accountant and part-time farmer. Young Alfredo went to primary school in Encarnación, but since the educational system was so backward there his father sent him across the river, to Posadas, Argentina, to attend high school. After graduation he entered the Military Academy in Asunción, in March 1929, at the age of seventeen.[11]

The Chaco War erupted while Stroessner was in his final year at the academy. The cadets would finish their training in actual combat with the Bolivians. Stroessner's baptism of fire came at the crucial battle of Boquerón, where the enemy's advance was smashed and routed. As head of a small mortar unit, Stroessner earned a medal for bravery and a second lieutenant's commission. By the end of the war he had won another medal and promotion to first lieutenant.

The postwar period was marked by political upheavals. The Liberal Party, which had been in power since 1904, was widely unpopular. Many army officers as well as intellectuals criticized it for its flabby prewar diplomacy over the Chaco and for its failure to adequately prepare Paraguay for war. Those who had been to the front had also come to admire the peasants who had fought so bravely in the war. A strong feeling had grown up through the ranks that the war would have to be followed by sweeping social and economic reforms. Thus, there was outrage when the Liberals demobilized the troops and sent the peasants back to their serfdom on the *latifundios* with no compensation, even for disabled veterans. Finally, when the Liberals began making concessions to Bolivia at the Chaco Peace Conference, a part of the army rose up in February 1936 and toppled the government. Then followed a series of short-lived regimes. First came a revolutionary regime led by Colonel Rafael Franco, one of the most dashing wartime officers. He initiated a land reform program and adopted a labor code. Squabbling inside the cabinet weakened Franco's government, however, enabling the Liberals to take power again through a counterrevolutionary coup in August 1937. But Franco's "February Revolution" had unleashed expectations of change that couldn't be ignored. The Liberals could hold on to power only by marginalizing their traditional wing and turning the government over to Marshal José Félix Estigarribia, the wartime army's commander in chief. He surrounded himself with a younger generation of "New Liberals" who were open to reform, but when he was killed in a plane crash, in 1940, the army replaced the New Liberals with General Higinio Morínigo, an extreme nationalist.

Throughout this turmoil, Alfredo Stroessner quietly ascended the army's career ladder while avoiding any partisan commitments. He was a spit-and-polish officer whose units always excelled on the parade grounds. With his fellow officers he was circumspect but popular, admired as much for his great strength and powerful physique as for his quick intelligence. He excelled at mathematics and chess, which indicated a cool, logical, and calculating mind. Sent to Brazil in 1940 for advanced artillery training, he impressed his instructors with his military bearing and his natural qualities as a leader. Upon returning to Paraguay he won Morínigo's gratitude by refusing to join a conspiracy against him and was rewarded by being sent to the Superior War School, a sign that he was destined for the command of large units. After completing the course of study he was appointed commander of Paraguay's artillery forces, with the rank of lieutenant colonel.

Meanwhile, in 1946 Morínigo began liberalizing his dictatorship. Under pressure from the United States, as well as from reformist officers in the Paraguayan military, he freed all political prisoners, lifted the ban on political parties, abolished censorship, and permitted exiles to return. His all-military government was replaced by a coalition of the old Colorado Party of General Bernardino Caballero and a new party built around Colonel Franco called the Febrerista Party (after the "February Revolution"). Excluded from the government, but still permitted to function openly, were the Liberals and the Communists. Lifting the political lid only released long-pent-up passions, however. The coalition government collapsed as Colorados and Febreristas fought to win the upper hand, while the Liberals and Communists plotted to bring down Morínigo. Morínigo was eager to divest himself of these annoying checks on his power, so he eventually dismissed the Febreristas and formed a cabinet of pro-Colorado military officers. But it was not so easy to put the lid back on. In March 1947 pro-Liberal and pro-Febrerista army units revolted, and a civil war was on. Only a minority of the officer corps remained loyal to Morínigo, but these were in key positions in and around the capital. Even so, he was forced to rely on the Colorado Party's peasant militia—and support from Juan Perón's sympathetic government in neighboring Argentina—to keep from being defeated.

The civil war raged for nearly six months, during which time Stroessner sided with the government. When a navy revolt broke out in the capital, Stroessner's artillery forces were called in to crush it by shelling the naval base. Next, Stroessner distinguished himself by suppressing rebel activity in the south and by knocking out two heavily armed rebel gunboats that were steaming toward the capital. When the rebellion was finally crushed, Stroessner found himself to be one of only a handful of victorious loyalist officers. But Morínigo was no longer firmly in control. His increasing reliance on the Colorados left him at their mercy after the war. Stroessner, sensing the shift in power, joined a coup that removed Morínigo from office in June 1948.

The Colorados were divided, however, into personal factions whose leaders were bitter enemies. During the next year and a half four presidents went rapidly in and out of power. For the most part, Stroessner steered a skillful course through those treacherous currents, although he miscalculated once and had to dash for the border hidden in the trunk of a car. During the next coup, however, he slipped back into the country and made a sudden appearance at his old artillery regiment, where he was welcomed with cheers. The beneficiary of that coup, an elderly Colorado named Federico Cháves, promoted Stroessner to head the First Military Region, which encompasses Asunción. Next, he made him commander in chief of the army. In the end, none of that saved Cháves from being overthrown himself. The economy was in a shambles, for constant political turmoil had prevented any rebuilding after the civil war. Approximately a fourth of the country had fled into exile. Out of desperation, Cháves had signed a treaty with Perón by which the two countries would combine their economies—in effect, an Argentine takeover of Paraguay. To top it all, Cháves engineered his reelection in 1952, deeply disappointing many younger Colorados who had their eye on the job. Stroessner, ever sensitive to shifting currents, began meeting with one of the party's rising stars, Epifanio Méndez Fleitas, a former police chief and Central Bank president. On 4 May 1954 he made his move. Professing umbrage at some command changes Cháves had made without consulting him, he ordered his tanks to roll. Tomás Romero Pereira, head of the Colorado Party's executive committee, became provisional president and scheduled elections—which Stroessner won unopposed. His inauguration, on 15 August 1954, began a period of rule that would last nearly thirty-five years.

The Power Structure

None of the top Colorado leaders expected Stroessner to stay in power for long. He was only forty-one, had never really been a party man, and had no political following. Most army officers were pledged to one or another faction of the party. Stroessner himself had no charisma, was a boring speaker, and gave the impression of being big, dull, and plodding. Behind that prosaic exterior, however, lay the mind of a chess master—or a first-rate political tactician. One by one he played off the rival Colorado leaders against one another, exiling the losers and giving their followers the choice of either leaving the country too or attaching themselves to him. Since personal grievances prevented them from switching to another Colorado faction, most of them took the latter course and were rewarded with government jobs. After that they could never go back to their former leaders: they were permanently dependent upon Stroessner. Meanwhile, each uprooting of a Colorado faction was followed by a purge of the army officer corps and the replacement of disgraced officers by Stroessner's handpicked men. Not until 1966 was this process of consolidating power complete, but in the end Stroessner had two firm pillars on which to base his government: the army and the Colorado Party. The last step involved placing the Colorados under military discipline, so that factionalism was prohibited, all party offices were filled from a single list of candidates, and orders came only from the top. By the same token, all military officers had to belong to the Colorado Party.

Stroessner was now the center of a power structure embracing the government, of which he was president; the Colorado Party, of which he also was president; and the armed forces, of which he was commander in chief. This was a formidable combination of offices, but by itself it doesn't fully explain the longevity of his regime. To understand the rule of a traditional dictator like Stroessner—and also, by analogy, Trujillo or Somoza—one must take into account the political realities of traditional Latin American societies, especially in small countries like the Dominican Republic, Nicaragua, and Paraguay.

Let us use Paraguay as an example. In 1960 Paraguay's total population was about 1,722,000. But all of the people who really counted—politically, economically, culturally—lived in Asunción, whose population was estimated at 266,000, or 15 percent of the total. Now in 1960 women took almost no part in Paraguay's politics, yet they constituted half of the population, so that leaves a pool of 133,000 males as potential political factors. Just under half of those, however, were under the age of twenty-one and so had little political influence. Let us subtract 66,000 from Asunción's male population, leaving us with 67,000, or 3.8 percent of Paraguay's total population. But in a traditional country like this, only university-educated civilians and military officers have a chance at high political office. Paraguay's total military strength in 1960 was estimated at 20,000 men of all ranks, so top-level officers probably did not number more than 100 men—probably fewer. Moreover, the number of civilians attending university was only about 1 percent of the university-age population. I would estimate that the number of university degree holders in 1960 was only around 5,000. In sum, to govern Paraguay Stroessner had to control about 5,100 people out of a population of 1,700,000, or three-tenths of a percent of the whole.

Even that is too much for one person alone, so a dictator needs an apparatus to help him. Trujillo and Somoza used their military for that purpose, but Stroessner had an additional advantage in the Colorado Party. Unlike the artificial parties created by Trujillo and Somoza, the Colorados constituted a real political party with traditions, heroes, symbols, and mass loyalties whose roots reached back to its founding in 1887, and even beyond. Party identification is strong in Paraguay and is passed on from generation to generation. Most Paraguayans choose their friends, and even their marriage partners, from among the *co-religionarios* of the same party.[12] Therefore, by becoming the head of the Colorado Party and surrounding himself with prominent but dependent Colorados, Stroessner controlled a vast organization of fanatical followers who could be put to a variety of uses. They could fill up the streets with cheering crowds waving the red banners that were the party's colors; they could intimidate other parties and run up huge majorities at the polls; they could act as informers and spies. They staffed every government office and every other public job, including the schools and clinics. Every village in the interior and every neighborhood and city block in Asunción had its *sección* (cell). Every social group—women, youth, doctors, lawyers, intellectuals, peasants, workers, landowners, businessmen, and veterans—had its Colorado-sponsored ancillary organization that distributed special benefits to the members. Stroessner's ability to mobilize such mass support also helped to keep the military in check, in addition to the fact that the officers themselves were members of the Colorado Party, and therefore *co-religionarios* too.[13]

Unlike Trujillo, who kept shifting his top military and government personnel, Stroessner tended to keep trusted subordinates in place. Like Trujillo and Somoza, however, he gave those subordinates ample opportunities to supplement their salaries with graft. Paraguay's heavily forested borders with Argentina and Brazil made it an ideal location for smugglers, especially as those neighboring countries placed high luxury taxes on cigarettes, whiskey, lingerie, stereos, and television sets. There was a brisk trade in drugs and guns as well. Each of these rackets was assigned to a highly placed military officer or government official, who then charged international dealers an "in-transit tax" for using Paraguay as an entrepôt.

The legal side of Paraguay's economy also thrived during all but the last years of Stroessner's rule. Inflation was brought under control through austerity measures, under an agreement with the IMF. Until the 1980s, the country enjoyed a stable currency and relatively high growth rates. A new paved highway connected Asunción to Brazil, freeing Paraguay from much of its former dependence on Argentina. A new airport gave the country even greater opportunities to diversify its trading partners. Joint projects with Argentina and Brazil to build hydroelectric dams on the Paraná River brought in additional revenue from the sale of surplus energy to those neighboring countries. They also created full employment and lucrative construction contracts for people with the right connections. A tourist boom in the 1970s added to the general prosperity that was transforming Asunción from a sleepy colonial town into a bustling modern city. The Central Bank's foreign exchange reserves rose from only $18 million in 1970 to $462 million by 1980. The 1970s were also a time of political decompression. A confident regime, basking in prosperity, could afford to be generous to its opponents. Accordingly, the Liberals and Febreristas were allowed to return from exile and even to reopen their party headquarters and publish their party newspapers—so long as they did not criticize either Stroessner or the army. Moreover, they were allowed to participate in elections, although they had no chance of winning since the government counted the ballots. Nevertheless, they were allotted a minority of seats in the Congress, which allowed Stroessner to claim that Paraguay was actually a democracy. Only the Communist Party and the Popular Colorado Movement (MOPOCO), a coalition of Colorado factions that Stroessner had purged, were left out of the amnesty.

Although Paraguay was far from being a democracy, its dictatorship was actually popular. A neon sign over the Central Bank reminded nighttime strollers downtown, "Paz, Trabajo, y Bienestar con Stroessner" (Peace, Work, and Welfare with Stroessner). It was a vulgar boast, but even Stroessner's opponents admitted that he probably would win a free election, if one were held.

Change is inevitable, however, and, ironically, economic growth was changing Paraguay's society in ways that would undermine this seemingly stable regime and make Stroessner look like an anachronism. By 1980 the population had grown from 1.3 to over 4 million. Asunción was now a city of over 600,000, while many of the sleepy little villages of the interior had grown into urban centers where tens of thousands lived. Increased trade spurred the growth of large-scale commercial agriculture, squeezing small proprietors off the land. Many of the latter moved to the capital, where they huddled in squatters' slums along the riverbank, eking out a living as occasional, unskilled laborers. When the last hydroelectric dam was completed in 1980 unemployment rose even further. Meanwhile, an urban middle class of small industrial and commercial entrepreneurs had expanded during the 1960s and 1970s boom years. Then they had been Stroessner supporters, but as the economy contracted in the 1980s they became vociferous critics. After two decades of economic growth, Paraguay was a far more complex society than it had been in 1954, and far more difficult to manage. Moreover, the stability of the regime depended heavily on the man who headed it, and as the 1980s drew to a close Stroessner was perceptibly aging and his health was beginning to deteriorate.

As the Colorado Party prepared to hold its convention in 1987, to nominate Stroessner for an eighth presidential term, speculation was rife about what the regime's future would be when its leader departed the scene. One faction, calling itself "the traditionalists," argued that the party must shore up its popular base for the coming power struggle by pushing for reforms: cleaning up corruption, ending censorship, and purging the regime's more retrograde figures. By doing so, the party would survive in power, even with Stroessner gone. Opposed to them was a faction called "the militants," who were the regime's hardliners. They placed loyalty to Stroessner ahead of loyalty to the party, and their contingency plan was to prepare Stroessner's younger son, Gustavo, an air force officer, to succeed him. Stroessner fell in with their plan to create a dynasty, so on the opening day of the convention the traditionalists found themselves barred from entering. The militants then took over the Colorado executive committee.

This was a blunder, for the militants had little support outside of the presidential palace, whereas the traditionalists were more in touch with the Colorados' mass base. The traditionalists also had a powerful friend in General Andrés Rodríguez, the army's commander in chief. Rodríguez had been Stroessner's protégé and even *compadre*, since Stroessner's elder son, Hugo, had married Rodríguez's daughter. But Hugo turned out to be a drug addict, the marriage had broken up, and the two families became more distant. Now Rodríguez found his subordinates in a spirit of revolt over the militant faction's choice of Gustavo Stroessner as the future president, for Gustavo was known among his colleagues as "La Coronela" because of his homosexual proclivities. The army refused to accept him, and Stroessner's insistence that it do so eventually produced an open break.

In the early morning hours of 3 February 1989 tanks and infantrymen surrounded the luxurious home where Stroessner had spent the night with his mistress. After a bloody battle between the soldiers and Stroessner's Presidential Escort Battalion the dictator surrendered and signed his resignation. At the age of seventy-six, he had been in power for nearly thirty-five years, longer than any other Paraguayan leader in history. Now in humiliation he departed the country for Brazil, while crowds at the airport shouted, "Death to the tyrant!"

Notes

1. On Trujillo's rise to power, see especially Robert Crassweller, *Trujillo: The Life and Times of a Caribbean Dictator* (New York: Macmillan, 1966), 55–86; and Howard J. Wiarda, *Dictatorship and Development: The Methods of Control in Trujillo's Dominican Republic* (Gainesville: University of Florida Press, 1968), 26–31.

2. Jesús Galíndez, *La era de Trujillo* (Buenos Aires: Editorial Americana, 1958), 120.

3. Galíndez, *La era de Truijillo*, 166. The translation is mine. Also, Wiarda, *Dictatorship and Development*, 48–50.

4. Galíndez, *La era de Trujillo*, 129; Crassweller, *Trujillo*, 118.

5. Crassweller, *Trujillo*, 205, 287–90.

6. Bernard Diedrich, *Somoza and the Legacy of U.S. Involvement in Central America* (Maplewood, NJ: Waterfront, 1989), 35.

7. Crassweller, *Trujillo*, 261–62.

8. Diedrich, *Somoza*, 42.

9. For Somoza's early life and background, I have relied mainly on Diedrich, *Somoza*, 2–20.

10. For Somoza's rise to power, see especially Knut Walter, *The Regime of Anastasio Somoza, 1936–1956* (Chapel Hill: University of North Carolina Press, 1993), 14–26. Also, Diedrich, *Somoza*, 14–20.

11. Bernardo Neri Farina, *El Último Supremo: La crónica de Alfredo Stroessner* (Asunción: Editorial El Lector, 2003), 37–39.

12. Byron Nichols, "Las espectativas de los partidos políticos en Paraguay," *Revista Paraguaya de Sociología* 2 (December 1968): 22–61.

13. On the structure of power in Stroessner's regime, see Paul H. Lewis, *Paraguay under Stroessner* (Chapel Hill: University of North Carolina Press, 1980); and Carlos R. Miranda, *The Stroessner Era: Authoritarian Rule in Paraguay* (Boulder, CO: Westview, 1990).

CHAPTER EIGHT

The Marxists

The Cuban Utopia

On 2 December 1956 a group of revolutionaries, led by Fidel Castro, disembarked on the southern coast of Cuba from their ship, the *Granma*, which had carried them from Mexico. After surviving some clashes with the Cuban army, they made their way to the Sierra Maestra mountains. There they began a guerrilla campaign against Cuba's dictator, Fulgencio Batista, which would end on New Year's Eve, 1958, with Batista's sudden flight into exile and Castro's assumption of power.

The bearded guerrillas, clad in combat dress, called themselves the 26th of July Movement, after an earlier attempt by Fidel, in 1953, to seize one of Batista's army barracks. He had gone to prison but then had been pardoned. Soon after his release he went to Mexico and began plotting once more. Now crowds lined the street to cheer him and his followers as they marched into the capital to take over the government. Against overwhelming odds they had defeated a professional army and brought down one of Cuba's most corrupt and brutal dictatorships: a truly dramatic, even romantic, odyssey. A triumphant Fidel promised to bring social justice to Cuba and to end its traditional dependence upon the United States, its close neighbor, only ninety miles away.

Almost immediately there followed a series of events that alarmed the United States about Castro's intentions. First came the show trials and public executions of Batista's top officials. Then came the May 1959 Agrarian

Reform Law that forbade foreign ownership of land and expropriated all holdings over 1,000 acres. Between August and October all remaining American property in Cuba was nationalized. In January 1961 President Eisenhower broke diplomatic relations with Cuba, but Castro already was moving toward placing his country under the protection of the Soviet Union. In April 1961 the United States made a bungled attempt to oust him by supporting an invasion by Cuban exiles at the Bay of Pigs. Many of the invaders were killed, the others were taken prisoner, and their supporters inside Cuba were rounded up. On 2 December 1961 a triumphant Castro announced, "I am a Marxist-Leninist, and will be one until the last day of my life." To solidify this new relationship with the Russians, he allowed them to construct intermediate-range missile sites in Cuba, targeted at the United States. On discovering this, the United States blockaded the island and pressured the Soviet government to withdraw the missiles, in exchange for a similar withdrawal of U.S. missiles from Turkey and a pledge not to invade Cuba. With the crisis averted, President Kennedy lifted the naval blockade, only to replace it with a travel and trade embargo that remains in effect today, more than forty years later.

Such were the chief proximate events that brought about a permanent rupture between the United States and Cuba, and the latter's incorporation into the Soviet communist orbit. But the real roots of Cuban radicalism go back further, at least to the founding of the Republic in 1902.

Under the Shadow of the Eagle
The Cuban Revolution's radicalism may be interpreted as the extreme expression of a long-repressed nationalism.[1] Cuba was the last of the Spanish American colonies to gain its independence. Its revolt against Spain broke out in 1895, but in 1898 that struggle became subsumed as part of the Spanish-American War, which ended with the United States taking over Puerto Rico, Guam, and the Philippines, while also invading and occupying Cuba. Although Cuba became nominally independent in 1902, its constitution had to be approved in Washington and contain a provision, known as the Platt Amendment. Under it, Cuba promised not to incur any unpayable foreign debts, to lease a naval base at Guantánamo to the United States in perpetuity, and to recognize the right of the United States to intervene militarily if law and order were to break down. The marines left in 1902 but were back four years later and stayed until 1908, after fraudulent elections provoked uncontrolled violence. A third U.S. intervention came in 1917, to suppress a revolution, and lasted until 1922. With each occupation, hatred of the United States grew.

It did not help, either, that the United States eventually turned to a "strongman," Gerardo Machado, to impose order on his fellow Cubans. The United States already had turned Cuba into an economic colony with the 1903 Reciprocal Trade Pact, granting Cuban sugar growers prices above the world market for sending raw sugar to U.S. refineries, while keeping out processed sugar. During Machado's rule (1925–1933), however, there was a great influx of direct U.S. investment in Cuba, most of it in sugar production and the remainder in the railroad, utilities, and banking sectors. This investment brought about a period of prosperity in the 1920s that made U.S. imperialism and Machado's heavy-handed rule tolerable, if not popular; but when the Depression hit, resistance began to mount. An underground movement calling itself the ABC Society, drawing support from the middle class, students, and labor, fought back against Machado's thuggery with riots, strikes, and violence. The United States, under the newly elected administration of Franklin D. Roosevelt, also withdrew its support, as part of the "Good Neighbor Policy." Even the army deserted Machado, who finally fled the country in August 1933.

Three weeks later another upheaval surprised the Machado-appointed army officers who took over the government. Reform-minded noncommissioned officers, led by a sergeant named Fulgencio Batista, revolted and seized power. Their choice for president was Ramón Grau San Martín, a university professor popular with student revolutionaries. The United States considered him too radical, however, and refused to grant the new government diplomatic recognition. Batista shopped around then for an innocuous figurehead—indeed, he moved seven such puppets in and out of the presidency over the next seven years, after which he called a convention that wrote a democratic constitution for Cuba. Not surprisingly, the first president elected under the 1940 constitution was Batista. What really was surprising was his stepping down at the end of his term and allowing free elections.

From 1944 to 1952 Cuba was governed democratically, first under Grau San Martín and then under Grau's protégé, Carlos Prío Socarrás. Unfortunately, under their administrations democracy came to be associated with unprecedented graft, corruption, and gangsterism. As the 1952 elections approached, Batista announced his candidacy for president. Polls showed him running a distant third in the race, however, so on 10 March 1952, he put himself at the head of a military coup. Once back in power he abolished all of the political parties, exiled their leaders, and suppressed their gangs. The universities were closed after the students protested, and the press was tightly censored. Corruption was still common, but more centralized.

Castroites like to insist that the revolution rescued Cuba from poverty, illiteracy, and American exploitation, which had reached new depths under Batista—but those are myths. Cuba in the 1950s had a large middle class made up of small businessmen, professionals, white-collar workers, and small independent farmers. According to the 1953 census, these groups, taken as a whole, constituted about 35 percent of the population. The addition of skilled workers would have brought the proportion up to about half.[2] Moreover, the living standards of those people were among the highest in Latin America (and indeed the world) according to measures such as per capita income; literacy rates; infant mortality rates; the number of physicians and dentists per capita; the per capita consumption of meat, vegetables, and cereals; the number of automobiles, telephones, and radios per capita; the availability of electric power; and the level of industrial production.

Nor was American capital so dominant in the 1950s as it had been in the 1920s. In the area of sugar production, which accounted for three-fourths of Cuba's exports, U.S. ownership had been declining since the 1930s, so that while it accounted for two-thirds of all production in 1929, by 1958 it was Cuban owners who produced two-thirds of the output. Moreover, Batista had earlier protected the interests of small growers under the 1937 Law of Sugar Coordination. Small producers were granted the right of permanent occupancy, if they were tenant farmers, and sugar mills had to take a certain quota of sugar from each small producer. As with sugar, so with banking. In 1929 three-fourths of all bank deposits were in foreign (usually American) banks, but by 1958 two-thirds of deposits were in Cuban-owned banks. True, American capital still dominated the manufacturing and utilities sectors, but Cubans controlled retail trade and services.

Batista was a corrupt and ruthless tyrant, but he was no mere right-wing throwback. One of his achievements was to persuade the Americans to withdraw the Platt Amendment. Moreover, the populist sergeant, a mulatto child of farm workers, had a long history of tolerance for the Popular Socialist (Communist) Party, going back to the 1930s. The Cuban Labor Confederation (CTC) was established in 1939 as a compromise between Batista, who sought labor support, and the Communist Cuban National Labor Confederation (CNOC), whose origins went back to 1925. Organized labor always enjoyed high wages under Batista, and during his last period in power (1952–1958) real wages rose by 14 percent. Small wonder that neither the Communists nor the CTC would agree to help Castro overthrow Batista. They ignored Fidel's call for a general strike against the dictatorship in April 1958.

Nevertheless, despite Cuba's relatively high living standards, important sectors of the population—rural labor and unskilled urban workers—lived in poverty and insecurity. About one-third of the labor force was either unemployed or worked at part-time, poorly paid jobs. Once the sugar crop was harvested, seasonal unemployment soared in the rural areas. The 25 percent of the population classified as rural labor seldom went beyond the third grade at school and had an illiteracy rate of almost 42 percent. Their housing lacked running water, electricity, or indoor toilets. They were undernourished, suffered from intestinal parasites, and had almost no access to health care.[3]

But it was Batista's own stubborn refusal to restore democracy to an essentially middle-class society, rather than the social injustices suffered by a minority, that eventually led to his downfall. His coup in 1952 had disrupted the country's political development, for although the Grau and Prío governments were corrupt, most Cubans nevertheless subscribed to the ideals embodied in the 1940 constitution. Moreover, Batista was not even an efficient dictator, as Trujillo, Somoza, and Stroessner were. His attempt to legitimize his rule through fraudulent elections in 1954 was done so farcically as to provoke contempt. Press censorship and the repression of political opposition were inconsistent and lackadaisical: just enough to antagonize his enemies but not enough to crush them. Perhaps his most serious mistake was to neglect the army, always the main prop of a dictatorship. He resisted pressure from the United States to upgrade military training because he feared that a more professional officer corps might try to replace him. As it was, both officers and conscripts were demoralized by the corruption that permeated the armed forces, and by their involvement in Batista's increasing resort to repression to keep himself in power. Caught between the middle classes' widespread hostility to the regime and the apparent moderation of the rebel forces—the Revolutionary Student Directorate, operating in the Escambay Mountains, and the 26th of July Movement in the Sierra Maestra—whose manifestos essentially called for a restoration of democracy, the army showed little inclination to fight. Desertions were common. Even the United States became convinced that further support for Batista was useless and finally cut off its military aid. By the time Batista boarded his New Year's Eve plane for the Bahamas, his regime had all but evaporated.

Marxist Morality

Fidel Castro came to power convinced that Cuba must have a radical social revolution that would liberate it once and forever from American economic, military, and cultural influence. The old bourgeois parties, the old dependent-capitalist order with its parasitic elites, and the corrupt armed forces had to be eliminated in order to clear the way for a new kind of society. A powerful revolutionary state would undertake the wholesale expropriation of wealth, while economic planning would focus on raising the living standards of Cuba's rural and urban poor. Planning would also aim at changing the old monocultural economy, with its heavy reliance on sugar, by diversifying agriculture and encouraging import-substituting industrialization.

It is important to emphasize that this was not a cool, rationally calculated strategy but more of a moral crusade. Partly inspired by national resentment against U.S. imperialism, and partly by disgust at Cuba's corrupt past, the young revolutionaries considered capitalism to be an evil, and socialism to be the remedy. As moralists, they placed social justice ahead of economic rationality. Postponement of crucial political decisions on economic grounds made little sense to leaders whose basic aim was to advance the power of the state over private interests in order to abolish the system of property, wealth, and class that the revolution was committed to destroy. Supply and demand did not matter. Who lost what did not matter. What the economic costs might be down the road did not matter. What was crucial was furthering the revolutionary process, doing rather than thinking, moving rather than standing still.[4]

The revolutionaries got busy right away by promulgating the First Agrarian Reform Law in May 1959, which expropriated all landholdings of over 400 hectares (approximately 1,000 acres). The National Institute for Agrarian Reform (INRA), created by the same law, then distributed the expropriated land into some 600 peasant cooperatives and 500 state farms (Farm Units under Direct Administration) by the end of 1961. The cooperatives would be abolished in 1963 and turned into state farms, still leaving about 63 percent of all arable land in the private hands of small and medium-sized farmers. The latter, however, would have to join a state-controlled farmers' organization and sell their produce, at government-fixed prices, to INRA.

After that, Castro turned his attention to the urban sector. In December, large Cuban-owned businesses were taken over by the state. Then in July 1960 the American-owned oil refineries were seized, without compensation. That was followed by a quick process, which lasted from August to October, in which the remaining American and other foreign businesses were nationalized. Also in October, the Urban Reform Law put all urban commercial real estate—such as hotels, department stores, and rental property—under state ownership.

A crusading state motivated by such moral passion would naturally resent obstacles to its forward motion. The old armed forces were dissolved, as were Batista's police, to be replaced by Castro's followers. Some 400 of the former regime's top military and police officials were executed, after show trials. Labor unions, which were tainted by their refusal to take a stand against Batista, saw their leadership purged. The Labor Ministry required all unions to obtain official recognition in order to be legal, and to join the government-controlled Confederation of Cuban Workers (CTC). Strikes were forbidden. Similar requirements were placed on other professional organizations representing doctors, lawyers, engineers, teachers, or journalists. By the end of 1960 all opposition newspapers had been closed down and the state had assumed control of all radio and television stations. The new revolutionary government also took over the educational system, purging teachers and professors. Private and religious schools were shut down. Meanwhile, the regime launched a literacy drive that combined learning to read with indoctrination in Marxism-Leninism. Officially, literacy rates rose to over 90 percent, although the quality of instruction was quite low.

As relations with the United States deteriorated and those with the Soviet Union became friendlier, Castro came under criticism from former allies and colleagues. They too were dealt with harshly. The Revolutionary Student Directorate was forced to merge with the 26th of July Movement and the Communists' Popular Socialist Party (PSP) to form the Integrated Revolutionary Organization (ORI), as the first step in the process of creating an official regime party. That process culminated, in 1965, in the establishment of a completely restructured Communist Party of Cuba (PCC), with Fidel Castro as its head. Moderates who resisted the drift toward communism were purged and arrested. Major Huber Matos, one of the heroes of the revolutionary struggle, was charged with treason and replaced as commander of the revolutionary army by Fidel's brother, Raúl. Besieged by enemies inside the revolution as well as outside of it, Castro announced, in September 1960, that he was setting up "a system of revolutionary collective vigilance, so that everybody will know everybody else on his block, what they do, what relationship they had with the [Batista's] tyranny, what they believe in, what people they meet, what activities they participate in." These committees for the defense of the revolution (CDRs) were first created as block committees in Havana, but they soon spread to other towns on the island. Other vigilance committees were organized in factories, stores, administrative offices, and schools. Within the next few years there would be over 100,000 such committees, embracing about 2 million members—or about one-fourth of Cuba's 8 million people. Tightly controlled from the top by the National Directorate, the CDRs were, in addition to spying on their fellow citizens, supposed to participate in mass meetings and demonstrations sponsored by the regime. By their example they would encourage others to adopt revolutionary values and participate as well.[5]

The departure of many potential dissenters, who chose exile, also made political control easier. The first wave of exiles were the few thousand Batista supporters who left immediately after the dictator's fall. A second wave, composed mainly of the former economic, social, and party elites, began in mid-1960 and continued until the missile crisis. A third wave lasted from late 1965 to 1972 and consisted mainly of skilled workers who resented Castro's takeover of their unions. While all of these people were leaving Cuba, others of course were returning to join in the revolution. The net loss of population, however, was calculated to be almost 585,000 by 1974.[6] By allowing the main potential sources of opposition to leave, the regime made it less likely that it would face any serious internal revolt. On the other hand, this exodus was economically disruptive and deprived the country of much-needed skills. For Castro and his top officials, this was a small price to pay for creating a truly socialist society.

The constant threat of U.S. intervention forced Castro to seek the protection of the Soviet Union. During a crucial visit to the USSR in April 1963 he succeeded in getting Cuba admitted to the Soviet Bloc, which guaranteed him military protection and economic aid. Although Russia itself was a major producer of sugar, it agreed to buy most of Cuba's sugar—at prices above the world market—which it would then resell to its Eastern European satellite states. It would also supply Cuba with all of its oil needs. In return, Cuba would give preferential treatment to imports of Soviet industrial goods. In appearance, at least, Cuba had merely switched masters and would still be tied to a monocultural sugar economy. But that was not how Fidel and his industry minister, Ernesto "Che" Guevara, viewed it. Both men were dedicated to creating a more "humanistic" type of communism than the Soviet version. Like all Marxists, they rejected private property, the profit motive, and individualism; but they hoped to avoid building up a totalitarian bureaucracy such as the Soviets had. Ultimately, they wanted complete independence from both the United States and Russia, although in the short run their dependence on the latter was increasing every day. The trade deficit between Cuba and Russia had to be financed by the Soviets to the amount of around $3 million a day.

Guevara's solution, which Fidel endorsed, was to begin immediately to create "the New Communist Man" by indoctrinating the people to adopt moral, as opposed to material, incentives to motivate their work. For Guevara, "It is not a matter of how many kilograms of meat one has to eat, nor of how many times a year someone can go to the beach, nor how many pretty things from abroad you might be able to buy with present-day wages. It is a matter of making the individual feel more complete, with much more internal richness and much more responsibility." Guevara believed that "the society of communist man" would replace individualism through the work of the Ministry of Education and the Communist Party's "informational apparatus." Youth brigades, organized to back up the army as a "popular militia" and to contribute "voluntary labor" in the cane fields at harvest time, would breed a sense of camaraderie, a new consciousness, a new set of values under the pressure of which the individual "tries to adjust himself to a situation that he feels is right and that his own lack of development had prevented him from reaching previously." Youth was to be targeted especially, "because it is the malleable clay from which the new man can be built without any of the old vestiges."[7]

The mobilization and indoctrination of Cuban youth was undertaken by the party's Union of Communist Youth, which in turn controlled a variety of organizations that reached out to young people of all ages: the Federation of University Youth, the Federation of Secondary School Youth, and, for grade-schoolers, the Cuban Pioneers. For young workers not attending the university there was the Youth Labor Organization. Membership was compulsory in each of these groups for all eligible youth.

The party extended its control to other groups as well. Over two million women were enrolled in the Cuban Women's Federation, which trained them to enter the labor force and encouraged them to do more "voluntary" after-hours work. The party also took over the old Confederation of Cuban Workers, which proved to be the most resistant to Guevara's "moral incentives." Despite that resistance, strikes were eliminated, wages were held down, and overtime pay was eliminated. Indeed, workers were forced to go to the countryside to contribute their "voluntary" unpaid labor during the sugar harvest. Similar resistance by small farmers to INRA's fixed prices took the form of sporadic revolts in 1961, provoking a crackdown by the regime in the form of the Second Agrarian Reform Law (1963). This time all farms of more than 165 acres were expropriated and turned into state farms. At the same time, the peasant collectives created by the First Agrarian Reform Law were abolished and transformed into state farms as well. The remaining small farmers were forced to join the official National Association of Small Peasants (ANAP). ANAP provided the credits, seeds, fertilizers, and implements the small farmers required. In return, the farmers were told which crops to plant and were forced to sell all their produce to INRA at prices set by the government. In March 1968 the government launched its "Revolutionary Offensive" against the remaining small businesses in the cities, in order to hasten the disappearance of all residues of the former capitalist society.[8]

The committees for the defense of the revolution were important in this process of tightening the government's control over society. They too contributed their "voluntary" after-hours labor to mass literacy campaigns, blood donation campaigns, and "agitprop." They also organized neighbor-hood "popular tribunals" to handle "politically deviant behavior," which might range from petty theft to quarrelsome behavior or an "oppositionist" attitude toward the authorities. Penalties also might vary in severity, from a mere warning to compulsory "socialist reeducation" through community service, or even six months in jail and the confiscation of the offender's personal property.

The Turning Point

The supreme test of the "moral economy" came in 1970, when Fidel an-nounced that Cuba would produce a ten-million-ton sugar harvest, by far the largest in the country's history. Such an achievement would show the world the Cuban people's enthusiasm for the revolution and the power of moral in-centives. Moreover, it would establish Cuba's "moral economy" as the lead-ing model for all other communist states to imitate, as opposed to the USSR's dreary bureaucratic totalitarianism, and that would make it more indepen-dent of the Russians. Since the average harvest over the past eighteen years had produced only about 5.4 million tons, Fidel essentially was calling for a doubling of the country's sugar output. It would require a massive effort. Nonetheless, he warned, "We shall not be satisfied with anything less than 10 million tons. One pound under 10 million tons would represent a moral defeat." Those were the words of a confident guerrilla chief who had con-quered power against great odds and now was certain that the same revolu-tionary willpower would overcome any economic obstacles.[9]

The harvest began in November 1969 and lasted until the following April. The weather was good and during the peak months there were about 350,000 workers in the cane fields, of whom all but 80,000 were unpaid vol-unteers. Over the entire six months around 1.2 million workers from the nonsugar sectors of the economy—out of a total labor force of 2.2 million—participated in cane cutting. That is to say, Fidel was able to mobilize over one-half of the civilian labor force to carry out his project. In addition, a huge assemblage of trucks and other vehicles were commandeered to carry the cut cane to the mills.

By Fidel's own standards, this enormous effort was a failure, for although 8.5 million tons of sugar were produced (a record), that was far below the goal he had set. Moreover, that record harvest came at the expense of lower output in almost every nonsugar sector of the economy—in other agricul-tural goods such as meat, poultry, dairy products, cooking oils, fruit, and veg-etables; and in industrial goods like cement, rubber tires, clothing, canned foods, soap, and textiles.

There was a host of reasons for the shortfall in sugar. The old technicians and administrators at the sugar mills had been dismissed for their lack of revolutionary ardor and replaced with inexperienced people. The new revolutionary management had ignored good business practices like replacing antiquated machinery, paying attention to maintenance, and storing up replacement parts. Thus, there were breakdowns and delays, causing the cut cane to lay in idle heaps for days, while it lost much of its sugar content. In addition, there was a shortage of experienced cane cutters, many of whom had moved to the cities or had left the country. That left the "volunteer" workers, who composed about 80 percent of the labor force. Most of them failed to respond to moral incentives. Since they weren't being paid, they were inefficient and careless in their work.

To his credit, Castro admitted that "the heroic effort to increase sugar production resulted in imbalances in the economy, in diminished production in other sectors and, in short, in an increase in our difficulties. . . . Our enemies say we have problems and in this our enemies are right." Moreover, he accepted the failure of moral incentives. The revolutionaries had mistakenly believed that "a world that for thousands of years had lived under the law of retaliation, the law of the survival of the fittest, of egoism and deceit, the law of exploitation, could, all of a sudden, be turned into a society in which everybody behaved in an ethical, moral way."[10] Moral incentives were abandoned during the course of 1971.

The Sovietization of Cuba

Instead of Cuba becoming the new model for the world's communist systems, it now accepted its dependence on Soviet aid, advice, and supervision. Russian advisers were assigned to reorganize all of the ministries dealing with the economy, as Cuba was to be integrated into the Soviet Bloc, along with the Eastern European satellites. A central planning agency (JUCEPLAN) gathered statistics from state farms, factories, and government ministries, after which it constructed an overall plan, replete with targets for each sector of the economy. Labor, machinery, and materials were carefully allocated to each enterprise. Managers of those enterprises were also told what wages they could pay and what prices to charge. Each economic unit was expected to be profitable and self-financing; unprofitable units would be shut down.

Worker productivity was encouraged by the use of piece wages, or payment by unit produced, instead of hourly wages, wherever possible. Each factory or farm was assigned a production quota. If it exceeded that quota, the manager and workers would be rewarded with a bonus. If it fell below the quota there would be an investigation from the supervising ministry as well as from the local party organization. The CTC, now under firm party control, was supposed to exhort its members to work to their utmost, and factory courts were set up to punish individual workers for absenteeism, disobedience, or negligence.

Sovietization, with its material incentives, meant that the regime now accepted the inequality of incomes. Productive workers would earn more than the less productive and could even top up their incomes with bonuses and overtime pay. On the other hand, the emphasis on profitability put pressure on managers to trim their payrolls, with the result that unemployment—previously eliminated by the revolution—reappeared as a social problem. However, the 1971 Anti-Loafing Law threatened the unemployed with jail unless they quickly found new jobs. One alternative for them was to enlist in the armed forces and be sent abroad as "volunteers" to fight in Soviet-backed "liberation movements." Some 50,000 Cubans were thus sent to Angola, another 24,000 were sent to Ethiopia, and an estimated 1,500 helped the Sandinista revolution in Nicaragua.

As in the Soviet Union, peasants were allowed to own small plots. These accounted for only 30 percent of all farmland, yet they produced about half of all fruit and vegetables. Peasants could sell any surplus above their assigned quota through "unofficial" markets, which assured the towns of an adequate—though not abundant—supply of food. On the whole, however, material incentives failed to produce great gains in productivity because, even with wage differentials, there were so few consumer goods available. One reason for this was that almost all state investment was now concentrated upon sugar production. Another reason was the government's heavy expenditure on the armed forces, which had swelled from just over 29,000 men under Batista to 300,000 under Castro. Under Soviet influence, the Revolutionary Armed Forces (FAR) were trimmed back to just over 100,000, with perhaps an equal number in the reserves. Troop levels started rising again toward the end of the 1970s, however, reaching over 200,000 in 1980–1981, with another 90,000 reservists and 118,000 men and women serving in the Militia and Territorial Troops (MTT), a civil defense organization that also sent work teams into the sugarcane fields.[11]

Like the Soviet Union, Cuba's Ministry of the Interior operated a large internal security apparatus whose powers of surveillance reached into every corner of the nation's life, thanks to the vigilance of the committees for the defense of the revolution. In any given year there were about 20,000 political detainees being held, and tortured, under inhuman prison conditions.[12] In addition, intellectual and artistic life, which had flourished so brilliantly during the revolution's early phase, was now smothered by a ubiquitous censorship and an incessant barrage of propaganda.

Castro went along with Cuba's "sovietization" with growing discontent. For him, the use of material incentives was leading away from the "new communist man," and he especially resented his own reduced role as the charismatic "Supreme Leader." Also, the USSR's own mounting economic problems were resulting in cutbacks in economic and military aid. Finally, when Mikhail Gorbachev introduced perestroika and glasnost, aimed at liberalizing the Soviet system, Fidel struck back by convoking a convention of the Cuban Communist Party in December 1986, at which he introduced his "rectification program." He rejected any movement toward opening the Cuban system to criticism or accepting the formation of dissident groups. Nor would he accept market reforms. In fact, he moved quickly to close down the "unofficial" peasant markets. Material incentives were scrapped. In the name of equality, highly paid workers found their wages reduced, while the lowest paid were granted raises. There were higher work norms and quotas, while microbrigades of "vanguard workers" sent out by the party descended upon lagging factories to set an example of dedicated work habits. There was also more after-hours "voluntary" labor, most of it focused on apartment house construction.

The final collapse of the Soviet Union, from 1989 to 1991, meant no more deliveries of oil, raw materials, or food. It meant no more replacement parts for factories or for military equipment. Without Soviet aid, the armed forces had to be reduced drastically, to around 65,000, although the MTT were expanded to over one million. The mass market for Cuban sugar suddenly disappeared, as did the Soviets' $3.5 million daily subsidy. The economic impact was excruciating: industrial imports (machinery, fuels, parts, vehicles) fell by one-fourth between 1989 and 1993, while Cuba's economic production fell by 35 to 40 percent. Rationing of food, pharmaceuticals, clothes, gasoline, and electricity—indeed, almost all consumer goods—was immediately imposed. About 40 percent of all buses were put out of service in order to save gas, so Cubans went to work on foot or bicycles. Meanwhile, the regime defaulted on some $11 billion in dollar-denominated debt, so no new loans were forthcoming from either Europe's "Paris Club" or the World Bank.

The regime had to make far-reaching changes to stay afloat. It shifted away from sugar production, which fell to unprecedented lows, and put its emphasis on tourism. To capture much-needed foreign exchange, in 1993 it allowed the dollar to circulate as legal tender along with the peso. Tourists without either currency were allowed to exchange their money at official *cambios* (exchange banks) at the rate of 1 dollar for 1 peso—although the black market rate was at least 1,000 to 1. Tourist hotels claimed the best of Cuba's rationed food supply, beaches were roped off for tourists only, and the regime reluctantly allowed some limited self-employment catering to tourists, such as small private restaurants and taxis. There were also state-run "dollar stores" where those with dollars, including Cubans receiving remittances from abroad, could buy better-quality food, clothing, and housewares. Parallel to all this was a vast underground economy where drugs, prostitutes of both sexes, and goods pilfered from the workplace were for sale.

Even so, there were still residues of support for the revolution: among the very poorest elements, among nationalists who resented the U.S. embargo, and among the political elites who enjoyed privileges from which most Cubans were excluded. The elites especially feared that the exiles in Miami would take revenge once the regime fell, and so they clung tenaciously to power. For those whom they ruled, who were unable to either protest or emigrate, life had become a cynical game of evasion in which one eked out a precarious existence in the underground economy: the dreary result of a utopian vision.[13]

The Rise and Fall of Allende's Chile

In the opening days of January 1966 Fidel Castro played host to the "Conference of Solidarity of the Peoples of Africa, Asia, and Latin America," which also became known as the "Tri-Continental Conference." Five hundred and twelve delegates from eighty-two countries or colonial territories attended. The governments of the Soviet Union, China, North Korea, North Vietnam, Algeria, Egypt, Tanzania, Ghana, and of course Cuba were represented. Most delegates, however, were from Marxist political parties, movements, or "front" organizations, such as the Vietcong, the Palestine Liberation Organization, and guerrilla groups from Angola and Mozambique. The Latin American contingent was similarly composed of small extremist parties and terrorist organizations, most of them with close ties to Cuba, which already was operating as a training ground for spreading revolution throughout the region. The Chilean delegation, headed by a senator named Salvador Allende, represented the Popular Revolutionary Action Front, a coalition of the Socialist and Communist parties, plus some smaller leftist parties. Unlike most of the other Latin American delegations, it enjoyed legal status in its home country.

One outcome of the "Tri-Continental" was the delegates' approval of Castro's proposal to extend "armed struggle" throughout Latin America. A second important outcome was a decision by the Latin American groups to meet again the following year to set up the "Organization of Latin American Solidarity" (OLAS), which would coordinate all revolutionary efforts. OLAS met, as scheduled, in Havana during August 1967. Once again, the meeting was composed largely of representatives of guerrilla organizations: Camilo Torres, the guerrilla priest from Colombia; Carlos Marighela, the Brazilian terrorist and chief theoretician of urban guerrilla warfare; a number of Argentines who would soon come together to form the Montoneros; and the Uruguayan Tupamaros. There were also participants from leftist, but legal, organizations, such as the Uruguayan Communist Party; the Chilean Communist Party; the World Council of Churches; black power advocate Stokely Carmichael; and the Chilean Socialist Party, represented by Salvador Allende, who presided over the general sessions. Another Chilean delegation represented the Movement of the Revolutionary Left (MIR), a terrorist organization in which Allende's nephew, Andrés Pascal Allende, was a leader. The high point of this OLAS meeting was the reading of a letter from Che Guevara, who was then trying to raise an insurrection in Bolivia. Although Guevara himself would fail and be killed in October, his ringing words, calling for uprisings around Latin America that would overwhelm the United States with "many Vietnams," remained inspirational to the delegates. Three years later, Salvador Allende was elected president of Chile.

Born in Valparaiso in 1908, Allende came from an upper-middle-class family that boasted of many prominent doctors and lawyers. His father and grandfather were active in the Chilean Radical Party and were well known as anticlerical Freemasons. Allende inherited this radical bent. When he entered medical school at the National University in Santiago, in 1926, he soon fell in with a student circle that would gather at night to read the works of Marx, Lenin, and Trotsky. At that time Chile was going through a constitutional crisis. Arturo Alessandri, the great reformer of his day, had resigned the presidency in 1925 to protest the scheming of his war minister, Colonel Carlos Ibáñez, who refused to renounce his candidacy in the upcoming elections. Alessandri's resignation served to block Ibáñez for the moment, and resulted in Emiliano Figueroa Larrain's election, but a year and a half later a coup brought Ibáñez to power anyway. The university students were outraged and took to the streets. Allende was arrested during a violent clash with the police and was temporarily expelled from the university. His punishment didn't last very long, however, for he received his medical degree in 1933.

In the meantime, Ibáñez had left office in 1931, under pressure from the Chilean oligarchy and the economic blows of the Great Depression. Shortly afterward another coup brought to power an air force colonel, Marmaduke

Grove, who proclaimed a "socialist republic." He, too, was soon to fall, but in the following year he brought together several socialist factions to form the single Socialist Party of Chile. The young Dr. Allende was an important participant in this process and came to head the party's Valparaiso branch and represent it in the Chamber of Deputies. In 1938 his political career took a big jump when the Socialists joined the Communists and Radicals to form the Popular Front, which elected Pedro Aguirre Cerda, a Radical, to the presidency. The Socialists won three cabinet seats, including the Ministry of Health, which went to the thirty-year-old Allende. In 1945 Allende was elected to the Senate, where he was to serve for the next twenty-five years, eventually becoming the president of that body. Nothing about him in those years presaged his turbulent end. Like many other members of Chile's upper-middle class, he was suave and sophisticated, an elegant dresser, and reputedly a connoisseur of fine wines, haute cuisine, modern art, and beautiful women.

By 1952 the Popular Front had long since disappeared, having first jettisoned the Communists and then the more radical Socialists. After fourteen years in power the Radical Party was a spent force. Although it had fomented a sizable manufacturing sector, including some heavy industry, and had greatly expanded the welfare state, generous government spending was becoming inflationary. Meanwhile, Chile's protected industries were inefficient. The resulting "stagflation" undermined the Radicals' popularity and led to an electoral backlash in the form of support for ex-dictator Carlos Ibáñez, who ran as a strong leader, and one who was "above politics." He promised to make Chile economically independent by intensifying the state's commitment to import-substituting industrialization. Ibáñez's candidacy caused the Socialists to divide over whether to support him. Although the party leaders decided to do so, Allende refused and led a breakaway faction that, together with support from the then illegal Communist Party, allowed him to make his first bid for the presidency. Although he received only 5.5 percent of the vote, he established himself as a national-level leader.

In 1956 Allende became the head of a formal Socialist-Communist alliance called the Popular Revolutionary Action Front (FRAP) and was its standard-bearer in the 1958 elections. This time he lost to the Right's candidate, Jorge Alessandri, by a mere 33,500 votes. Allende's third try at the presidency, in 1964, was less successful, however. Unable to succeed himself, Alessandri convinced the Right to support the Christian Democratic candidate, Eduardo Frei. Frei won easily with 56 percent of the vote.

Frei had run on the promise that he would bring about "a revolution within liberty," a democratic alternative to FRAP's Marxism. Once in office, however, he found himself squeezed between a right-wing congressional bloc determined to prevent change, and a left-wing bloc determined to criticize his every move as insufficiently revolutionary. Two main policy initiatives illustrate his dilemma. First, Frei embarked on a gradual nationalization of the American-owned copper mines, which were popular targets of nationalist resentment. The Chilean government would use its royalties from the mines to buy up the companies' stock, while in the meantime the companies promised to properly maintain the mines and their equipment. FRAP dismissed this program as being too generous to the foreigners, while the Right criticized Frei for enlarging the state enterprise sector.

Secondly, the Christian Democrats launched a long-overdue agrarian reform that expropriated approximately 1,300 *latifundios* and redistributed the land to the former tenants. Some 37,000 families were settled on small private farms, and another 30,000 were gathered into farm cooperatives. Small-farmer and cooperative unions then formed to represent these new owners. The Right naturally viewed all this as an attack on private property. The Left, on the other hand, thought that redistribution should have been in the form of state farms. Otherwise, the Christian Democrats were simply creating an agrarian petite bourgeoisie. Moreover, FRAP criticized Frei for having exempted large holdings that were being efficiently worked.

The Christian Democrats approached the 1970 elections exhausted and fragmented. Their liberation theology wing split off to form the independent Movement of United Popular Action (MAPU) and joined the Socialist-Communist coalition, now rebaptized as Popular Unity (UP). Other small groups on the Left, including a fragment of the old Radical Party, also joined UP, which increased its strength enough to put Allende in first place on his fourth try for the presidency. In a reverse of the 1958 election, he beat Jorge Alessandri with 36 percent of the vote to the latter's 35 percent, and the Christian Democrats ran third at 28 percent.

Since no candidate had a majority, Congress would choose the winner from between the top two. The Christian Democrats would have the deciding vote. At this juncture, the U.S. Central Intelligence Agency intervened in such a way as to throw public sympathy behind Allende. It began by trying to bribe the Christian Democrat congressmen to vote for Alessandri, which only insulted them. Then it participated in a clumsy plot to kidnap General René Schneider, the army's commander, who was insisting that the military remain neutral. Schneider was killed during the attempt, and in an act of revulsion against the Right a Christian Democrat convention voted to support Allende—on the condition that he agree to a "statute of democratic guarantees" that would bind him to respect (1) the freedom of the press,

(2) the autonomy of the three branches of government, (3) the freedom of assembly and association for all political parties and interest groups, (4) the right of private schools and universities to exist without interference from the state, and (5) the continued nonpartisan character of the armed forces.[14] Allende signed, on the advice of his Communist allies, although many of the more radical Socialists objected. It didn't matter; within three years he would violate every one of his pledges.

Initiating the Revolution

The Popular Unity government was divided over tactics from the very beginning. The Communist Party, drawing on the experience of the Spanish Republic before Franco, urged moderation. The government should avoid attacking the Catholic Church or frightening the middle classes, in order to retain the Christian Democrats' cooperation for as long as possible. The Socialists and MAPU, however, thought that the government had only a narrow window of opportunity and should move ahead fast to eliminate private property and destroy the bourgeoisie forever. This viewpoint won out. The foreign copper companies were quickly confiscated, without compensation, and when they demanded payment Allende levied an "excess profits tax" on them, to be applied retroactively. Some 282 domestic industrial, commercial, and financial companies were taken over as well. Some were purchased by the state development corporation (CORFO), while in other cases Allende used an old law from the Depression era that allowed the state to take over a firm if it ceased producing goods or services. The law originally was intended to preserve jobs, but in its current application the takeover was preceded by a strike deliberately called to shut down production. The Supreme Court ruled this to be unconstitutional, but Allende ignored the judges. Agrarian reform was pushed a step further by a decree expropriating all farms greater than 80 hectares (about 200 acres), whether they were being used efficiently or not. The newly expropriated land was then turned into state farms.

That still left about a quarter of the country's farmland under small private farms, many of which had been recently created by the Christian Democrats. These now came under scrutiny from the Corporation for Agrarian Reform (CORA), and those without clear land titles were taken over by the state. The rest were subject to *tomas* (invasions) by landless farm workers, armed and led by guerrillas from the Movement of the Revolutionary Left, while government officials denied any knowledge of the events. The victims of these *tomas* were then forced into communal farms.

MIR deserves special mention for its unofficial relationship to Allende's government. In fact, one of its top leaders was Andrés Pascal Allende, the president's nephew. It had started in 1965 as an offshoot of the Socialist Youth, committed to insurrection. After a series of bank robberies and arms thefts it was outlawed by the Frei government, but Allende restored it to legality by an amnesty after he took office. He even surrounded himself with bodyguards drawn from MIR. Even though it was not formally a part of the Popular Unity coalition, MIR spread its influence throughout the government. It had cells in the state farms, the nationalized companies, and throughout the industrial slums that ringed Santiago, Concepción, and Valparaiso, where slum dwellers were encouraged to invade and occupy empty buildings and apartments. These were "liberated zones" in which MIR stored up arms and prepared for a great general uprising.

Meanwhile, the Allende government was seeking to gain more popular support with an aggressive program of income redistribution whose centerpiece was a huge wage increase: 35 percent on the average, with raises of up to 50 percent for unskilled workers. Fringe benefits went up too, as did spending on social programs like pensions, health services, day care centers, family allowances, and school lunch programs. Nor did this require any increase in taxes, for Allende had inherited a full treasury from Frei.[15] There was also no need at first to worry about inflation or impose price controls because there had been a recession during Frei's last two years, and now heavy government spending reactivated idle industrial capacity. Unemployed workers were being hired back or else were finding newly created jobs in the nationalized companies or in expanded social programs. The GDP grew by a record 7.7 percent, and in manufacturing by 11.1 percent. Not surprisingly, the voters rewarded Popular Unity in the April 1971 midterm municipal elections, with 49.7 percent of the vote: more than 13 percentage points over its 1970 performance.

The Revolution in Trouble

If 1971 was a year of unprecedented growth in Chile, without inflation, 1972 saw a sudden, disastrous reversal on all fronts. Production fell in agriculture, manufacturing, and construction as farmers and businessmen refused to invest and squirreled their money abroad. Investment was down by 12 percent in agriculture, and by 40 percent in industry. There were shortages everywhere as ordinary consumer products disappeared from store shelves, not to be replaced—except, perhaps, in the black market. Meanwhile, heavy government spending had doubled the amount of money in circulation, creating a rise in consumer demand in the face of falling supply. Consequently, inflation, which had been held to an annualized rate of only 22 percent in 1971, exceeded 900 percent by the end of 1973. Meanwhile, a sharp fall in world copper prices prevented Chile from earning the foreign exchange that might have softened the economic crisis. The reserves that Allende had inherited from Frei had been used up to buy control of local banks and businesses, so now the government was forced to borrow from abroad, thus driving up the foreign debt.

Much has been written about U.S. culpability in socialist Chile's financial woes. There is no doubt that the U.S. government's refusal to supply more loans from the Export-Import Bank, or to refinance Chile's debt, caused disruption in the manufacturing sector, since Chilean factories were unable to buy replacement parts for machinery. The United States also put pressure on international financial institutions, such as the Inter-American Development Bank (IADB), the International Monetary Fund, and the World Bank, to deny loans to Chile as well. These moves were not decisive in bringing down the revolution, however.[16] Allende not only responded by repudiating his debts to the United States but was able to secure other outside help from the Soviet Union and communist China. A more effective U.S. policy was to provide the CIA with an $8 million secret fund to compensate business and farm organizations that withheld their goods from the market. Some of the money also was used to support striking unions, truck owners, shopkeepers, and professional organizations resisting the state's attempts to take them over.

U.S. interference was successful only to the extent that domestic opposition to Allende was on the rise. As early as December 1971 middle-class housewives were attracting media attention by marching through Santiago's streets, banging on empty cooking pots to protest shortages of food and household items. Shopkeepers were angered and humiliated by neighborhood *juntas de abastecimiento y precios* (price and supply boards), or JAPs, composed of vigilantes—many of them from MIR—whose job was to make sure that there was no evasion of price controls, or hoarding of goods in order to divert them to the black market. A merchant caught breaking the law, or a landlord found to be violating rent controls, could have his property seized by one of the boards. Out in the countryside, a right-wing guerrilla organization called Patria y Libertad (Fatherland and Liberty) was organizing small and medium-sized landowners to resist MIR-led invasions, and even to lead dispossessed farmers in violent *re-tomas* that restored them their farms. Allende's most serious opposition, however, came from the very working class that his government claimed to represent.

Runaway inflation undermined labor's living standards. Real wages already had eroded by nearly 100 percent by May 1972, provoking strikes among copper miners (May), construction workers (August and December), airline mechanics (September), chemical workers (October), and hospital employees (November). The most serious strike, which erupted in October, involved the truckers. Unlike the others, it was not about wages. The issue at stake was the government's intention to nationalize the trucking industry. Most of the truckers were owner-operators of vehicles that they had purchased with their savings. Because they were small, independent businessmen whose entire capital was invested in their rigs, when they perceived the danger they called a general strike of the entire trucking industry that quickly tied up the movement of goods and threatened to bring the economy to a halt. Within days sympathy strikes were declared by taxi and bus drivers, bank employees, gas workers, dentists, doctors, lawyers, engineers, shopkeepers, and Christian Democrat peasant groups.

Allende fought back by arresting the strike leaders and seizing some of Santiago's downtown stores, the opposition radio stations, and some of the factories that had shut down. Nevertheless, production and distribution remained paralyzed. After two weeks of stalemate Allende finally agreed to a cabinet shakeup that would incorporate leading figures of the military, which by now was the only institution trusted by both sides. On November 2 General Carlos Prats took over the Interior Ministry, Rear Admiral Ismael Huerta became public works minister, and Air Force Brigadier Claudio Sepúlveda headed the Ministry of Mines. The military immediately persuaded Allende to promise that he would abandon the scheme to nationalize trucking and would take no reprisals against the strikers. Requisitioned stores and factories were returned to their owners. On November 5 the opposition ended its strike.

Bringing the military into the government not only violated the Statute of Guarantees, but it was the first step toward politicizing the armed forces. General Prats promised, however, that the officers would stay on only until after the March 1973 congressional elections, in order to guarantee a fair count. The military did indeed oversee a free and fair election and returned to the barracks afterward; but the election results only deepened the political stalemate. The combined vote of the opposition parties was just under 55 percent, allowing them to claim majority backing, but they failed to win enough seats in Congress to impeach the government. Meanwhile, Allende's Popular Unity coalition, with just under 44 percent, increased its vote in comparison to the 1970 general elections, although it was below its April 1971 municipal elections total. Both sides claimed victory, but it was clear to the Popular Unity side that it would have to gain an outright majority to remain in power after the next general elections in 1976. Time was running out.

Allende's Fall

After the military's departure from the government Allende stepped up the campaign to undercut the bourgeois opposition by nationalizing industry and commerce. He ignored court orders to restore private property seized by the state, and, in May 1973, he clashed openly with the Supreme Court when it ordered him to stop requisitioning private radio stations. The Popular Unity press attacked the *viejos de mierda* on the court and called for abolishing life tenure for the justices. Allende suggested that they should be elected by Congress, with terms to coincide with the president's. Congress was also to be revamped as a unicameral legislature. Its members would be elected for a single six-year term. Although Allende never actually submitted these proposed schemes to subordinate the legislative and judicial branches as constitutional amendments, he kept drafts of them in reserve and threatened to place them directly before the people in a plebiscite. Had Popular Unity won a majority in 1976, they surely would have been at the top of his agenda.

Instead, Allende preferred to silence the opposition by harassing its newspapers, radio stations, and television channels with a variety of hostile tactics: withdrawing advertising by government ministries and state companies, opening investigations for tax evasion, pressing lawsuits for libel, and encouraging labor troubles. The principal opposition paper, *El Mercurio*, was raided by the police and its director arrested for tax evasion. On another occasion the government tried to foment a strike at the paper, so as to justify taking it over, but the workers refused to go along. Another pressure tactic was to try to control the supply of newsprint. It tried to buy control of Chile's one private newsprint company, La Papelera, but CIA funding allowed the company to outbid the state for any shares that stockholders wished to sell. Then the government tried to put the company out of business by raising prices on the raw materials it needed, while refusing to allow price increases on finished newsprint. Once again, CIA funding enabled La Papelera to keep going.

Even more controversial was Allende's plan to impose a national unified school curriculum on all of Chile's pupils, including those in private schools. All students would be required to learn "the values of socialist humanism" and all high school students would have to work in state-owned enterprises. The proposal raised a storm of protest from the Catholic Church and the Christian Democratic Party. Allende thereupon "postponed" implementing the plan but did not withdraw it.

All of these attacks on private property, the independence of the judiciary and Congress, the opposition media, and the private educational sector served to polarize the public as never before. The Christian Democrats had long since abandoned their middle-of-the-road stance and had joined the

National Party in passionate opposition to the government. By now neither side was willing to wait for the 1976 elections—still three years distant—to decide Chile's future. Politics had become an all-or-nothing contest, in which Chile's traditionally neutral military would be the final arbiter.

With inflation running at around 300 percent, labor troubles were inevitable, especially with the skilled workers, who were less favored by the government's wage adjustments. The miners at the El Teniente copper company struck in mid-April. When the government refused to bargain, they marched on Santiago, as they had done in the past, where they were met with violent resistance from the police. The strike finally was settled in the workers' favor in July but was renewed almost immediately when the government began to take reprisals against the union's leaders. Meanwhile, factory workers had begun occupying their places of work in June, raising the number of companies seized by the revolution from 282 to 526.[17] Out in the industrial belts surrounding Santiago, MIR guerrillas were stockpiling arms, imported from Cuba, in the occupied factories and preparing "people's militias" for a violent upheaval.

On July 25 the truckers went back on strike, accusing the government of deliberately holding up needed tires and spare parts so as to drive them out of business. The government then tried to seize the strikers' idle trucks, which then brought on a new wave of sympathy strikes by bus drivers, taxi owners, shopkeepers, and a wide number of professional groups. Once again, the economy was paralyzed. And once again General Prats and other military commanders entered the government, on August 9, to negotiate a peace.

This time, however, military officers were divided among themselves. Already, on June 29, a right-wing army regimental chief had attempted a coup, and although it was snuffed out quickly, Prats was rapidly losing support among his fellow officers. Two days before the military chiefs joined the cabinet, the navy discovered a plot by enlisted men to carry out a mutiny. Senator Carlos Altamirano, a close Socialist colleague of Allende's, boldly admitted that he had masterminded the plot. After navy officers interrogated some forty-three arrested sailors, marines, aided by air force personnel, raided MIR strongholds in the industrial suburbs around Santiago, Talcahuano, and Valparaiso. All of this eroded Prats's position as defense minister. Finally, after a majority of his own generals voted to request his departure, both from the government and as army commander, he resigned, on August 22. His replacement as head of the army was an apparently nonpolitical general named Augusto Pinochet.

On that same day the Chamber of Deputies passed a resolution, by eighty-one votes to forty-seven, calling on the military men in the cabinet to put an end to Allende's illegal suppression of the opposition press, his by-passing of Congress through executive decrees, his high-handed takeovers of private property, his refusal to comply with court orders, and his surreptitious support for left-wing guerrilla groups. The resolution stopped short of actually calling for a coup, but the armed forces heads were already planning one. As the hour approached, Senator Altamirano made a violent public speech, on September 9, threatening the military with "people's power . . . which nothing and nobody can contain."

When the coup finally came, on the morning of September 11, there was very little resistance, despite Altamirano's threats of civil war. Holed up inside the Presidential Palace, Allende broadcast a farewell speech to the public, saying that he was ready to die rather than resign. Since he refused to surrender, the air force bombed the palace. Finally, in the early afternoon, when Allende's political compatriots and medical personnel had left under a truce, the soldiers burst in. From that point, accounts vary. Some allege that Allende already had committed suicide; others say that he was killed in a hail of bullets. In either case, Chile's Marxist experiment was over.

Notes

1. For prerevolutionary Cuban history since independence, I have consulted especially the following: Jorge I. Domínguez, Cuba: Order and Revolution (Cambridge, MA: Belknap/Harvard, 1978), 11–133; Edward González, Cuba under Castro: The Limits of Charisma (Boston: Houghton-Mifflin, 1974), 27–65; and Marifeli Pérez-Stable, The Cuban Revolution: Origins, Course, and Legacy (Oxford: Oxford University, 1999), 14–60.

2. For estimates about the size of different occupational categories, see Cuban Republic, Tribuna Superior Electoral, Oficina Nacional de Censos Demográfico y Electoral, Censos de población, viviendas, y electoral: Informe general (Havana, 1953), 153, 196, 202. This is also a source of statistics on living standards. Domínguez, Cuba, 54–97 and 115–23, is another useful source.

3. Pérez-Stable, Cuban Revolution, 27–31.

4. Juan M. del Aguila, Cuba: Dilemmas of a Revolution, 3rd ed. (Boulder, CO: Westview, 1994), 50.

5. Richard R. Fagen, The Transformation of Political Culture in Cuba (Stanford, CA: Stanford University Press, 1969), 69, 71, 76–78, 81, 85, 88.

6. Domínguez, Cuba, 140–41.

7. Ernesto Che Guevara, "Socialism and Man in Cuba," in Socialism and Man in Cuba, 2nd ed., by Ernesto Che Guevara and Fidel Castro, 1–17 (New York: Pathfinder, 1989).

8. Domínguez, Cuba, 271–81, 298–301, 321–23, 438–60, 474–78, 494–504; del Aguila, Cuba, 174–78; Pérez-Stable, 135–42, 145.

9. Sergio Roca, *Cuban Economic Policy and Ideology: The Ten Million Ton Sugar Harvest* (Beverly Hills, CA: Sage, 1976), 7, 11.

10. Roca, *Cuban Economic Policy*, 36, 62.

11. In 1974 Cuba spent 6.44 percent of its GNP on the military and had 1.24 percent of its population in uniform, more than any other Latin American country. See Trevor N. Dupuy, Grace P. Hayes, and John A. C. Andrews, eds., *The Almanac of World Military Power*, 3rd ed. (New York: R. R. Bowker, 1974); and United States Arms Control and Disarmament Agency, *World Military Expenditures and Arms Transfers, 1967–1976* (Washington, DC: U.S. Government Printing Office, 1978), 40, 57.

12. Considerable evidence on the mistreatment of political prisoners was compiled by the Organization of American States during the first decade of the revolution. See OAS, *The Organization of American States and Human Rights, 1960–1967* (Washington, DC: Secretariat of the Inter-American Commission on Human Rights, 1972), 203–90; and OAS, *The Organization of American States and Human Rights: Activity of the Inter-American Commission on Human Rights, 1969–1970* (Washington, DC: Secretariat of the Inter-American Commission on Human Rights, 1976), 123–70. Domínguez, in *Cuba*, 254, concludes that Cuban prison conditions improved in the 1970s, but see also Armando Valladares, *Against All Hope: The Prison Memoirs of Armando Valladares* (New York: Ballantine, 1986), for a grim picture of the Cuban gulag.

13. Ben Corbett, *This Is Cuba: An Outlaw Culture Survives* (Boulder, CO: Westview, 2002).

14. Paul E. Sigmund, *The Overthrow of Allende and the Politics of Chile, 1964–1976* (Pittsburgh: University of Pittsburgh Press, 1977), 118–20; Robert J. Alexander, *The Tragedy of Chile* (Westport, CT: Greenwood, 1978), 127–28; Mark Falcoff, *Modern Chile, 1970–1989: A Critical History* (New Brunswick, NJ: Transaction, 1989), 41–42.

15. Falcoff, *Modern Chile*, 58; Alexander, *Tragedy*, 174.

16. Paul E. Sigmund, in "The 'Invisible Blockade' and the Overthrow of Allende," in *Chile: The Balanced View*, ed. Francisco Orrego Vicuña (Santiago: University of Chile, Institute of International Studies, 1975), argues that while no new loans were approved by the IADB and the World Bank, previously approved loans continued to flow into Chile. Moreover, "considerable" aid was furnished by the IMF and other foreign sources. He concludes that the argument for attributing Allende's downfall to an "invisible blockade" by the United States is "not persuasive."

17. Sigmund, *Overthrow*, 215.

CHAPTER NINE

~

Counterrevolutionaries

The Military Takes Power in the Southern Cone

The Cuban Revolution inspired a host of similar Marxist-influenced movements: the Nicaraguan Sandinistas, the Chilean MIR, the Armed Forces of
the Colombian Revolution (FARC), the Farabundo Marti National Liberation Front (FMLN) in El Salvador, the National Liberation Alliance (ALN)
in Brazil, the National Liberation Army (ELN) of Bolivia, and a couple of
especially well-funded and lethal Argentine organizations: the Montoneros
and the People's Revolutionary Army (ERP)—to name only some of the
most prominent examples. Many of their representatives had attended the
1966 Tri-Continental Conference in Havana and the following year's meeting to launch the Organization of Latin American Solidarity (OLAS), which
hoped to encourage "many Vietnams" throughout the region, so as to sap the
United States' strength and morale. By the same token, the Cuban Revolution also alarmed Latin America's bourgeoisie and military brass. The bloody
fate of Batista's officer corps was a clear warning to other military men of
what they could expect if a revolution were to triumph in their country.

Some of the sharper military minds began searching through the writings
of Mao Zedong and Che Guevara to try to understand the dynamics of revolutionary guerrilla warfare. Those who dug deeper also discovered a body of lit-
erature, much of it by French army officers who were veterans of colonial wars
in Vietnam and Algeria, that argued that a new kind of warfare was becoming
common. "Revolutionary war" did not follow the old rules. Its practitioners

did not wear uniforms, fly flags, or fight set battles. They blended in with the general population and attacked from ambush. Above all, modern revolutionary warfare emphasized ideology, which played on popular resentments against corrupt elites and perceived social injustices in order to enlist mass support. Such criticism of the status quo often was accurate, which meant that until the necessary reforms were made, subversion would most likely continue to spread throughout the system. Rapid economic and social development obviously was the solution, so military men became impatient with all those organized interests that seemed to block change: the old *latifundista* class defending its privileges, demagogic politicians, corrupt labor leaders, speculators. What was needed was a strong government with strong executive leadership capable of sweeping aside all resistance and pushing through changes that would enable Latin America to quickly industrialize and raise its living standards. This kind of argument convinced the officers that military rule was the proper temporary solution. They would hold down the lid on political dissent until economic development was complete. Then, and only then, would it be possible to allow democracy.

Political tensions were highest in the countries of southern South America, where import-substituting industrialization (ISI) had advanced the furthest during the 1930s and World War II. The urban middle and working classes had grown in size and importance and were wedded to the protectionist policies and redistributionist programs that undergirded ISI. However, as global commerce picked up again in the postwar period, ISI's fundamental weaknesses became obvious. First, most of the local industries produced consumer goods with inefficient, labor-intensive methods. To modernize and compete with foreign products they would have to invest heavily in building capital goods industries, or else import capital goods from abroad. There was not enough local investment capital to undertake the former option, so capital goods imports would have to be paid for by foreign exchange earned from exports. Since local industry was not competitive on the world market, that meant resorting to traditional agricultural exports. The second weakness in these domestic economies was that agriculture had been largely neglected since its collapse in the Depression. Local investment had gone into the booming industrial sector, resulting in stagnant agricultural production. Therefore, these semi-industrial countries faced the postwar period with a limited ability to export. To make matters worse, world agricultural prices tended to be low. Furthermore, since so many people had moved to the cities during the Depression, there was a greater domestic demand for the limited amount of agricultural produce available, which tempted populist politicians to require that farmers supply the domestic market first, and at controlled prices.

For all these reasons, both industrial and agricultural production stagnated in Brazil, Argentina, Uruguay, and Chile during the 1950s and 1960s. At the same time, however, populist governments continued to seek public approval by broadening social welfare programs, creating jobs through public works projects, and running deficits in state utility and transportation companies by keeping rates low. Inflation began its climb, and it would eventually reach levels of "hyperinflation." When combined with stagnant production the result was a new, typically Latin American phenomenon that came to be dubbed as "stagflation." People dependent on wages, salaries, or pensions were whipsawed. Strikes became more common, and more violent, as workers desperately tried to maintain their living standards, while employers found they had little room for compromise. As jobs dried up, young people coming out of the universities found fewer opportunities. They either remained unemployed or took low-paying, dead-end jobs. Small wonder that many of them became radicalized, especially since local politicians blamed foreign capital for the deteriorating situation.

The first major country to undergo a military takeover was Brazil. Vargas had begun the inflationary process when he returned to power in 1950. Inheriting a 6 percent annual inflation rate from General Dutra, he drove it up to 20 percent by the time of his suicide. Juscelino Kubitschek, a *getulista* elected in 1955, was less politically divisive than Vargas but also a greater spendthrift. Promising "fifty years of progress in five," he spent enormous sums of money, especially on the building of a new capital at Brasília. By the time he left office in 1960 inflation was up to 60 percent a year—a point at which it could be said to be "runaway inflation." The strains of this situation on the labor movement created openings for Communist infiltration. For years corrupt labor leaders, known as *pelegos*, had been co-opted into the *getulista* coalition, where they did relatively little for their followers. The Communists, by contrast, had nothing to lose by challenging the status quo. As the workers felt increasingly squeezed by inflation, militant Communists replaced the old *pelego* leadership.

The radicalization of labor caused a breakup in the old Vargas political coalition, as big business, big agriculture, and the military shifted to the right. For a brief period in 1961 it seemed that the process of decline might be reversed when the *anti-getulistas* succeeded in electing as president a charismatic candidate named Jânio Quadros who ran on a platform of orthodox economic reform. But Quadros was an unstable character who, upon being denied extraordinary powers by Congress, suddenly resigned. His vice president, elected on a separate ticket, was the dreaded João Goulart: Vargas's protégé and demagogic head of the Brazilian Labor Party (PTB). This surprising turn of events soured Brazilian conservatives on democracy. In 1964 the Brazilian armed forces, alarmed at what they perceived to be widespread Communist infiltration of the labor movement and also of the rural peasantry, overthrew Goulart.

Uruguay was the next country to fall under military rule. As in Brazil, a deteriorating economy had radicalized the labor movement, giving the Communists their opportunity to take over the leading trade union federation. In addition, the parties of the Left, previously small and unimportant, had managed to combine in a movement called the Frente Amplio (Broad Front), patterned after Allende's Popular Unity coalition in Chile. They won over 18 percent of the vote in 1971, thus posing a challenge to the two traditional parties, the Colorados and the Blancos. More alarming still was the rise of an urban guerrilla movement, the Tupamaros. Founded in 1963 by radical dissident Socialists, they slowly organized, armed themselves, and burst upon the scene in a series of spectacular robberies and kidnappings designed to raise money to expand their operations. One of their kidnap victims was Dan Mitrione, an employee of the U.S. Agency for International Development who was training the Montevideo police; he was murdered after the government refused to negotiate his release. Another victim was the British ambassador, Geoffrey Jackson, who was held for almost a year in a "people's prison" before being released. By February 1973 the Uruguayan armed forces, suspecting that some legislators were secretly aiding the Tupamaros, forced President Juan María Bordaberry to dissolve Congress. Three years later, they forced Bordaberry's resignation too and took power directly.

In the meantime, the armed forces had brought down Allende's government in Chile, in September 1973. Much to the surprise and chagrin of the Christian Democrats and the center-right Nationalist Party, General Augusto Pinochet decided not to turn power over to another civilian government but to use military rule to undertake a comprehensive reform of the economy and the political system.

Finally, Argentina succumbed to military rule in March 1976. After overthrowing Perón in 1955, the armed forces were unable to replace him with any government, civilian or military, capable of uniting the country or fostering economic growth. For the working classes all around Argentina, Perón was the only legitimate leader, and he, through extraordinary skill and a continuous stream of emissaries, kept control of his followers. Eight short-lived presidencies—five military, three civilian—in eighteen years reflected the country's extreme instability. As capital fled, production stagnated and inflation rose, which helped to radicalize politics. By the beginning of the 1970s guerrilla organizations began carrying out kidnappings, bank robberies, raids on military and police outposts, and some highly publicized assassinations. The largest of them, calling itself the Montoneros, after the irregulars who fought in the war of independence against Spain, claimed membership in the Peronist Movement. Perón encouraged the group as a battering ram that finally forced the armed forces to end their proscription of him and his movement. Elections in March 1973 resulted in the election of a hand-picked stand-in of Perón's, Héctor Cámpora. Before the end of the year Perón himself was back in the presidency, with his new wife, María Estela ("Isabel"), as his vice president. It was perhaps the most stunning comeback in Latin America's political history.

Having attained his long-sought goal, Perón ordered an end to the violence. The Montoneros were not to be so easily reined in, however. They expected Perón to lead a socialist revolution that would eliminate private property in Argentina, in accordance with the extreme rhetoric he had been issuing from exile for the past eighteen years. The other major guerrilla group, the People's Revolutionary Army (ERP), knew Perón for the pseudorevolutionary that he really was and had no intention of obeying him. When Perón's private secretary and minister of social welfare, José López Rega, began forming right-wing death squads (the Argentine Anti-Communist Alliance, or AAA) composed of former policemen, criminal elements, and labor union toughs, violence began once again to escalate out of control. Inflation, which price controls had temporarily brought down from 100 percent when Cámpora was inaugurated to only 30 percent when Perón took office, soon resumed its inexorable climb. Perón had learned nothing about economics during his exile and had quickly set about restoring the old state-centered corporatist system he had constructed in the 1950s, with predictable results. Perón himself was old and sick and had lost much of his former knack for politics. By the time of his death, at the beginning of July 1974, the Peronist Movement was badly split, and the Montoneros were preparing to go back underground. Worse, the government now devolved upon Perón's wife, Vice President Isabel Perón, an uneducated former nightclub dancer who had no talent for the job. López Rega, considered to be her éminence grise, was widely hated, by the Montoneros, the labor unions, and the military. ERP launched a rural guerrilla campaign in the mountains of the western province of Tucumán and also succeeded in infiltrating the industrial belt north of Buenos Aires to the extent that it threatened to paralyze the economy. The Montoneros stepped up their attacks in the cities. The emboldened guerrillas even began attacking army bases. As military casualties mounted, the armed forces demanded more forceful government action to suppress subversion; instead Isabel Perón vacillated, suffered nervous collapses, and finally was charged with a financial scandal that deprived her of all remaining authority. By the time the military removed her, on 23 March 1976, political violence was claiming lives at the rate of one every eighteen hours, the inflation level was at 920 percent, and the government was on the verge of defaulting on the foreign debt.

The Responsibilities of Power

The coups in Argentina, Brazil, Chile, and Uruguay were somewhat different in nature from the traditional Latin American *golpe de estado*. In the past, the most common type of military takeover was the "barracks revolt," in which some rebel unit, or units, usually positioned in or near the capital, rose up suddenly and removed the government before it could react. A variant on this might be called "the executive coup," in which an incumbent president would conspire with some army units to increase his power by overthrowing the constitution and dissolving the congress. Yet another variant would be the *pronunciamiento*, in which a regional garrison would proclaim itself in revolt and call upon other units to join in. All of these coups put a great deal of emphasis on secrecy and surprise. The modern-day coup, as developed in the Southern Cone, differed in that it was a gradually negotiated process by which all three branches of the armed forces agreed to act in unison—and only after they had each carefully consulted, and enlisted, their middle-range and lower-level officers. Secrecy was not so important, nor was surprise, since the government knew that the blow was being prepared and could do little to prevent it. This new "consensus coup" aimed at challenging the government with such overwhelming force as to make any resistance impossible. If done correctly, the resulting takeover would be bloodless, or nearly so.

Consensus was aided by the spread of a compelling counterideology to that of Marxism-Leninism: the so-called national security doctrine. The development of this ideology proceeded earliest in Brazil, at the Superior War School (ESG), set up in 1949 by some of the veterans of the Brazilian Expeditionary Force (FEB) with advice from the U.S. Army. Attended by both senior military officers and prominent civilians, its participants engaged in intensive courses on geopolitics, economics, mass psychology, social organization, and strategy. The underlying ideology, as developed by its leading military intellectual, General Golbery do Couto e Silva, began by placing Brazil—and the rest of Latin America—into the Cold War context. The region was part of the Christian West, he argued, and therefore must follow the military and diplomatic lead of the West's leading power, the United States.[1]

The national security doctrine further argued that the nuclear stalemate between the United States and the Soviet Union made a "hot war" unlikely. Instead, the Communists would seek to promote "wars of liberation" among the less-developed nations, with the aim of overthrowing their pro-Western governments. The process had begun already in Latin America with Cuba, and it would spread unless confronted by energetic resistance inspired by an equally compelling ideology. The first order of business was to uproot subversion, wherever it existed and in all of its forms: not only guerrillas and terrorists, but also their allies in various "front organizations" such as labor unions, student groups, and extremist political parties. Their sympathizers in Congress, the courts, the press, the bureaucracy, educational and cultural institutions, and "human rights" advocacy organizations had to be silenced as well.

By itself, however, repression would not suffice unless real reforms were made. Corrupt politicians, grinding poverty, and glaring inequalities in living standards created the conditions for communism to find a receptive audience. Political institutions had to be cleansed and rapid economic growth achieved. Strong military leadership would impose order and eliminate all obstacles to growth. Partisan politics would be suspended in the name of national unity, and private interests would be forced to subordinate their claims to the good of the whole. Private capital, both domestic and foreign, would be encouraged to shoulder the main investment burden. Once economic growth became self-sustaining, democracy could be restored.

Such were the broad outlines of the military's purpose. Soon, however, the officers found themselves divided as to the details. One potential source of conflict was the allocation of positions in the new governments among the various service branches. That was not a problem in Brazil or Uruguay, where mandatory retirement rules were strictly followed, as were periodic, routine transfers of military commands. In all four countries the army, as the largest service branch, assumed the presidency of the revolutionary junta, whose duty it was to oversee the entire reform process. Also, with one exception, the presidency of the government, which carried out the junta's policies, was entrusted to an army officer. In Uruguay the military kept up the pretense of civilian rule after deposing Bordaberry in 1976. Civilian presidents served as figureheads until 1981, when the new army commander, General Gregorio Alvarez, took over. In Argentina a power struggle broke out between the army's General Jorge Videla and the navy's Admiral Emilio Massera. Massera wanted the presidency for himself and sought to confine Videla to the role of army commander. Videla thwarted him by holding on to the junta's presidency and promoting a friend, General Roberto Viola, to head the army. Even so, Massera kept the junta in turmoil and blocked many of Videla's attempts to liberalize the Argentine economy. Chile's General Pinochet was similarly challenged by General Gustavo Leigh, the air force commander. Leigh failed to win support from any of the other military commanders, however, and was forced out of the junta in 1978. Pinochet thereafter consolidated his grip on both the junta and the government until he left power in 1989.

Much more common than interservice rivalries was the division between moderates and hard-liners. Moderates wanted to put a time limit on military rule. Remaining too long in power, they reasoned, would politicize the armed forces. There would be disagreements over policy, and even personal rivalries, leading to factions. Unlike civilian politics, however, these would be armed factions. Conspiracies and clashes would disrupt the principles of order, hierarchy, and obedience, which lie at the heart of military life. Rather than that, the armed forces should turn power over to the civilians as soon as possible and return to the barracks. Hard-liners, on the other hand, saw the task of rooting out subversion, cleansing the political system, and achieving economic development as a lengthy process that only the military could undertake. To surrender power before the goals were achieved would leave untouched the root causes of the current crisis. If that happened the crisis would erupt again in a few years. Thus an indefinitely long period of military rule was unavoidable.

In Brazil, the military moderates from the ESG came to power immediately after the 1964 coup, behind the leadership of General Humberto Castelo Branco. Failing to get Congress's approval for the sweeping purges they intended, the officers arrogated plenary powers to themselves through an executive decree known as the First Institutional Act. Under its provisions former presidents Kubitschek, Quadros, and Goulart were stripped of their political rights for ten years, as were dozens of former cabinet ministers, congressmen, state governors and legislators, judges, civil servants, labor leaders, educators, journalists, and student leaders. Government recognition was required for political parties to exist, and their number was sharply reduced to three by new electoral rules. Stagflation was tackled through a package of free market reforms that lowered tariffs, lifted price controls (to encourage production), imposed wage controls, increased rates for public services, and slashed government subsidies. This brought inflation down from 100 percent to only 20, but it also produced bankruptcies among firms that were unable to suddenly face the rigors of a free market, and it brought about higher levels of unemployment. Unaware of how unpopular these measures were, the Castelo Branco government scheduled gubernatorial elections for October 1965. To its surprise and chagrin, the *getulista* parties won big in the key urban states of Minas Gerais and Guanabara, discrediting the moderate officers in the eyes of the hard-liners. The latter now insisted on more purges and the replacement of the old political parties by new ones approved by the regime. In the 1967 general elections the senior hard-line general, Artur da Costa e Silva, won the presidency at the head of the government's official National Renovating Alliance (ARENA).

A similar shift to the hard-liners occurred in Argentina. After serving for five years, General Videla was able to pass on the presidency to General Viola, but the latter was unfortunate enough to take office just as the economy plunged. Moreover, Viola's plans to gradually return the government to civilian rule were upset when his friend and head of the Unión Cívica Radical, Ricardo Balbín, died. Finally, when Viola suffered a heart attack and had to be hospitalized, the hard-line military saw an opportunity to remove him from office and take power. The hard-liners' leader, General Leopoldo Galtieri, now became president. He quickly made it clear that there would be no elections in the near term.

Uruguay's junta proceeded in much the same manner as Brazil's. Believing that the old democratic system had been permeated by corrupt politicians, or else by Marxist subversives, the military stripped hundreds of citizens of their political rights. Legislators, judges, labor union leaders, teachers, and journalists were especially targeted. Congress was replaced by the Council of the Nation, composed of top military officers and selected civilians. Like the other military regimes in the Southern Cone, the Uruguayan government viewed stagflation as the source of societal breakdown and was determined to replace the system that Batlle created with a free market economy. In contrast to the other Southern Cone countries, Uruguay's military was not so clearly divided into moderate and hard-line factions. Given the country's strong democratic traditions, the new rulers were quick to assure their fellow citizens, in August 1977, that the armed forces had a timetable by which they were committed to an eventual return to civilian government. A plebiscite for approving a new constitution was scheduled for November 1980. The draft constitution that finally emerged provided only for a "limited democracy," however. The military would retain a tutelary role over civilian governmental institutions by way of a national security council, while military courts could review and overrule the decisions of the regular judiciary. However, Uruguayan voters rejected the proposed constitution by a wide majority of 57 percent to 43.[2]

In Chile, General Pinochet was free of pressure from the military as well as from civilians. As head of the army he quickly forced the retirement of

more than half of the generals, including all those closest to him in senior-
ity. As commander of the largest service branch, he not only headed the revolutionary junta but also claimed for himself the presidency of the new military government. None of his officer colleagues on the junta, except for
General Leigh, questioned his leadership. As for civilians, the Left was
smashed and the Right had been greatly weakened by Pinochet's predecessors. The landed upper class had been destroyed by agrarian reform under Frei
and Allende, while domestic and foreign business elites were undermined by
the expropriations undertaken by the Popular Unity government. Of all the
regimes in the region, Pinochet's had the cleanest slate to write on. A hard-
liner, Pinochet aimed to stay in power indefinitely by holding a carefully
managed plebiscite on his rule in October 1978. In contrast to the
Uruguayan military's defeat in its plebiscite, 75 percent of the voters supported him. He then followed up this "success" by preparing a new constitution that would keep him in power at least until 1989—and even beyond, if
the voters so chose. This too was submitted to a plebiscite and "approved" by
a two-thirds majority.

Terror and Reform

The rise of military hard-liners to power in Brazil began an era, from 1967
to 1974, characterized by the most severe repression on the one hand, and
a simultaneous growth in the economy that was so impressive as to be called
"the Brazilian miracle." As the Costa e Silva government closed off every
avenue of legal opposition, angry radicals began thinking in terms of armed
resistance. One of those was Carlos Marighela, a Communist militant who
had attended the meeting in Havana that founded OLAS in August 1967.
On returning to Brazil he broke with the Communist Party leaders, who
were urging a cautious approach, and gathered several of the party's youth
wing into a guerrilla band called the Ação Libertadora Nacional (ALN). In
early 1968 they began robbing banks to get money for weapons. In mid-1968
a second guerrilla outfit, the Vanguarda Popular Revolucionária (VPR),
made its appearance and soon gained notoriety by assassinating a U.S. army
captain, Charles Chandler. Throughout 1969 and 1970 the ALN and VPR
carried off a series of kidnappings of American, European, and Japanese
diplomats that forced the Brazilian government to pay ransoms and release
some political prisoners.

In mid-1969 the military government also faced a succession crisis when
General Costa e Silva suffered a stroke that left him incapacitated. The revolutionary junta of commanding officers quickly moved to block the civilian

vice president from taking charge, but the officers were divided among themselves as to whom they would accept as the new president. One candidate was General Afonso Albuquerque Lima, but his nationalist and populist views placed him too near the old *getulista* tradition, so he was ruled out. Nevertheless, he had enough support that the junta had to move slowly. Not until October was it finally able to name General Emilio Garrastazu Medici, an even firmer hard-liner than Costa e Silva, to the presidency. Medici took office just a month after the ALN kidnapped the U.S. ambassador, Charles Burke Elbrick, and forced the government to release fifteen prisoners and provide them safe passage out of the country. The hard-liners were humiliated but bowed to U.S. pressure. With Medici in power, however, they began a systematic campaign to uproot the guerrilla organizations, using a variety of "dirty war" methods—electric shocks, near drownings, mock executions, and the witnessing of loved ones being tortured—to quickly extract information from captured suspects. Though the methods were brutal, they paid off: by 1972 the guerrilla threat was reduced to a minor nuisance, and by 1975 it had been eliminated entirely.[3]

Simultaneously with political repression went a surge in Brazil's economic growth. Orthodox austerity policies under Castelo Branco had succeeded in bringing down inflation, but at the cost of high unemployment and complaints that too many Brazilian companies were going bankrupt and being taken over by foreign capital. Under Antonio Delfim Neto, the hard-liners' economics minister, emphasis was shifted from decreasing demand to increasing the supply of goods. Inflation was to be controlled by "indexing" prices, wages, interest rates, and pensions to the cost of living. Rather than abandoning import-substituting industrialization, the state would lead the way to making Brazil independent in capital goods by directly investing in "strategic" areas of the economy (such as steel, oil, mining, chemicals, hydroelectric energy, and banking) and by entering into joint ventures with foreign capital in other areas requiring advanced technology (motor vehicles, machinery, engines, rubber, pharmaceuticals, and large appliances). In the latter areas, the aim was to encourage industrial exports, which would earn the foreign exchange necessary to cover the heavy borrowing that would finance the growth of the state enterprise sector. Domestic private capital would be left mainly with the role of producing nondurable consumer goods, and the government aimed at greater efficiency there as well. It would audit the production costs of local firms, and only those that showed productivity gains would be allowed to raise their prices. Agriculture, too, was encouraged to modernize and diversify production. The government guaranteed prices for new crops such as wheat and soybeans, while also providing tax credits for purchasing new machinery, pesticides, and fertilizers. Such incentives made relatively little impact in the traditional north, but in the south small farms were bought up and turned into mechanized, highly productive agribusinesses. By the mid-1970s coffee was no longer "king." Indeed, Brazil had become an exporter of industrial goods. Between 1967 and 1973 the GDP grew by an average of 11 percent a year, and manufacturing—especially of capital goods and durable consumer goods—led the way.

The benefits of growth were not equitably distributed, however. Between 1960 and 1970 the poorest half of the population saw its share of the total national income decline, while the richest 20 percent increased its share considerably. That was a deliberate policy of the regime, to encourage the investor class. At the same time, heavy borrowing from abroad led to increasingly large balance-of-payments deficits and ran up the national debt in 1973 to almost four times what it had been in 1967. Despite those negative signs, the "economic miracle" achieved its primary goal of laying down a heavy capital goods industrial base. The urban population grew as large numbers of people moved from the agricultural sector into manufacturing, construction, commerce, and services.

Repression in Argentina was far more ubiquitous and terrifying than in Brazil, in large part because the guerrilla organizations there were much larger, better armed, and, in the case of the Montoneros, often encouraged and protected by some of the provincial Peronist governments. When, in 1977, the military discovered that one of Argentina's leading bankers was laundering money for the Montoneros its suspicions embraced almost the entire civilian population. For years the police and military intelligence had been collecting names and photographs of militant radicals involved in strikes, riots, and protest demonstrations. After the coup such people, along with their friends and family, were rounded up in dragnets and taken to clandestine interrogation centers where they were tortured for information. Anyone named by the victims was also brought in for questioning, even though some were later found to be innocent. Those "sucked in" by the repressive apparatus were known as the "disappeared." Some of them became collaborators with the military, riding about in cars with their captors to point out guerrilla hideouts and identify people on the street as former underground *compañeros*. This was a particularly effective way of uprooting terrorism. If the military determined that a prisoner was innocent, or only tangentially involved in subversion, he might be released—with orders not to talk with anyone about his experiences. But those who had been deeply involved in ERP or the Montoneros were usually marked for death. Some were dumped into unmarked graves, or strewn around a field as though they had been killed in a battle with the security forces. Others were drugged, placed aboard airplanes, flown out over the South Atlantic, and dropped into the sea. Estimates on the total number killed range from 6,000 to 20,000, although it is impossible to verify either figure. An official investigation held after the return to civilian rule put the number at 8,961—although many people rejected that calculation as being too low.[4] Whatever the real figure might be, these "dirty war" tactics unquestionably succeeded in crushing the guerrilla organizations. By the end of 1977 they had practically ceased to exist, except for a lucky few who escaped abroad. The Montoneros tried to disrupt the World Cup soccer tournament being hosted in Argentina in 1978 by launching some bomb attacks, and in 1979 they tried a last "guerrilla offensive." That brought on another bout of repression so effective in uprooting their remnants in Argentina that their exiled leaders formally dissolved the Montonero "army."

The Argentine armed forces were much less successful in managing the economy. General Videla's economics minister, José Martínez de Hoz, came to office with the intention of shrinking the state and opening up the economy to foreign competition, but he was constantly blocked by Admiral Massera and army hard-liners. There was some trimming of the public payrolls, but none of the big state enterprises were privatized. Indeed, during the period the government acquired a foreign-owned electric company, a private airline company, and several other private firms that were going bankrupt. Fearful of driving the workers into the arms of the leftist guerrillas, the military put a priority on full employment. Inflation proved recalcitrant too. Raising interest rates and freezing wages only caused sales to drop and some businesses to close, while other businesses maintained their high prices simply by cutting back production and creating scarcities. Frustrated, Martínez de Hoz announced that he would institute a series of currency devaluations that would allow cheaper foreign goods into the Argentine market, but this required constant "fine-tuning." In practice, devaluations always lagged behind inflation, resulting in an overvalued peso that hurt the country's exports. Worst of all, runaway military spending made it impossible to balance the government's budget. Between 1978 and 1983 over $10 billion was spent acquiring military equipment for an impending war with Chile over some islands in the Beagle Channel, between the tip of the continent and Tierra del Fuego.[5]

In Uruguay, the Tupamaro guerrillas proved relatively easy to defeat with "dirty war" tactics. By the end of 1972 their leader, Raúl Sendic, was in prison and the organization had creased to function. Their combatants and supporters, along with leaders of the Communist-led National Confederation of Workers (CNT), filled the jails. "At the height of the repression, in the mid-1970s, the regime held more than seven thousand political prisoners; it was claimed that Uruguay had the highest ratio of prisoners of conscience to total population of any country in the world." The rest of the civilian population was classified into three categories: A-type civilians were trustworthy, B-types were those with questionable attitudes, and C-types were people who were suspected of having contacts with subversives. People in the last two categories were excluded from holding jobs in the government, the state enterprises, and the educational system.[6]

Uruguay's economic record closely paralleled Argentina's. The first economics minister, Alejandro Végh Villegas, found himself blocked by nationalist military officers when he tried to privatize the state enterprise sector. Nor was he allowed to make drastic cuts in the government's payroll. His attempts to bring down inflation from nearly 100 percent in 1972 were only partly successful because of increased spending on the military and police, which accounted for about half of the budget. Inflation dropped to about 46 percent but fell no further. In addition, the government embarked on a policy of subsidizing "nontraditional" industrial exports. Despite a series of mini-devaluations the currency remained overvalued, however, and exports suffered. Meanwhile, low wages restricted consumer demand, forcing several businesses to close. High interest rates and tight credit added to the rising number of bankruptcies as the 1970s ended.[7]

In Chile, the coup was followed by a wave of terror. The military junta immediately shut down Congress, banned all political parties, dissolved the Communist-led labor federation, and imposed press censorship. The entire country was placed under martial law. Although radicals on the Left had threatened a violent mass uprising if the Popular Unity government were attacked, when the coup came there was little actual resistance. Thousands of leftists were rounded up in dragnets and put into makeshift prison camps; others sought diplomatic asylum in foreign embassies. An estimated 1,500 people died in the first few months: MIR guerrillas killed in shootouts, prisoners tortured to death or executed by firing squads, or victims of revenge by private vigilantes. Not content with merely overthrowing the Marxist regime, the military was intent on rooting out the causes of its existence. In June 1974 it set up the National Intelligence Directorate (DINA) and gave it a free hand to use any methods it deemed necessary for the "total extermination of Marxism" in Chile. Using "dirty war" methods like Argentina's, and with the same sinister efficiency, DINA smashed the underground remnants of MIR and the Communist Party. It even reached out beyond Chile's borders to eliminate prominent exiles, such as Orlando Letelier, a former Allende diplomat, who was killed in Washington on 21 September 1976 when a bomb went off in his car. As many as 1,000 people may have "disappeared" in DINA's secret interrogation centers from the time it was founded until its growing notoriety from the Letelier case led to its closing in late 1977.[8]

The Chilean military inherited an economy characterized by large numbers of state-owned banks and businesses, a large public payroll with strong public sector unions, big government deficits, and price and credit controls that failed to control inflation. The officers took power just before the OPEC oil cartel decreed drastic cuts in production that caused oil shortages throughout the West and sent inflation soaring. In Chile, it was running at an annualized rate of 900 percent, but production was stymied—the worst possible stagflation scenario. Still, the junta's first steps were timid, because the officers shared the skepticism of most Chileans about the advantages of free markets. They removed some of the price controls, froze wages, and cut government spending to reduce the money supply. Inflation dipped somewhat, although at 340 percent in 1975 it was still too high; meanwhile, the country plunged into a recession. The officers were then faced with three options, all of them distasteful: (1) to return to civilian rule and the old import-substituting economy; (2) to continue the authoritarian system with a corporatist, import-substituting economy; or (3) to make a radical break with the past and introduce a free-market, export-oriented economy that would incorporate lots of foreign investment. After a visit by the Nobel Prize–winning free-market guru, Milton Friedman, in March 1975, the officers, prodded by Pinochet, adopted the third approach. A new economic team, headed by Sergio de Castro, took over. Since many of the economists had studied with Friedman at the University of Chicago, they were called "the Chicago Boys."

The Chicago Boys' recipe was orthodox monetarism, and it probably could have been implemented only by a dictatorship like Pinochet's. They drastically reduced the size and scope of the public sector, cutting the budgets for education, health, and housing and dismissing large numbers of government employees. Not only were farms and businesses that had been expropriated by Allende returned to their former owners, but state enterprises created earlier and administered under the Corporación de Fomento (CORFO) holding company were quickly privatized.[9] The new team also eliminated tariffs, abolished controls on prices and interest rates, lowered wages, and struck at union power by instituting right-to-work laws. Rather than an immediate improvement in the economy, there was a transition period during which certain local capitalists with privileged access to foreign (mainly U.S.) bank loans snapped up the privatized state companies and formed them into three large conglomerates. Each conglomerate had a core of banks and investment companies, which were then surrounded by agribusinesses, food-processing plants, and trading companies specializing in exporting agricultural and forestry products. By 1977 the Chilean economy began to experience noninflationary growth of around 8 percent a year, which lasted until 1982. During this period Pinochet's Chile became a showplace for free marketeers throughout the West. Chileans involved in the export economy were enthusiastic about the new policies; however, businesses supplying the domestic market, blue-collar workers, and politicians from the Christian Democrat and Socialist parties were much less so.

Retreat to the Barracks

In all four of the Southern Cone countries the military justified its rule on two principal grounds: that it alone could uproot guerrilla terrorism and also rise above petty special interests to make healthy, overdue economic reforms. In all four countries it certainly performed the first task quickly and efficiently. Economic reform was more problematic. The Argentine and Uruguayan armed forces were never united behind a common economic policy, and therefore they failed to carry out any significant or coherent reforms. By contrast, the "Brazilian miracle" and the Chicago Boys' programs, while different, were radical departures from the past—and quite successful for a time. Their success bolstered the military's belief in the superiority of its leadership; but when things started going wrong, as they did in the early 1980s, the military lost confidence in itself and began a slow retreat to the barracks.

Brazil offers a textbook example of how a military dictatorship begins to unravel when its economic policies go wrong, and how factors beyond any government's control can disrupt a booming economy. In 1973 Brazil was dependent on imports from the Middle East for 85 percent of its oil needs, and in that same year the OPEC oil cartel decided to punish the pro-Israeli West by drastically cutting back production. Brazil's economy reacted as a speeding car does when it hits a stone wall. Between 1973 and 1974 the direct cost of importing oil more than tripled; the indirect costs, reflected in higher prices for other imported goods, doubled from $6 billion to $12.6 billion; the trade balance went from a positive $7 million to a negative $4.7 billion; loans contracted to meet the new costs drove up the foreign debt from $12.5 billion to $17.1 billion; the inflation rate more than doubled, from 15 to 35 percent; and the economic growth rate fell from 14 to 9.5 percent. Between 1974 and 1981 it would average around 5 percent.[10]

Five percent a year growth was still not bad, and indeed between 1974 and 1979 the regime managed in some years to get the rate back up to 7 percent. To do so, however, it had to resort to heavy foreign borrowing, so that by 1979 the debt had risen from $17.2 billion to $50 billion. Moreover, real wages, which had been rising during the "miracle" years, were 8 percent below their 1973 levels because the government was insisting upon keeping adjustments below the actual rise in the cost of living. This proved ineffectual as an anti-inflation device. By 1979 inflation had doubled again, to 80 percent a year. That was also the year that OPEC sent a second "oil shock" throughout the world. By 1981 the GDP growth rate was a negative 1.9 percent, the foreign debt was over $60 billion, and inflation was approaching 100 percent—and would go to 230 percent by 1985.

This turnaround in its fortunes robbed the military of its self-confidence, and also of its allies. Industrial strikes, unknown since the 1964 coup, suddenly broke out again in São Paulo. Instead of clinging to the regime in the face of such militancy, much of domestic private industry criticized the military government for driving down wages and thus shrinking the market for nondurable consumer goods. It wanted more credits from the government in order to expand and create jobs, and it called for wage increases to stimulate consumption. Local businessmen, who for some time had felt squeezed between the growing state enterprise sector and the favorable treatment accorded to foreign capital, now demanded protectionism for themselves and restrictions on the foreign companies' repatriation of profits. Furthermore, they criticized the government for its heavy foreign borrowing, much of which went to prop up state-owned companies that—so they argued—ought to be privatized.

A political realignment was in process. As local merchants and industrialists deserted to the antigovernment side, so did the urban middle classes, which were wracked by inflation. The Catholic Church also turned against the regime, arguing that the austerity programs aimed at fighting inflation were worsening the plight of Brazil's poorest classes. It also pointed to a host of human rights abuses. As these groups began shifting their allegiances, the government's official party, ARENA, began losing ground to what previously had been thought of as a tame, tolerated opposition party, the Brazilian Democratic Movement (MDB). In 1970, for example, ARENA, with 48.4 percent of the vote in that year's congressional elections, had twice as much support as the MDB, which attracted only 21.3 percent—which was less than the null and blank votes, whose combined total was 30.3 percent. By 1978, however, the MDB and ARENA were practically tied: the former garnered 39.3 percent to the latter's 40 percent. The null and blank vote had declined to 20.7. In 1982 the military tried to split the MDB by reintroducing proportional representation and changing ARENA's name to the Social Democratic Party (PDS). The ploy almost worked. The MDB did break up into several smaller parties, but most of these got back together to form the new Party of the Brazilian Democratic Movement (PMDB) and gave the regime a severe shock at the polls, winning 48.2 percent of the vote to the PDS's 36.7. Again, the null and blank vote fell, to 15.1 percent, as the possibilities for a PMDB-led opening for the return of civilian rule became more evident. And indeed, in the 1985 presidential elections it was the PDS that split, as one faction, called the Liberal Front, joined the PMDB to give the latter's candidate, Tancredo Neves, an old *getulista* senator from the pre-1964 era, a victory. The military bowed to the result and turned over power.

Economic mismanagement also undermined the Argentine military regime. In March 1980, a year before General Videla handed over power to General Viola, the jerry-rigged economy that Martínez de Hoz had somehow kept going finally collapsed in a record number of bank failures. The Viola administration, having inherited a bleak situation, made it worse by two sharp devaluations intended to increase Argentina's exports and improve its trade balance. Unfortunately, so many Argentine companies had acquired dollar-denominated loans that the devaluations made it impossible for them to repay. Instead, they went bankrupt. Buffeted by a hurricane of criticism, Viola suffered a heart attack that hospitalized him in November 1981. The hard-line military officers, who suspected Viola of wanting to turn Argentina back over to civilian rule, took that opportunity to launch a coup and replace him with General Leopoldo Galtieri. The new president made it clear that the military intended to stay in power indefinitely. However, even he was sensitive to the fact that military rule had become unpopular, so he devised a scheme to reverse that.

Nine hundred miles southeast of Buenos Aires lie the British-owned Falkland Islands, or—as they are known in Argentina—the Malvinas. Argentina claims them as a legacy from Spain, but the British seized them in 1833, thus creating an ongoing diplomatic dispute that has inflamed generations of Argentine nationalists. General Galtieri decided to win the affection of his fellow citizens by invading the Malvinas and reincorporating these cold, damp, treeless, and sparsely populated islands. His instincts were partly right, for when he announced, on 10 April 1982, that his troops had landed on the islands, there was a massive outpouring of public support that packed the Plaza de Mayo. On the other hand, he had calculated wrongly when he expected the British to cave in, because their "Iron Lady" prime minister, Margaret Thatcher, quickly dispatched a war fleet to the scene. On June 15 Galtieri was forced to announce to another huge gathering in the Plaza de Mayo that the

Argentine forces in the Malvinas had just surrendered. This time the crowd roared in anger and surged forward to attack the Casa Rosada. Although forced back by the soldiers, the mob nevertheless broke several windows and then went on a rampage through the adjacent streets. Two days later the army removed Galtieri and replaced him with General Reynaldo Bignone, whose task was to hand over power gradually to an elected civilian government. General elections were held in October 1983. Raúl Alfonsín, a human rights lawyer, was elected president at the head of the Radical Party's ticket.

Uruguay's transition back to democracy began after the 1980 referendum, when the voters turned down the military's proposed constitution. That rejection, plus a rapidly deteriorating economy, sapped the military's desire to remain in power. The Colorado and Blanco parties were allowed to hold primary elections in 1982, as a first step. In both cases strong antiregime factions won huge majorities, further underlining the military's unpopularity. Against an increasingly ominous background of labor strikes and street demonstrations, the military scheduled general elections for November 1984; but it still was unclear which parties and factions would be permitted to run. Two prominent civilian leaders, Wilson Ferreira Adulante, head of the Blancos' largest faction, and General Liber Seregni, head of the leftist Frente Amplio, were in jail. By excluding both when the elections finally were held, the military paved the way for the Colorados' Julio Sanguinetti, a man of the Center-Right who favored a civil-military reconciliation.

In Chile, the Pinochet regime's economic progress under the "Chicago Boys," like Brazil's "miracle," was thrown into confusion, by the second OPEC "oil crunch," in 1979. As in Brazil, much of the growth had been fueled by easy foreign loans taken out by the three big capitalist conglomerates that now dominated the economy. As the United States raised its interest rates to curb inflation, future loans became more expensive and harder to get. At the same time, a deepening global recession caused a drop in Chile's exports, which meant that the big agribusinesses were unable to repay loans to the banks that formed the conglomerates' core. Those banks, in turn, were forced to default on loans to their U.S. creditors. A string of spectacular bank failures and collapsing businesses brought unemployment up to 30 percent. For the first time since Allende's fall there were mass street protests. As in Brazil, local business leaders, united in the new Confederation of Production and Commerce (CPC), demanded a new set of policies.

Fearing that the businessmen would desert his government, as had happened in Brazil, Pinochet sacrificed Sergio de Castro and the "Chicago Boys" in April 1982. After some months of tinkering with the economic crisis, he finally intervened in the conglomerates in January 1983 and began pursuing a more Keynesian approach. The government began pumping money into the economy, through public works, home building, easier credit, and export subsidies. Exchange rates were revised to make imports more expensive and give protection to local industry. Gradually, the economy began to revive, and by 1985 Chile was once again enjoying prosperity. With that, Pinochet made another shift in his economic policies, to a position that Eduardo Silva has termed "pragmatic neoliberalism."[11] The banks were reprivatized and the conglomerates were sold to foreign creditors in debt-for-equity swaps. Local capital continued to enjoy moderate levels of protection from foreign imports.

In 1988 the military junta nominated Pinochet for another nine-year presidential term; but, as required by his own constitution, this would have to be submitted to the public for approval in a plebiscite. That was scheduled for October. Pinochet was confident of winning, since the Chilean economy was performing well. In the meantime, however, the Christian Democrats and the Socialists had formed an opposition coalition, which now pledged itself to maintaining the "pragmatic neoliberal" economy, if elected. Shunning any hint of class conflict, the coalition concentrated instead on appealing to Chile's long tradition of civilian government. When the votes were counted, Pinochet's bid to extend his personal rule was defeated, by 55 to 43 percent. There were rumors afterward that he might nullify the results, but since even his supporters conceded victory to the other side, general elections were set for December 1989, with the winner to take office in March 1990.

Though defeated at the polls, Pinochet had accomplished a capitalist revolution in Chile, which even the moderate parties of the Left accepted. The economy was export oriented, not based on import-substituting industrialization. Moreover, copper, which in 1970 had accounted for three-fourths of all export earnings, now brought in less than half, while nontraditional exports like fruit, seafood, wine, and processed food accounted for nearly as much. Inflation seemed under control, there was much less government involvement in the economy, and many fewer people had government jobs. Instead, Chile had developed a modern business culture that was competitive in international markets. There were nagging problems, however. Unions were weaker, wages were lower, and there was less job security. Officially, there was little unemployment, but there was also a large "informal" sector of nonunionized labor that worked for less than the minimum wage, was uninsured, and collected no social security. Wealth was much more concentrated. The richest 10 percent of the population received more of the national income at the end of Pinochet's rule than it had at the beginning, whereas the poorest 40 percent received less.[12]

Politically, the transition to civilian democracy was still incomplete. The 1980 constitution remained in effect, giving the president enormous powers without any effective check by Congress. Above the president, however, re-mains the tutelary power of the military, exerted through the National Secu-rity Council, which is composed of both officers and civilians. That, in turn, influences the composition of the Constitutional Tribunal and also the ap-pointment of nine senators, in addition to the thirty-eight elected ones. The electoral system also provides for allocating seats to runner-up parties, which increases the representation of the Right.[13] Thus, in both economic and po-litical matters, the Pinochet era continues to influence Chilean society.

Notes

1. Albert Stepan, *The Military in Politics: Changing Patterns in Brazil* (Princeton, NJ: Princeton University Press, 1971), 176–83.

2. Martin Weinstein, *Uruguay: Democracy at the Crossroads* (Boulder, CO: West-view, 1988), 74–76.

3. Thomas E. Skidmore, *The Politics of Military Rule in Brazil, 1964–85* (New York: Oxford University Press, 1988), 117–26.

4. See Paul H. Lewis, *Guerrillas and Generals: The "Dirty War" in Argentina* (Westport, CT: Praeger, 2002), 147–78.

5. Paul H. Lewis, *The Crisis of Argentine Capitalism* (Chapel Hill: University of North Carolina, 1990), 448–62.

6. Henry Finch, "Uruguay since 1930," in *Cambridge History of Latin America*, vol. 8, ed. Leslie Bethell (Cambridge: Cambridge University Press, 1991), 219; We-instein, *Uruguay*, 53.

7. Weinstein, *Uruguay*, 55–68.

8. Pamela Constable and Arturo Valenzuela, *A Nation of Enemies: Chile under Pinochet* (New York: W. W. Norton, 1993), 90–107.

9. One exception to privatization was the copper industry. The removal of large foreign capital from this pivotal sector of the economy was too popular for even Pinochet and the Chicago Boys to try to undo.

10. Regis Bonelli and Pedro S. Malan, "Industrialization, Economic Growth, and Balance of Payments: Brazil, 1970–1984," in *State and Society in Brazil: Continuity and Change*, ed. John D. Wirth, Edson de Oliveira Nunes, and Thomas E. Bogenschild, 13–47 (Boulder, CO: Westview, 1987); Luis Bresser Pereira, *Development and Crisis in Brazil, 1930–1983* (Boulder, CO: Westview, 1984), 162–76.

11. Eduardo Silva, *The State and Capital in Chile: Business Elites, Technocrats, and Market Economics* (Boulder, CO: Westview, 1996), 173–214.

12. Javier Martínez and Alvaro Díaz, *Chile: The Great Transformation* (Washing-ton, DC: Brookings Institution, 1996).

13. Peter M. Siavelis, *The President and Congress in Postauthoritarian Chile: Institu-tional Constraints to Democratic Consolidation* (University Park: Pennsylvania State University Press, 2000).

CHAPTER TEN

~

The Prospects for Democracy

The Latin American republics emerged in the wake of the American and French revolutions, so it is not surprising that their constitutions usually have expressed democratic sentiments. Those constitutions typically provide for periodic elections, the classic tripartite separation of powers, and guarantees of free speech and free press. Unfortunately, in the approximately 180 years that have passed since independence, few Latin American countries have achieved stable polities based on free elections and effective checks on the abuse of executive power by an independent legislature, judiciary, and press. Even when the outward forms of democracy are present, popularly elected presidents often show contempt for constitutional procedures by rewriting constitutions, packing the courts, and legislating through executive decrees. Such majoritarian tyrannies usually end with a backlash in the form of military rule, during which the armed forces try to suppress all politics. In the past fifty years every Latin American country except Costa Rica has experienced either one-party rule, military dictatorship, or a domineering president unrestrained by checks and balances.

From time to time observers in the region, as well as in the United States, have claimed to see the dawn of real democracy. The Mexican Revolution was greeted with optimism, at first, but eventually it evolved into a corrupt one-party regime. After World War I the popularly based governments of Argentina, Chile, and Uruguay seemed to be heading toward democracy, but then came the Great Depression of the 1930s, and with it a swing of the pendulum back to authoritarianism. The victory of democracy (and communism) over the fascist powers in World War II seemed to give another push in the direction of democracy. During the 1940s dictatorships and oligarchies gave way to popular governments in Guatemala, Costa Rica, Venezuela, Peru, Chile, Uruguay, and Brazil. That momentum slowed down in the 1950s. Guatemala and Venezuela reverted to dictatorship, although the latter returned to something resembling democracy in 1958. Somoza's assassination in Nicaragua changed very little, since his family continued to rule. Perón's fall from power in Argentina raised hopes for democracy there but never satisfied them. The Bolivian and Cuban revolutions also began with promises to sweep away all the oppressive and corrupt practices of the past, only to sink into tyranny. In Colombia, General Rojas Pinilla installed a populist dictatorship that, in some ways, might have been more progressive than the oligarchic "democracy" that preceded it; but the oligarchs closed ranks and soon deposed him. General Alfredo Stroessner came to power in Paraguay, launching a tight, efficient dictatorship that would last almost thirty-five years.

The 1960s were even more disillusioning. They began with Trujillo's assassination, but his one-man rule was replaced by a one-party state headed by his protégé, Joaquín Balaguer: a much less terrifying situation, but no democracy. Argentina and Peru had brief democratic interludes but soon returned to military rule. Brazilian democracy, which had begun with Vargas's fall in 1945, came to an end with the military coup of 1964. In that same year Eduardo Frei was elected president of Chile. His Christian Democratic administration was expected to provide an attractive "revolution in liberty" as an alternative to the Cuban Revolution's march toward communist totalitarianism. By the end of the decade Frei had disappointed most Chileans, split his party, and opened the way for Salvador Allende to steer Chile in the same direction as Cuba—albeit behind a temporary facade of democracy. The 1970s were the cruelest decade, as Chile, Argentina, Bolivia, Guatemala, and Uruguay succumbed to military regimes whose mass arrests and executions gave rise to the term "state terror." The seventies closed with the Sandinistas overthrowing the Somoza dynasty in Nicaragua: another false dawn for democracy that ended with left-wing oppression replacing right-wing oppression.

By the mid-1980s military regimes began returning to the barracks: in Argentina in 1983; in Uruguay, Brazil, and Guatemala in 1985; in Chile in 1989. Bolivia's last military coup was in 1980, after which it had a series of weak civilian governments. A military coup deposed General Stroessner, Paraguay's perennial strongman, in 1989. The 1990s witnessed an extension of this trend. The decade opened with the Nicaraguan Sandinistas calling an election that they fully expected to win, only to be voted out of power. In neighboring El Salvador, a long, vicious civil war came to an end in 1992, to be followed by more or less free elections. Mexico's one-party regime began crumbling, as opposition parties began to win state and municipal elections from 1995 on. The process culminated with the victory of opposition candidate Vicente Fox, of the Partido Acción Nacional, in the 2000 presidential elections. Something similar happened in Venezuela when outsider Hugo Chávez won the 1998 presidential elections, bringing to an end the cozy and increasingly corrupt two-party oligopoly based on Acción Democrática and the Christian Social Party, COPEI (Comité de Organización Política Electoral Independiente). Down in Uruguay a new party, Encuentro Progresista/Frente Amplio (EP/FA), mounted a serious challenge from the Left to the Blancos and Colorados. By 1999, only a change in the electoral laws requiring a runoff if no candidate received a majority enabled the country's two traditional parties to avoid a victory by the EP/FA's Tabaré Vásquez in the presidential elections. The third-place Blancos threw their votes to the second-place Colorados and subsequently accepted cabinet posts in the Colorado administration. Nevertheless, the old system was wobbling. Elsewhere, the 1996 elections ousted the old political machine that Joaquín Balaguer had built in the Dominican Republic; and in 1999 the military bowed to civilian rule after elections in Honduras and Panama. By the end of the decade, every country in Latin America had an elected government, with the exception of Cuba.

Do these trends signal the long-awaited advent of democracy, or just another false dawn?

It is well to remain skeptical and recall that, with the exception of Costa Rica, none of the Latin American countries since 1945 has escaped military rule. If democracy is indeed emerging in the region, these are still democracies without deep roots.

Furthermore, the absence of military rule and the use of elections are not by themselves sufficient to guarantee effective democracy. Mexico, most of Central America, Colombia, Bolivia, Paraguay, and Ecuador have civilian rule, but those countries are so riddled with violence and corruption that their governments are either fragile or ineffectual. Brazil is somewhat better off, having impeached one corrupt president and peacefully turned over the presidency to Luis Inácio "Lula" da Silva, the trade union head of the leftist Labor Party (PT), without polarizing the country. One reason for that may be that the 1988 constitution distributed so much power away from the national government to state and local political machines. Thus, corruption and patronage politics still rule the grassroots. Something similar is taking place in Mexico, where the privatization of hundreds of state companies and the breakdown of the old PRI corporatist system has given more autonomy to state and local political bosses—and given the national government less control over crime, drug trafficking, and police corruption.

Even free and fair elections do not guarantee that the winning presidential candidates will act democratically. In many ways the old *caudillo* politics of clientelism, plunder, and lawlessness has reinvented itself in the form of new populist presidents, both of the Left and the Right, who rewrite constitutions to suit themselves and brush aside restraints posed by legislatures and courts. Carlos Menem (Argentina), Alberto Fujimori (Peru), and Hugo Chávez (Venezuela) are examples of this new version of a traditional leadership style. All three came to office through elections, yet all three sought to perpetuate themselves in power by changing the rules. All three weakened the fragile democratic institutions of their respective countries and undermined the rule of law.

The Menem Decade in Argentina

Carlos Saúl Menem, born of Syrian immigrant parents in the distant province of La Rioja, had risen gradually through the ranks of the local Peronist party to become governor just before the military took power in 1976. He was held a prisoner under military rule for five years, and although not severely mistreated he nevertheless emerged a hero. With the return of civilian rule he was reelected governor of La Rioja and became a leading figure in the "Renovationist" faction of Peronism, which aimed at institutionalizing the party, now that its charismatic leader was dead, and to give it a more democratic image. Menem was a good speaker who enjoyed mingling with the masses. The masses adored him too: he liked to box, play soccer, and drive fast sports cars. He also was macho, very much a "ladies' man." In 1988 he won the party's presidential nomination by defeating Antonio Cafiero, who was considered to be too close to the labor union bosses. In 1989, as the economy crumbled and inflation rose to nearly 5,000 percent, voters decided they had had enough of Radical Party governance and swept Menem into office. Overwhelmed by mounting troubles, the incumbent president, Raúl Alfonsín, resigned and turned over power early to Menem.

Although he had campaigned as a populist, Menem shrewdly calculated that hyperinflation would wreck his administration as it had Alfonsín's unless the economy were put in order. Every class in society, from top to bottom, was suffering and desperate. It was now widely recognized that the old system of import-substituting industrialization had reached its dead end. Menem thus had a mandate to fix the system and he used it to justify a 180-degree turn in his politics. The top economic positions in his administration would be filled by businessmen, not populists. Furthermore, he insisted upon, and received, extraordinary powers from Congress to deal with the emergency.[1]

First, the "Law of Economic Emergency" allowed the president to dismiss government employees, cancel government contracts, and end subsidies by simple executive order. Second, the "Law of State Reform" enabled the president to issue executive orders to privatize state companies and abolish subcabinet agencies. Third, the "Law of Reform of the Supreme Court" increased the number of justices from five to nine and gave the president the power to name the additional four. That gave Menem a majority on the court and freed him from any concern that his acts might be declared unconstitutional. Beyond these formal grants of power, Menem claimed others, which were not challenged by his congressional majority. In the name of fighting inflation with balanced budgets he asserted his right to exercise a line-item veto. Moreover, he claimed, and often exercised, the "right" to issue decrees "of necessity and urgency" to deal with any resistance to his reforms.

Armed with these powers, Menem embarked on a neoliberal reform program that his opponents condemned as "savage." Between 1989 and 1995 more than 400 state-owned enterprises were privatized, including those that previously had been considered "untouchable," such as the railroads, the oil company, telephones, airlines, gas, electricity, and the merchant fleet. In most cases, foreign capital, especially Spanish and French, bought them up. Menem also reduced or privatized the social security system, unemployment insurance, and workplace health and accident insurance. The military's budget was slashed too. Industries previously run by the army, navy, and air force were sold off. An attempt by extremist elements—the so-called *carapintada*—to overthrow the government in December 1990 provided an excuse to purge the officer corps, while the overall size of the armed forces was greatly reduced in 1994 by abolishing the draft. At the same time, Menem pleased moderate officers by pardoning the former junta leaders who ruled from 1976 to 1983.

Success came slowly. The representatives of Argentine "big business" who composed the first economic team were more interested in securing favorable government treatment for their companies than in real reforms. They were replaced at the end of 1989 by a new team of cronies brought in from La Rioja. Though personally loyal to Menem, these men were so unscrupulous that another cabinet shuffle was required at the beginning of 1991 to clear the air of scandal. This time a Harvard-trained economist, Domingo Cavallo, took over as economics minister and announced the radical "Convertibility Plan." Under this plan, the Argentine peso was pegged to the dollar at one to one, with free convertibility. That meant that the Central Bank could only put into circulation as many pesos as there were dollar reserves.

In the past, Argentine governments had simply printed as many pesos as they needed to cover their current deficits. Now the various official agencies had to either limit their spending or increase their revenues in order to stay within their budget. That struck directly at the chief cause of inflation, which did in fact drop, from 2,300 percent in 1991 to only 4.3 percent by 1995. Meanwhile, the apparent soundness of Argentina's currency plus the market opportunities created by privatizations brought in over $30 billion in foreign investment. From 1991 to 1995 the economy grew by over 7 percent a year. This dramatic turnaround in the economy brought enormous popularity to the Menem government. Before Cavallo's first year was up the Peronist Partido Justicialista made gains in the September 1991 congressional elections and then added to those in the October midterm elections. Riding high in the polls, Menem was able to force the opposition Radicals to agree to a constitutional convention, which, in 1994, resulted in a new constitution that allowed him to run for a second, consecutive, term. He won easily in the May 1995 presidential race.

Menem's luck turned during his second administration, revealing the moral and structural flaws in his system. Scandals had plagued him from the start. In mid-1990 his wife, Zulema Yoma, accused him of gross infidelity with numerous women and separated from him, taking their two children. A few months later the American ambassador accused several cabinet ministers of extorting bribes from U.S. companies, including the Swift meatpacking firm. It was "Swiftgate" that led to the cabinet shakeup that brought Cavallo to the fore. "Swiftgate" was quickly followed by "Yomagate," a scandal involving Menem's in-laws. His sister-in-law, "Amira," who had been his appointments secretary; her ex-husband, who was in charge of customs at the international airport; and two of her brothers were under indictment in a Spanish court for drug trafficking and money laundering. Simultaneously, Menem's brother, Munir, was accused of being the partner of a notorious Syrian arms smuggler. Though embarrassing, none of these were fatal blows to Menem's prestige while he was bringing down inflation and restoring growth, but when the economy turned down again almost immediately following his reelection the public was less forgiving.

During 1995 Argentina suffered a recession as part of a rippling effect from Mexico's economic troubles, which had resulted in the devaluation of the Mexican peso. On Wall Street, managers of "emerging markets" funds began pulling money out of Latin America. An emergency IMF loan kept the crisis from worsening, while Cavallo raised taxes, cut spending, and laid off government workers in order to regain investor confidence. It worked in the short run, but it also raised political problems. Labor, Peronism's traditional mass base, was on the verge of revolt. Privatizations and trimmer government payrolls had already increased the number of unemployed; now the 1995 recession and further austerity measures boosted the level to 20 percent of the workforce. Nearly a fourth of the population was said to be living below the poverty line, in a country that had once boasted of being the wealthiest in Latin America. Even the middle class was affected, as small businesses, dependent on consumer buying, went bankrupt. Worse still, even with all his austerity measures, Cavallo could not close the government's budget deficit. On the revenue side, the tax system remained unreformed and evasion was rife. On the spending side, Menem was committed to feeding the Peronist party's patronage machine, which spread throughout the provinces, down to the municipalities, and even to the neighborhoods. At every level party bosses and "fixers" were expected to deliver favors.

The federal administration greased the cogs of this machine by sharing revenues. For example, the governor of Buenos Aires Province, Eduardo Duhalde, was given $1 million a day to distribute to his clientele through the dubious "Fund for the Historic Preservation of Greater Buenos Aires." In poverty-stricken Tucumán Province there were 10,000 federal employees and another 80,000 people on the provincial or municipal payrolls, out of a total workforce of around 400,000. In Formosa Province half of all people employed worked for either the federal, provincial, or municipal governments. Many of them only showed up at work to collect their paychecks. A typical provincial or municipal government spent almost its entire budget on salaries, and very little on services. At the topmost level salaries were quite generous. In Tucumán the average provincial legislator was paid the equivalent of $300,000 a year, and annual raises were expected. Such waste had been easily funded with money coming in from privatizations, but now there was nothing left to privatize, so Cavallo's austerity measures signaled an end to the free ride. There were riots in some of the provinces, and roadblocks on the highways, as the unemployed, the unpaid, the ruined, and the parasitic joined in protest. Unable to persuade Menem to close the patronage tap, Cavallo turned to foreign borrowing, running up the dollar-denominated debt from $60 billion in 1992 to $100 billion in 1996, after which he finally resigned, exhausted from fending off demands to "re-Peronize" the economy. Menem, having achieved his goal of a second term, no longer defended him. In fact, Menem was looking ahead to changing the constitution again to permit himself a third term, and he needed the support of Peronist governors and congressmen.[2]

Cavallo didn't leave quietly, however. In a public speech before Congress he denounced the network of corruption emanating from the Casa Rosada. Judicial investigations into various aspects of the administration, such as the social security system and the customs services, supported Cavallo's accusations. A great deal of sordid evidence also emerged about bribery and influence peddling in the sale of the state companies to private investors. More serious still was the revelation that the Ministry of Defense and the army's commander in chief had illegally sold weapons to Ecuador and Croatia—the latter in contravention of a United Nations embargo. Three secret executive orders, signed by Menem, had authorized the sales. Finally, investigations into drug trafficking pointed increasingly to a close friend of Menem's, Alfredo Yabrán, who headed a business empire that included private mail delivery; courier services; air cargo delivery; the printing of official documents, automobile registration documents, and banknotes; the duty-free shop at the airport; and private security services. As early as 1994 Cavallo had raised an alarm about Yabrán's involvement in the narcotics traffic and had been saved from dismissal only by the pressure brought to bear on Menem by the businessmen's and bankers' associations, and the American ambassador. An investigation into the grisly murder of a journalist who had been digging into Yabrán's dealings eventually compiled enough evidence to result in an indictment against this sinister figure, driving him to suicide. In the course of the investigation it was revealed that Yabrán and Menem had been frequently in touch by telephone.[3]

This piling up of scandals happened against the background of another economic crisis, which began in early 1999 when Brazil devalued its currency. Argentina, Brazil, Paraguay, and Uruguay were partners in a free-trade zone called MERCOSUR, set up in 1991. Argentina already had been suffering trade losses with Europe because of its overvalued currency, but the Brazilian devaluation cost it its single most important market. By now Menem's approval ratings had sunk to 15 percent, and his hopes for a third term were blocked by a rival: Eduardo Duhalde, the governor of Buenos Aires Province. Congress, following the polls, refused to amend the constitution. Desperate to have some public office, Menem tried running for the Buenos Aires governorship, only to be outflanked by his vice president, Carlos Ruckauf, who won the prize. As he stepped down from the presidency, Menem left behind a fiscal deficit of $7 billion and a foreign debt of $170 billion.

The 1999 elections were won, not by Duhalde, but by Fernando de la Rua, who headed an alliance of Radicals and left-wing dissidents. De la Rua's fate was to suffer the collapse of the corruption- and debt-riddled system Menem left behind. As a Peronist congressional majority blocked any more attempts at austerity, foreign lenders refused more loans and wise investors began with-drawing their money from local banks. Riots, the sacking of grocery stores, and a freeze on bank withdrawals preceded de la Rua's resignation on 20 December 2001. Three very short-lived presidencies followed, until Congress finally settled on Eduardo Duhalde as provisional president. He declared a default on the foreign debt but kept the freeze on bank deposits. By that time the GDP had shrunk by 11 percent, inflation had risen by 40 percent, unemployment had risen to a fourth of the workforce, and an estimated one-half of the population was living below the poverty line.

Menem was not allowed to retire into obscurity. During the early part of 2001 he was indicted for authorizing illegal arms sales to Ecuador and Croatia and placed under house arrest. He subsequently was found guilty and sentenced to ten years in prison, but he escaped when an appellate judge—a friend from La Rioja—dismissed the case on a technicality. With his usual irrepressible self-confidence, Menem entered the 2003 presidential elections against Duhalde's picked candidate, Néstor Kirchner, the governor of Santa Cruz Province. More scandals erupted during the race. Menem, it was revealed, had two Swiss bank accounts. One of them was said to contain $10 million that the government of Iran had paid to him for successfully obstructing the investigation of a 1994 terrorist bombing of a Jewish community center in Buenos Aires. Despite this, Menem came in first in the initial voting, but he had far from a majority. Because his calculations showed that all the other candidates would back Kirchner, he dropped out of the race before the runoff. It was the end of the line, after almost fifty years in politics.

The Fujimori Phenomenon

Unlike Carlos Menem, who had worked his way up the Peronist party hierarchy over many years, Alberto Fujimori was a virgin in politics when he unexpectedly won the Peruvian presidential election in 1990. Born in 1938, the son of Japanese immigrants, he was an agricultural engineer by profession. At the time he formed his campaign organization, called "Change 90," he was dean of the science faculty at the Agrarian National University. His only brush with politics had been as a television talk show host, where he sometimes expressed his expert opinions about Peru's social and economic problems. Starting with little name recognition, Fujimori campaigned vigorously in the poor urban barrios and in hundreds of remote mountain villages, insisting that his agronomy background could provide solutions to poor people's problems. This grassroots approach worked. The Peruvian Left was badly split after Alan García's disastrous administration, allowing Fujimori to qualify for a runoff against the Right's candidate, the famous novelist Mario Vargas Llosa. The latter, a descendant of Peru's traditional elite, lacked the popular touch. Fujimori, the quintessential "outsider," won easily.[4]

García had left Peru with a daunting set of problems: hyperinflation running at 7,650 percent, a shrinking GNP, and an escalating level of violence from two left-wing guerrilla movements: Sendero Luminoso (Shining Path) and Tupac Amarú. Within a few weeks after taking office Fujimori began attacking inflation by lowering tariffs, making state companies cover their deficits by raising rates, deregulating wide areas of the economy, devaluing the currency, and slashing government spending. At the same time he gave the armed forces a free hand to deal with the guerrillas. Many of these initiatives were taken without consulting Congress, where Fujimori lacked majority support. He also ignored judicial decisions declaring his measures to be unconstitutional. The opposition, whose principal voice was ex-president García, accused him of abusing the president's executive decree powers and of sanctioning human rights abuses.

Fujimori responded, on 5 April 1992, by dissolving Congress, purging the Supreme Court and lower courts, and imposing press censorship. He justified this executive coup, which the armed forces supported, on the grounds that the opposition was deliberately subverting the government's fight against the guerrilla terrorists. Although there was an outcry from the international community, including the United States, Fujimori's popularity rose inside Peru as he projected an image of strength and decisiveness. Furthermore, his actions seemed to bear fruit when, in September 1992, the police captured Abimael Guzmán, the Shining Path leader, and most of his inner circle.[5]

Nevertheless, Peru's status as an international pariah, cut off from all economic and military aid, finally convinced Fujimori to schedule elections for a constitutional convention. Many of the opposition leaders, citing government intimidation, refused to participate, which enabled Fujimori's "Change 90" party to win a majority of seats and write a new constitution that was to his liking. Freed to run for immediate reelection, he won by a landslide in 1995.

The president's popularity hit its peak in 1997–1998. Inflation was on its way down and would hit a low point of 6 percent in 1998. More dramatically, in April 1997 Fujimori sent soldiers into the Japanese ambassador's home where Tupac Amarú guerrillas, having broken into a diplomatic soiree, were holding some seventy-two people hostage and demanding the release of some of their imprisoned comrades. Fujimori refused to negotiate. As television cameras rolled the soldiers freed all but one of the hostages, killing all fourteen guerrillas and suffering two losses themselves. Fujimori was on the scene to make it clear that he was in charge.

Although Peru nominally had returned to democracy, the president's style became increasingly authoritarian. Human rights violations continued, even after the guerrilla threat subsided. Press criticism often was silenced, as when the government shut down the independent television station Frecuencia Latina in 1997. Indeed, there was a well-coordinated campaign to silence all opposition by tapping the telephones of journalists and politicians, and collecting compromising information about their private lives and business dealings. The sinister figure orchestrating this—Fujimori's equivalent of Yabrán— was Vladimir Montesinos, head of the National Intelligence Service (SIN) and a man with a shady past. He once had been dishonorably discharged from the army, and sent to prison for a year, for selling military secrets to the CIA. After leaving prison he had become a criminal defense lawyer with contacts in the narcotics underworld. Despite that, or perhaps because of it, he eventually found a job with the SIN. During Fujimori's first political campaign Montesinos signed on as an adviser. His reward was to be appointed head of the SIN and also, through his brother-in-law, a general, Fujimori's liaison with the army. He was said to be the mastermind behind the 1992 coup.[6]

Fujimori's popularity eroded quickly after he announced, in 1999, that he would stand for a third term in the next year's presidential election. The 1993 constitution limited the president to two terms; but Fujimori argued that since Peru had a new constitution, his first term, under the old constitution, didn't count. The opposition took the matter to the Supreme Court, but when the judges found against him Fujimori simply purged the court again. Similarly, he blocked the opposition's attempt to submit the issue to a national referendum.

History seemed about to repeat itself in the April 2000 election when, to his surprise, Fujimori was forced into a runoff by a little-known economist named Alejandro Toledo. Polls showed Toledo winning easily on the second ballot, but Fujimori and Montesinos, disregarding protests from opposition spokesmen and international election observers, pulled out their bagful of dirty tactics to ensure the president's reelection. Toledo withdrew in protest. A victorious Fujimori ignored the massive street demonstrations mounted against him.

The government's triumph was short lived, however, for in September a Lima television station ran a videotape showing Montesinos bribing an opposition congressman. That was too blatant for even Fujimori to ignore, so he suspended his SIN chief. Then more revelations came out about Montesinos: he had more than $100 million stashed away in various overseas bank accounts, most of it drug money, according to the testimony of imprisoned drug lords in Brazil and Colombia. Further investigation turned up evidence that Fujimori might be involved in those underworld dealings. In November, Fujimori suddenly fled the country and took asylum in Japan. A caretaker government then scheduled new elections, for April 2001. They were won by Alejandro Toledo.

Venezuela's "Man of the People"

Throughout the Cold War Venezuela's democratic system of government was held up as a model by the United States, as an alternative to communist Cuba. Following the overthrow of Marcos Pérez Jiménez's military dictatorship, in 1958, two middle-of-the-road parties contended for office. The center-left Acción Democrática (AD) elected the first two presidents, Rómulo Betancourt (1959–1964) and Raúl Leoni (1964–1969); the right-of-center Christian Social Party (COPEI) elected the third, Rafael Caldera (1969–1974). These first governments carried out an agrarian reform, won substantial concessions from the foreign oil companies, and fended off attempts to subvert democracy by both the diehard Right and the *fidelista* Left. Much of their popularity stemmed from rising oil prices, which brought in ever-larger revenues that could be spent on development projects.

Starting in 1974, a worldwide cutback in oil production staged by OPEC quadrupled Venezuela's revenues. AD's new president, Carlos Andrés Pérez, was the beneficiary of this immense windfall. He promised "to sow the oil" and spent lavishly, buying out foreign investors in the oil and iron industries, and creating a host of new state companies to pursue his ambitious plans for import-substituting industrialization. As with similar schemes elsewhere in Latin America, the new industries created economic problems, and some of them had to be abandoned. The most ambitious projects were not export-competitive because they still had to import technology and capital goods, which raised their costs. At the same time, because of Venezuela's small middle class and great mass of poor people, the domestic market was inadequate to sustain a large industrial sector. Private investors were also reluctant to risk their money in a system where so many economic decisions were based on political considerations and where the state frequently changed the rules to suit itself. Corruption was endemic. Much of the money allocated to development projects simply disappeared into offshore accounts.[7]

Just as rocketing oil prices in the 1970s had led to this spending orgy, so the fall in oil prices in the 1980s brought on a deep recession. Capital fled, the GDP shrank, wages fell. Inflation, unemployment, and the foreign debt all rose. The country was shocked in 1983 when the government was forced to devalue the currency. Even greater shocks occurred in February 1989. After sitting out two terms, the free-spending Carlos Andrés Pérez returned to the presidency—only this time he announced (after taking office) that Venezuela was bankrupt and would require extreme measures to restore its economy to health. Two weeks after his inauguration Pérez began applying the bitter medicine: a rise in charges for state goods and services such as telephones, gas and oil, and electricity; higher interest rates; lower tariffs. The immediate reaction was three days of rioting throughout the country that left over 300 persons dead.

Undeterred, Pérez went ahead with his austerity program. The outbreak of the Gulf War in 1990 gave him some breathing room by temporarily boosting oil revenues, but a tight government budget inevitably caused a deterioration in public services such as health, sanitation, schools, and transportation. The privatization of several state companies was another blow to a public accustomed to believing that Venezuela was inexhaustibly rich. The military felt the pinch too, especially the junior officers who lacked the opportunities that senior officers had to supplement their salaries with "kickbacks" from defense contractors. In February 1992 their anger boiled over in a coup attempt that nearly succeeded. The coup's leader, Lieutenant Colonel Hugo Chávez, was sent to prison. As for Pérez, fresh evidence of corruption in his administration, gathered by the attorney general and certified by the Supreme Court, resulted in the Senate's forcing his resignation in May 1993. New elections, held later that year, returned another ex-president, COPEI's Rafael Caldera, to office. By this time, however, the public was thoroughly disgusted with both of the traditional parties, so that nearly 40 percent of the eligible voters stayed away from the polls.[8]

The public's perception that COPEI and AD offered no real choice was confirmed during Caldera's presidency by their close collaboration in Congress and by Caldera's continuation of Pérez's austerity program. As the 1990s wore on the two parties' vote declined steadily as factions broke away and set up competing parties. At the same time, absenteeism increased, as did the number of people telling pollsters that they had no party identification or interest in politics. Finally, the chance to break with the past came in December 1998 when Lieutenant Colonel Hugo Chávez, released from prison by Caldera, threw his hat into the ring for the presidency. His rhetoric electrified the public. He ran as a man of the people, the son of humble small-town schoolteachers, who felt the masses' rage against the "rancid oligarchs" who stole from them. Alarmed, AD and COPEI closed ranks behind a single candidate, but to no avail. Backed by a coalition of leftist parties, including the Communists, Chávez stirred up enough popular passion against the old system of *partidocracia* to win easily.

244 ⁓ Chapter Ten

Chávez moved quickly upon taking office. During his inauguration, in February 1999, he had called the existing constitution of 1961 "moribund." He pushed through a referendum in April to call a constitutional convention, and although only 39 percent of the eligible voters participated, it passed by a large majority. In the July elections for convention delegates Chávez supporters won 122 out of 131 seats. As soon as they assembled, in August, Chávez declared that Venezuela was in a state of "social emergency" and dissolved both Congress (where his supporters were in a minority) and the Supreme Court. The new constitution, approved by another referendum in December, increased the president's powers, lengthened his term from five to six years, and permitted him to run for an immediate second term. Congress, now renamed the National Assembly, was much reduced in power. A fourth branch of government, called Citizen Power, was added to the other three. It combines the attributes of public prosecutor, auditor, and ombudsman.

The core of Chávez's support was the desperately poor shantytown dwellers in the hills above Caracas, whom he gradually organized into armed "Bolivarian circles," similar to Cuba's "committees for the defense of the revolution." These would be his shock troops against the organized elements of the old civil society: the businessmen, labor unions, the Catholic Church, and the privately owned media—all of whom look upon him as a throwback to *caudillo* politics. The military was another crucial element. Its commands were reshuffled, and officers suspected of disloyalty were forced into retirement. Chávez's friends, on the other hand, were put in charge of key garrisons, and many of them were given important positions in his government. In a move to deprive the opposition of its largest component, in December 2000 Chávez held another referendum, this time on whether the top echelons of the Confederation of Venezuelan Workers (CTV) should be dismissed. It passed, though turnout was only 23 percent, and the old union leadership had to resign. Nevertheless, 80 percent of the former CTV leaders were returned to their posts in the new union elections.

Despite his undemocratic tactics, Chávez showed little inclination to make sweeping economic changes. His "revolutionary" behavior was confined mainly to foreign affairs, where he staked out a strong anti-U.S. position, praising Fidel Castro as a "champion of liberty," allowing Colombia's guerrillas to use Venezuelan territory as their staging ground, and urging the raising of oil prices at OPEC meetings. To solidify his international reputation as a revolutionary, Chávez made frequent trips to Cuba and agreed to supply it with 50,000 barrels of oil a day, at cut-rate prices. In return, Castro sent doctors, teachers, sports trainers, and intelligence agents to Venezuela.[9]

None of that helped to grow the domestic economy or reverse the spread of poverty, which gradually engulfed about 80 percent of the population. Corruption persisted. A fiscal deficit of $9 billion represented almost 10 percent of the GNP.

Some of Chávez's left-wing support began to drop away as 2001 began. Stung into action, he rushed through the Rural Development and Land Law in September, then followed that with decrees raising taxes on foreign oil companies, firing the management board of the state oil company (PDVSA) and replacing it with his own cronies, and giving the state majority control of all other companies having contracts with the oil industry. Despite these moves, polls showed the president's popularity falling to dangerously low levels. Capital flight accelerated. In December the backlash came, spearheaded by the employers' association, Fedecamaras, and the labor unions' CTV. Work stoppages and massive street marches demanded Chávez's resignation. They were answered with counterdemonstrations by the Bolivarian circles. Tensions escalated through January, February, and March of 2002, and so did the size of the street marches. When the Catholic clergy supported the protesters Chávez attacked them as "devils in skirts." Finally, the CTV, backed by Fedecamaras, called a general strike that was to bring the economy to a halt and was to last until the military removed Chávez. The armed forces themselves were divided, especially when the protesters mobilized an estimated half million people on Thursday, April 11, to march on the Presidential Palace.

Much has been written, pro and con, about the events of April 11, their causes, and their consequences.[10] Out of the confused and often contradictory reports some things appear certain, however. The protest marchers were fired upon as they approached the palace, by national guardsmen and by well-armed men from the Bolivarian circles, some of whom were positioned on the rooftops of nearby buildings. A horrified Army General Staff demanded Chávez's resignation the next day and even placed him under arrest. A few hours later the head of Fedecamaras, Pedro Carmona, announced that he had the army's backing to form a provisional government. Had Carmona limited himself to that, the coup might have succeeded; however, he went on to demand revenge on all the top figures in the Chávez administration, many of whom were military officers. Almost immediately the army's mood shifted, and indeed the opposition itself split, as some of the unions distanced themselves from Carmona, whom they considered a right-wing extremist. The following day the military shoved Carmona aside and restored Chávez to power.

Though jubilant at his restoration, Chávez owed his position to a very divided military, which could change its mind again at any time. Meanwhile, businessmen, labor unions, Church leaders, middle classes, and independent media were still ranged against him. In August 2003 they organized a recall effort and claimed to have collected three million signatures to force a referendum on whether Chávez should resign. His handpicked National Elections Council dismissed the petition, however, on the grounds that most of the signatures were fraudulent. More riots ensued, involving hundreds of thousands of protesters. Eight were killed, hundreds were jailed. In December the oil workers' union went on strike, seriously disrupting the economy. Chávez dug in. By February the strike had collapsed and the workers were back on their jobs. In the meantime, however, the opposition had successfully organized another recall petition. On 15 August 2004 Venezuelans went to the polls to decide whether Chávez would serve out his term or be forced to resign and call new general elections within thirty days. Exit polls showed the opposition's "yes" option gaining 58 percent support, but when the votes were actually counted it was Chávez who won with 58 percent. Foreign election observers confirmed the count, but opposition leaders charged the government with committing massive fraud. Polarized and without stable political parties or governing institutions that commanded respect, Venezuela seemed headed for a protracted stalemate.

Retrospect and Prospect

The Spanish and Portuguese colonies in America achieved their independence during the first two decades of the nineteenth century. Among their leaders were men, influenced by the Enlightenment, who tried to establish republican governments that would uphold "the rights of man." Few of them were democrats in the modern sense of the word, but most of them believed in "progress," in the sense that education and expanding economic opportunities would eventually produce a citizenry capable of self-governance. Nevertheless, the political norm in Latin America has been for strongmen, backed by armed supporters, to seize power and rule as dictators—or for local political bosses to combine and rule as an oligarchy.

Latin American authoritarianism has evolved along with the material and social conditions of the region. The internal dynamics of *caudillo* politics led to the consolidation of nation-states, under the rule of either national dictators or oligarchic machines. With political stability came economic growth as the new states attracted foreign investment and became involved in the world economy. This new order was sanctioned by the ideology of liberalism, which in Latin America had an authoritarian twist. Latin American liberalism accepted the doctrines of free trade and comparative advantage borrowed from Adam Smith and David Ricardo, but on the political side it blended the Postivism of Auguste Comte with the Social Darwinism of Herbert Spencer. The result was an era of economic progress that brought material improvements, rapidly growing cities, expanding commerce, and the appearance of urban middle and working classes as increasingly important political actors. These new classes demanded greater participation in the benefits of economic progress. Political parties, emerging to press their claims, provided opportunities for a new type of *caudillo*: the charismatic party leader.

The era of mass politics retained the old authoritarian tradition, however. The new *caudillo* may embrace an ideology such as communism or fascism, but like the old variety he is impatient toward any restraint, disdainful of tradition, and contemptuous of institutions. He makes up his own rules as he goes along. His first concern is to break with the past, which is condemned—often with reason—as being corrupt and unrepresentative of "the People's" *true* interests. He promises "real democracy," for the first time ever in the country's history: a fresh beginning that allows "the People" finally to come into their birthright. Whereas the old *caudillo* distributed plunder among his relatives, friends, and clients, the new *caudillo* nurtures his following with the "renewable resources" of the state, buying votes with jobs, contracts, welfare, and graft. Behind the facade of the revolutionary regime or the corporate state, however, lurks the Iberian tradition of personal rule, military-type organization, and crusading intolerance. The usual antidote to the modern *caudillo* is the modern oligarchy, in which the upper classes turn to the armed forces for protection.

Those who argue that recent trends toward democracy in Latin America are eroding the old authoritarian culture still have to grapple with the examples of excessive presidential power, as illustrated by Carlos Menem, Alberto Fujimori, and Hugo Chávez. Moreover, since excessive presidential power stunts the development of strong democratic institutions, there is a tendency, should public opinion turn against the president, for authoritarianism to give way to anarchy. Popular riots may embolden the opposition and eventually force the president from office, or prevent him from extending his period of rule. In the last fifteen years presidents have been forced out of office in Brazil, Bolivia, Ecuador, Guatemala, and Paraguay. It happened to Menem's successor, Fernando de la Rua, in Argentina, and to Hugo Chávez's predecessor, Carlos Andrés Pérez, in Venezuela. Chávez himself might end that way. In some cases the fallen leader was caught engaged in criminal behavior and so had it coming to him; but in other cases he simply was pursuing unpopular policies. Even when justice is done, it is too often mob justice, or partisan justice, rather than the impartial application of the law.

To be sure, there are heartening examples of progress being made toward democracy in several of the republics. Still, democratic institutions everywhere throughout the region have shallow roots. Corruption is common, criminal behavior is on the rise, and there is a constant temptation to ignore the law in the name of expediency or partisan advantage. Menem's Argentina, Fujimori's Peru, and Chávez's Venezuela also show how globalization, impacting on Latin America economies, puts emerging democracies under pressure. The carefully protected state-nurtured systems created by import-substituting industrialization are being forced to open up to global competition, with painful consequences for established interests. The neo-liberal reforms initiated by Menem and Fujimori, for example, required firing thousands of people who worked for state companies, canceling contracts with private companies doing business with the state, exposing other private companies to foreign competition, deregulating prices, ending subsidies, and raising taxes. Those changes not only bore down heavily on the working classes but were a serious blow to many people in the middle classes: small entrepreneurs, government employees, professionals, and white-collar workers in the private sector. Taken together, these are the "popular classes" on which a democracy must rest; but they are also the same classes that today are taking to the streets to protect their jobs and status. When constitutional procedures fail them, they look to men like Hugo Chávez—charismatic leaders who promise a "third way" between "savage capitalism" and communist totalitarianism. That "third way" is but a reversion to *caudillo* demagoguery, which opposes the creation of those strong institutions that are necessary to sustain real democracy.

So, the authoritarian culture persists under new guises. Material conditions change, new classes emerge, new ideologies clash with each other across the region; but all are transformed locally into familiar shapes whose roots reach back for centuries. This does not mean that Latin America is incapable of achieving democracy; no one would deny that some progress has been made. Especially in Costa Rica, Chile, and Uruguay, democracy seems to be more or less stable. Moreover, contemporary Spain and Portugal—the mother countries—have evolved into democracies, proving that the Iberian authoritarian tradition can be overcome. Spain and Portugal have been guided toward democracy by the European Union, however. The Latin American republics, lacking such an outside force to guide them, will have a more difficult path to follow.

Notes

1. Carlos H. Acuña, "Politics and Economics in the Argentina of the Nineties (Or, Why the Future No Longer Is What It Used to Be)," in *Democracy, Markets, and Structural Reform in Latin America*, ed. William C. Smith, Carlos H. Acuña, and Eduardo Gamarra, 31–73 (New Brunswick, NJ: Transaction, 1993); Atlio Borón, "Menem's Neo-Liberal Experiment," in *Problems of Democracy in Latin America*, ed. International Congress of Americanists, 8–34 (Stockholm: Institute of Latin American Studies, Stockholm University, 1996); Artemio Luis Melo, *El primer gobierno de Menem: análisis de los proceso de cambio política* (Rosario: Editorial de la Universidad Nacional de Rosario, 2001); and Vicente Palermo and Marcos Novaro, *Política y poder en el gobierno de Menem* (Buenos Aires: Grupo Editor Norma, 1996), are my chief sources for Menem's first administration.

2. On Menem's relations with Peronist provincial governors, see Melo, *Primer gobierno*, 39, 47, 113, 183, 212, 223, 227; Palermo and Novaro, *Política y poder*, 317–18, 437–38, 440–42; Kent Eaton, "Political Obstacles to Decentralization: Evidence from Argentina and the Philippines," *Development and Change* 32, no. 1 (January 2001): 101–27; and Jorge R. Vanossi, "¿Es viable el estado federal en la Argentina?" *Foro Político* (Buenos Aires) 31 (April 2001): 13–40.

3. On the arms trafficking scandal, see Daniel Santoro, *Venta de armas, hombres del gobierno* (Buenos Aires: Editorial Planeta, 1998); and Santoro, *Venta de armas, hombres de Menem* (Buenos Aires: Editorial Planeta, 2001). On the Yabrán business empire, its connection to Menem, and the murder of the journalist José Luis Cabezas, which led to Yabrán's suicide, see Enrique O. Sdrech and Norberto Colominas, *Cabezas: Crimen, mafia, y poder* (Buenos Aires: Editorial Atuel, 1997); and Alejandro Vecchi, *El crimen de Cabezas: Radiografía de un país mafioso* (Buenos Aires: Editorial Biblos, 2001). Domingo Cavallo expanded upon and published his denunciation of corruption under Menem in *El peso de la verdad* (Buenos Aires: Editorial Planeta, 1997).

4. For Fujimori's background and entry into politics, see James D. Rudolph, *Peru: The Evolution of a Crisis* (Westport, CT: Praeger, 1992), 137–52; and "Alberto Fujimori: Biography, history of Peru since 1990," June 2000, www.cosmopolis.ch/english/cosmo7/fujimori.htm.

5. On Fujimori's governing style and the 1992 coup, see Alvaro Vargas Llosa, *The Madness of Things Peruvian: Democracy under Siege* (New Brunswick, NJ: Transaction, 1994); Francisco Sagasti and Max Hernández, "The Crisis of Governance," in *Peru in Crisis: Dictatorship or Democracy?* ed. Joseph S. Tulchin and Gary Bland, 23–34 (Boulder, CO: Lynne Rienner, 1994); Fernando Rospigliosi, "Democracy's Bleak Prospects," in Tulchin and Bland, *Peru in Crisis*, 35–61; Carlos Iván Degregori, "Shining Path and Counterinsurgency Strategy since the Arrest of Abimael Guzmán," in Tulchin and Bland, *Peru in Crisis*, 81–100; and Maxwell A. Cameron, "Political and Economic Origins of Regime Change in Peru," in *The Peruvian Labyrinth: Polity,*

Society, Economy, ed. Maxwell A. Cameron and Philip Mauceri, 37–69 (University Park: Pennsylvania University Press, 1997).

6. On Montesinos, see Vargas Llosa, *Madness*, 12–15, 27; and "Montesinos, Fujimori, Toledo and Peru's future: Biography and analysis," 10 November 2000, www.cosmopolis.ch/english/cosmo11/peru.htm.

7. Daniel Hellinger, *Venezuela: Tarnished Democracy* (Boulder, CO: Westview, 1991), 121–54; and Fernando Coronil, *The Magical State: Nature, Money, and Modernity in Venezuela* (Chicago: University of Chicago Press, 1997), 237–360.

8. José E. Molina V. and Carmen Pérez B., "El fin del bipartidismo en Venezuela: Las elecciones venezolanas en la década de los noventas," in *Urnas y desencanto político: Elecciones y democracía en América Latina, 1992–1996*, ed. Juan Rial and Daniel Zovatto G., 443–66 (San José, Costa Rica: Instituto Interamericano de Derechos Humanos, 1998).

9. Fundació CIDOB (Barcelona), *Biografías de Líderes Políticos: Hugo Rafael Chávez*, 14 April 2002, 1–15; and Mark Falcoff, "Venezuela: It's Not Over Yet," *AEI Latin American Outlook*, May 2002, www.aei.org/lao, 1–4.

10. For example, see Antonio Frances and Carlos Machado Allison, eds., *Venezuela: La crisis de abril* (Caracas: Ediciones IESA, 2002).

~

For Further Reading

Barman, Roderick J. *Citizen Emperor: Pedro II and the Making of Modern Brazil, 1825–91.* Stanford, CA: Stanford University Press, 1999.

Burns, E. Bradford. *A History of Brazil.* New York: Columbia University Press, 1980.

Bushnell, David, and Neil Macaulay. *The Emergence of Latin America in the Nineteenth Century.* New York: Oxford University Press, 1994.

Collier, Simon, and William F. Sater. *A History of Chile, 1808–1994.* Cambridge: Cambridge University Press, 1996.

Coronil, Fernando. *The Magical State: Nature, Money, and Modernity in Venezuela.* Chicago: University of Chicago Press, 1997.

Hamil, Hugh H., ed. *Dictatorship in Spanish America.* New York: Alfred A. Knopf, 1965.

Haring, Clarence H. *The Spanish Empire in America.* New York: Harcourt, Brace & World, 1963.

Lambert, Jacques. *Latin America: Social Structures and Political Institutions.* Berkeley: University of California Press, 1967.

Lewis, Paul H. *The Crisis of Argentine Capitalism.* Chapel Hill: University of North Carolina Press, 1990.

———. *Guerrillas and Generals: The "Dirty War" in Argentina.* Westport, CT: Praeger, 2002.

Lockhart, James, and Stuart B. Schwartz. *Early Latin America: A History of Colonial Spanish America and Brazil.* Cambridge: Cambridge University Press, 1983.

Lynch, John. *Caudillos in Spanish America, 1800–1850.* Oxford: Oxford University Press, 1992.

MacLachlan, Colin M., and William H. Beezley. *El Gran Pueblo: A History of Greater Mexico.* Upper Saddle River, NJ: Prentice Hall, 1994.

Palmer, David Scott. *Peru: The Authoritarian Tradition.* New York: Praeger, 1980.

Rock, David. *Argentina, 1516–1987*. Berkeley: University of California Press, 1987.

Skidmore, Thomas E. *Politics in Brazil, 1930–1964*. New York: Oxford University Press, 1967.

———. *The Politics of Military Rule in Brazil, 1964–85*. New York: Oxford University Press, 1988.

Wiarda, Howard J., and Harvey Kline, eds. *Latin American Politics and Development*. Boulder, CO: Westview, 2000.

Wolf, Eric, and Edward C. Hansen. "Caudillo Politics: A Structural Analysis," *Comparative Studies in Society and History* 9, no. 2 (January 1967).

Index

~

About the Author

Paul H. Lewis earned a B.A. degree in political science from the University of Florida in 1960 and a Ph.D. from the University of North Carolina in 1965. He is an emeritus professor of political science at Tulane University, where he has taught since 1967. Lewis is the author of several books on Latin American politics, including *Paraguay under Stroessner* (1980), *The Crisis of Argentine Capitalism* (1990), *Political Parties and Generations in Paraguay's Liberal Era* (1993), and *Guerrillas and Generals: Argentina's "Dirty War"* (2002).